ALL NEW 100

LITERACY HOURS

- Follows the NLS medium-term planning
- Photocopiable extracts
- Differentiated lesson plans

YEAR 5

Chris Webster

CREDITS

Author
Chris Webster

Editor
Roanne Charles

Assistant Editor
Victoria Paley

Illustrations
Ray & Corrine Burrows Illustrators

Series Designer
Joy Monkhouse

Designer
Erik Ivens
Catherine Mason

Text © Chris Webster
© 2005 Scholastic Ltd

Designed using Adobe InDesign

Published by Scholastic Ltd
Villiers House
Clarendon Avenue
Leamington Spa
Warwickshire CV32 5PR

www.scholastic.co.uk

Printed by Bell and Bain Ltd, Glasgow.

3 4 5 6 7 8 9   6 7 8 9 0 1 2 3 4

ACKNOWLEDGEMENTS

The publishers gratefully acknowledge permission to reproduce the following copyright material: **The Book Trust** for the use of an extract from Michael Morpurgo's diary which appeared on www.childrenslaureate.org (c) The Book Trust. **Faber and Faber** for the use of 'Nessie' by Ted Hughes from *Moon-bells and Other Poems* by Ted Hughes © 1978, Ted Hughes (1978, Chatto & Windus; 1986, The Bodley Head). **Jane Grell** for the use of *Nyangara the Fire Python* © 2005, Jane Grell (previously unpublished). **David Higham Associates** for the use of an extract from *Arthur, High King of England* by Michael Morpurgo © 1994, Michael Morpurgo (1994, Pavilion Books) and for the use of extracts from *Kensuke's Kingdom* by Michael Morpurgo © 1999, Michael Morpurgo (1999, Egmont). **James and James (Publishing) Limited** on behalf of the Estate of Jame MacGibbon for use of the poem 'Angel Boley' by Stevie Smith from *The Collected Poems of Stevie Smith* by Stevie Smith © 1983, The Estate of James MacGibbon (1983, W W Norton). **Tony Mitton** for the use of 'Write-a-Rap Rap' by Tony Mitton from *The Moonlit Stream and Other Poems* by Tony Mitton © 2000, Tony Mitton (2000, Oxford University Press). **Jack Ousbey** for the use of 'Gran Can You Rap?' by Jack Ousbey from *All in the Family* edited by John Foster © 1993, Jack Ousbey (1993, Oxford University Press). **Campbell Perry** for the use of *Amul and The Drum* by Campbell Perry © 2005, Campbell Perry (previously unpublished). **Campbell Perry** for the use of 'Fairground' by Campbell Perry © 2005, Campbell Perry (previously unpublished). **Celia Warren** for the use of 'Cold Morning' by Celia Warren © 2005, Celia Warren (previously unpublished). **A P Watt Limited** on behalf of The National Trust for Places of Historic Interest or Natural Beauty for the use of 'Old Mother Laidinwool' by Rudyard Kipling from *The Collected Poems of Rudyard Kipling* © The National Trust for Places of Historic Interest or Natural Beauty (1994, Wordsworth Editions Limited).

British Library Cataloguing-in-Publication Data
A catalogue record for this book is available from the British Library.

ISBN 0-439-971-691
ISBN 978-0439-971690

The right of Chris Webster to be identified as the author of this work has been asserted by him in accordance with the Copyright, Designs and Patents Act 1988.

Extracts from The National Literacy Strategy © Crown copyright. Reproduced under the terms of HMSO Guidance Note 8.

Contents

ALL NEW 100 LITERACY HOURS: YEAR 5

About the series

The books in the updated *All New 100 Literacy Hours* series offer a set of completely new term-by-term lesson plans, complete with objectives and organisation grids and accompanied, where relevant with photocopiable texts and activity sheets. The series offers a core of material for the teaching of the English curriculum within the structure of the Literacy Hour, but now perfectly matches the recent NLS *Medium-Term Plans*, *Grammar for Writing*, and *Speaking, Listening and Learning* guidelines. The series also builds on current teaching ideas including the provision of activities to match children's preferred learning styles.

Using this book

The units of work

This book provides 100 literacy hours for Year 5 based on the National Literacy Strategy Medium-Term Plans, which either form a core scheme of work or can be used to supplement your existing planning. This core should be extended in several ways. For example:

● Repeating the sequence of lessons, but with different texts, for example the activities, Term 1, Unit 3, Aspects of narrative, could usefully be followed by a classic text on the 'island' theme, for example *Treasure Island*.

● Adding additional texts, for example, Term 1, Unit 4, Poetry, is based on a small anthology of poetry, which could be usefully doubled in length to exemplify a wider range of verse forms.

● Giving extra time for the drafting and redrafting process. This is essential if it is to be done with the thoroughness recommended in NLS exemplification, for example, Improving Writing: Writing Flier 1.

● It is also well worth allowing more time for final presentation. An example is Term 2, Unit 4, How Things Work, where the unit culminates in a class booklet.

In addition to the above, tried-and-tested resources from previous schemes of work, other publications, or the original 100 Literacy Hours series, can be used to supplement the new materials.

The lesson plans

The lesson plans should be seen as a source of ideas, not as a straitjacket, and should therefore be used flexibly. Most lessons plans can easily be adapted for rotational use by rotating the independent and guided activities. The number of guided activities that are possible in one week will depend on the number of available adults. When planning rotation, it is important to ensure that all children experience the key activities throughout the week. If following the linear model, guided activities will usually need to involve a guided version of the independent activity, otherwise children may miss out on key experiences.

INTRODUCTION

Organisation of teaching units

Each term is divided into teaching units comprising between five and ten hours. Each of the units cluster the NLS text-, sentence- and word-level objectives. The units are organised as follows:

Unit overview

Introduction
Overview of each unit including ideas for extending units.

Organisation grid
Outlines the key activities for each lesson.

Key assessment opportunities
A bulleted list of key assessment opportunities. These will help you to plan assessment opportunities throughout each unit.

Unit lesson plans

Each unit of lesson plans is written with the following headings:

Objectives
NLS objectives including Speaking and listening emphases.

What you need
Provides a list of resources required for each lesson.

Shared work
Sets out the shared text-, sentence- and word-level work in each lesson. Some of these objectives are taught discretely, while others are integrated into the theme of the unit as the NLS recommends.

Guided work and Independent work
Every unit contains at least two suggestions for guided work to be used if the lessons plans are reorganised on a rotational basis. The lessons also include ideas for independent group, paired or individual activities. In some units, you may wish to re-organise these, along with the suggestions for guided work, on a rotational basis, for example, when a group set of books is being shared around the class.

Plenary
Sets out what to do in the whole-class plenary session.

Differentiation
Ideas for supporting more or less able children including ideas for peer and other adult support.

Links to the NLS Medium-term plans

The units provide clear links to the requirements of the NLS *Medium-Term Plans.* Genres are matched exactly with appropriate texts for the age group and the range of objectives covered, as shown on the grid for each term. Some of the word- and sentence-level objectives identified in the *Medium-Term Plans* have been relocated from the specified units to meet the needs of specific texts and the running order of the selected units.

Differentiation

In every lesson plan, suggestions for supporting the less able and stretching the more able are given. However, it is important to use these advisedly as a child may be 'less able' in some aspects of literacy, but 'more able' in others. These suggestions should be applied when appropriate to the individual child and not be automatically given to a predetermined group. Other important considerations are children's different learning styles, and the concept of 'multiple intelligences'. Children also need to experience working individually, in pairs, and in a range of larger groups, organised in different ways to meet different educational objectives. The number of groups will depend on class size, spread of ability and learning style. Try to ensure a balance of gender and personality type in each group, and don't hesitate to separate children who cannot work well together.

Assessment

Each unit includes a list of bullet points to help with the children's ongoing assessment. It is important to note that, these are not intended to replace National Curriculum assessment, but represent the 'bottom line' that all the children should have achieved by the end of the unit. If a number of children have failed to achieve satisfactory standards in any of the bulleted areas, then the unit may need to be revisited (with different resources).

Using the photocopiable resources

Where there is instruction to copy material from copyright texts, it is important that you ensure this is done within the limits of the copying licence of your school. If the children are using their own exercise books or paper for their answers, then all of the photocopiable resources are available for reuse.

Usually, the best way to share a resource with the class is to make a display version for an overhead projector or data projector. However, try to avoid this becoming routine. An effective alternative is to sit with the children in a circle and work together with a hard copy of the text, so that, where possible the children can engage with actual books.

Interactive whiteboard use

Permission is granted for those pages marked as photocopiable to be used in this way. Where third party material is used, permission for interactive whiteboard use must be obtained from the copyright holder or their licensor. This information can be found at the front of the book in the acknowledgements section.

Annotations

The methodology of analysing texts by annotation is used in this book. Annotations to texts are given in one margin only, without lines pointing to the textual features they describe. In this manner, the resource can be used both as an exemplar of annotations and as a blank resource on its own.

● To make blank resources, cover or fold back the annotations when photocopying. The annotations can be used in several ways:

● Write them 'live' on an enlarged version of the blank resource, adding lines from notes to text as appropriate, to demonstrate how to annotate a text.

● Read a text with the annotations covered, discuss key points, then reveal the annotations.

● Annotate the first part of a text for demonstration purposes then ask the children to complete the annotations for the rest of the text in the independent session.

● In an independent reading session, give the children a jumbled up version of the annotations and ask them to link them to the appropriate text features.

● In a plenary session, display the text and notes together at the same time and ask the children to add lines from notes to text as each point is raised in discussion.

Speaking and listening

When speaking and listening is one of the main focuses of the lessons, links are made to the Primary National Strategy's *Speaking, Listening and Learning* (DfES, 2003), and to the speaking and listening emphases within the *Medium-Term Planner*. These links are also highlighted in the objectives grid through the use of a logo ⌐.

Children will use speaking and listening as a process skill in every lesson. To encourage this, particular emphasis is given to children working with 'talk partners'. When a larger group is needed, 'talk partners' can join into fours. Groups of this size are ideal for discussion and collaborative work as they provide a range of opinion and yet are not too large to make full participation difficult. It is important to vary group organisation so that children experience working with different partners with different approaches or abilities.

Creativity

Recent reports have emphasised the importance of creativity, and creativity is embedded within many of the lessons this book. Creativity can also be encouraged by using some of the following ideas:
● Children as Real Writers - encourage children to see themselves as real writers writing for real purposes. This means giving them a strong sense of audience and purpose, using redrafting techniques and finding a way of 'publishing' completed work.
● Writing Journals - encourage the children to write something in their journal every day. This can be anything they like - diary entry, story, poem, exploration of a problem, and so on. This is the one place where grammar, and punctuation do not matter. The aim is to develop writing fluency, such as, a free flow between thought and written page.
● First-Hand Experiences - many NLS writing tasks are responses to texts. Balance this by using stimulating 'real-life' starting points such as visits, visitors, artefacts, and so on.
● Experimentation - encourage the children to play with ideas, and explore alternatives. Positively encourage them to suggest alternative tasks.
● Writing Materials - provide inspiring media such as paper in various colours and sizes; a variety of pens and pencils (for example, felt-tipped pens, calligraphic pens); rulers; scissors; glue; DTP and presentation software; a clip art library; a colour printer.

Learning styles

Researchers have identified three different learning styles: auditory, kinaesthetic and visual. Most children will use a mixture of all three styles, but in some children, one style will predominate. Many lessons in this book offer specific opportunities for different learning styles.

Media and ICT

There have been major advances in media and ICT. We need to give more emphasis to media education and ICT in the primary classroom. This can be done by showing film versions of books and documentaries on non-fiction topics, and by ensuring that, every time writing takes place, at least one group is writing on a word-processor and that children take it in turns to do their research via the Internet.

Medium-term planner	All New 100 Literacy Hours unit	Text level	Sentence level	Word level	No of hours	Text(s)	Links to GfW, S&L	Outcomes
Narrative structure	The Ghostly Wedding	1, 2, 9, 11, 15	5, 6, 7	10	5	'The Ghostly Wedding' by Chris Webster (retelling of 'The Spectre Bridegroom' by Washington Irving)	GfW 34. S&L 42	Dramatic performance of story. Plan and draft of own story
Plays	Trisha turns veggie	5, 9, 15, 18, 20	5, 6, 7	10	5	'Trisha Turns Veggie' by Chris Webster	GfW 36. S&L 42, 51	Personalised playscript. Additional scenes
Aspects of narrative	A class novel	2, 3, 9, 10, 13, 14, 15	1, 2, 4, 7, 8	3, 7	10	*Kensuke's Kingdom* by Michael Morpurgo	GfW 35	Creative responses and interpretations. Own story with similar setting.
Poetry	Poetic forms	1, 7, 8, 16, 17	1, 3, 6	1	5	Haiku, clerihews and limericks; 'Stately Verse' by Anon; 'Cold Morning' by Celia Warren; 'Nessie' by Ted Hughes	GfW 34, 35, 37. S&L 42	Own jokes and word play poems. Own expressive poems. In-depth analysis.
Note-taking and recount	Children's Laureate newsletter	21, 24, 26	3, 4, 6, 8	1	5	Michael Morpurgo's sixth web report as Children's Laureate		Mini-biographies and recounts developed from notes.
Instructions	Fantasmagoria	22, 25	3, 5, 9	6	5	Safety leaflet	GfW 34 S&L 39, 50, 55	Evaluating instructions. Writing and following directions. Group presentation.

Medium-term plan	All New 100 Literacy Hours unit	Text level	Sentence level	Word level	No of hours	Text(s)	Links to GfW, S&L	Outcomes
Traditional stories and fables	Scientific Sleeping Beauty	1, 2, 3, 11, 16, 17	5, 6	3, 5, 9, 12	10	'Amul and The Drum', a tale from India; 'Scientific Sleeping Beauty' by Chris Webster; fables; urban legends	S&L 42, 44	Modern fairy tales, fables and urban legends. Story about modern myth.
Poetry	Narrative poetry	4, 5, 6, 7, 12	4, 6, 10	3, 6, 10, 11	5	'The Mystery of Sir Roger's Tomb' by Chris Webster; extracts from narrative verse	GfW 39. S&L 53, 57	Additional verses. Story adapted from poem. Anthology. Choral reading.
Myths and legends	The Odyssey and King Arthur	1, 2, 3, 8, 11, 14	3, 10	4, 7, 8, 11	10	'The Odyssey' by Chris Webster; 'Morte d'Arthur' by Thomas Malory; 'Idylls of the King' by Tennyson; *Arthur, High King of Britain* by Michael Morpurgo	GfW 35. S&L 48	Additional episodes and updated versions.
Note-taking and explanation texts	How things work	15, 17, 19, 20, 22, 24	2, 3, 6, 8	9	5	'Volcano' by Chris Webster		Class book. Simplified book for younger audience.
Non-chronological report	Ancient Greece	15, 17, 19, 20, 22	3, 8	9	5	'Homeric Greece' by Chris Webster	S&L 53	Class display of double-page spreads.

Medium-term plan	All New 100 Literacy Hours unit	Text level	Sentence level	Word level	No of hours	Text(s)	Links to GfW, S&L	Outcomes
Narrative: empathy/point of view	Customs and cultures	1, 2, 3, 10	3, 4, 5	13	5	'Nyangara, the Fire Python' by Jane Grell; 'The Man in the Moon' by Chris Webster	GfW 42. S&L 46	Presentation and written response to cultural differences in stories. Rewritten story.
Poetry	A poetry performance	4, 5, 6, 11		5, 9, 12	5	'Fairground' by Campbell Perry; 'Old Mother Laidinwool' by Rudyard Kipling; extracts from dialect poems; 'Gran Can You Rap?' by Jack Ousbey	S&L 40, 44, 60.	Performance of poetry. Additional verses.
Narrative: author style	A classic novel	6, 7, 8, 19	2, 7	5, 8, 9, 11	5	*The Secret Garden* by Frances Hodgson Burnett	GfW 35	Reading journal. Discursive essay.
Persuasion 1	Stop animal testing!	14, 15, 16, 19	2, 7		5	Mock leaflet from anti-vivisection campaign group	GfW 35, 43. S&L 50, 55	Debate. Magazine article.
Persuasion 2	Wind farm simulation	12, 13, 14, 16, 17, 19	6	12	5	Formal letter	S&L 52, 54–56	Letter of complaint. Role-play debate.
Persuasion 3	Naughty or nice?	13, 14, 15, 18	2, 6, 7	2	5	'Food fascists ban 'naughty' foods' by Chris Webster	GfW 43	Balanced newsletter article. Persuasive web page or poster.

UNIT 1

Narrative structure

This unit is based on a simplified version of *The Spectre Bridegroom* by Washington Irving (1783-1859). A 'box' method is used to explore narrative structure and provide opportunities for children to evaluate and experiment with different beginnings, endings and ways of developing the story. Hour 5 introduces a writing task that will require additional time to finish, edit and present. Hour 1 links to Unit 34 in *Grammar for Writing*.

Hour	Shared text-level work	Shared word-/ sentence-level work	Guided reading/ writing	Independent work	Plenary
1 The basic story	Reading *The Ghostly Wedding*, focusing on genre features.	Noting how punctuation helps reader.	Re-reading story and discussing plot.	Annotating text for genre and structure features.	Reiterating genre features; suggesting subtitles for different parts.
2 Beginnings	Comparing other possible story openings.	Examining dialogue punctuation.	Re-reading to include new beginnings.	Trying out new beginnings – agreeing as a group; drafting own beginnings.	Discussing choices of openings. Sharing first drafts.
3 Endings	Comparing possible endings.	Discussing direct and indirect speech.	Playing a game around reported speech; turning direct speech to indirect.	Trying out new endings; drafting own endings.	Discussing choices of endings. Sharing first drafts.
4 Dramatic development	Re-reading the story with new beginning and ending.		Discussing and annotating story to develop it for performance; improvising and taking notes for improvement.	Discussing and annotating story to develop it for performance; improvising and taking notes for improvement.	Acting the story, with comments.
5 A final version	Looking at different story structures.	Using synonyms of said in dialogue.	Looking at features of good dialogue.	Planning and drafting stories, making use of drama work.	Sharing plans and work so far.

Key assessment opportunities
● Can the children plan and structure stories?
● Can they write stories with interesting beginnings and satisfying endings?
● Do they write varied dialogue with correct layout and punctuation?

The basic story

Objectives

NLS
T2: To compare the structure of different stories, to discover how they differ in pace, build-up, sequence, complication and resolution.
S6: To understand the need for punctuation as an aid to the reader.

What you need

- Photocopiable page 17 (with annotations removed)
- box 2 from photocopiable page 17 with all punctuation, capitalisation and layout features removed.

Shared text-level work

- Explain to the children that they are going to read a story called *The Ghostly Wedding*. Ask them what kind of story the title leads them to expect.
- Display photocopiable page 17 and read the story aloud to the children. Tell the children that although it is a modern version, the story is written in the style of a traditional story or folk tale. Explain that it has been boxed here to show the story structure. Ask the children: How is the style of this story different from a modern story? (Traditional characters and setting, simple narrative style with little description and dialogue.)
- After reading, ask the children if they enjoyed the story and if they have any ideas about what will happen next.
- Now go through the text in detail and demonstrate how to write brief notes in the margins (based on the full version of photocopiable page 17). Focus on the traditional tale features and the plot structure. Point out other features, such as vocabulary if appropriate, but keep the children's attention on the main focus of genre and structure.
- Building on this discussion, write class-inspired versions of the following points on the board:

> - Traditional opening
> - Not much description of characters or settings
> - Not much dialogue
> - Structure – beginning, build-up, complication, resolution (we don't know this yet).

Shared sentence-level work

- Ask the children how punctuation helps the reader. Demonstrate the problem by displaying the amended box 2. Work together to replace the punctuation.

Guided and independent work

- For a guided reading activity re-read the story with a group, focusing on further understanding of the story and how the plot is developing. ● Discuss structure, pace, clues that all is not well, what might happen next.
- Ask the children to independently work in pairs to produce their own annotated version of the text, focusing on two things: features of traditional story style and the structure of the plot.

Plenary

- Display photocopiable page 17 and restate the key features of traditional story style.
- Recap on the narrative structure by asking the children to identify the parts of the story in each box (beginning, build-up, complication) and to suggest a subtitle for each box, such as *Leonora's arranged marriage, The wedding, Henri mysteriously disappears*.

Differentiation

Less able
- Ask children to highlight punctuation in the text using different colours, for example red for full stops, orange for commas, green for speech marks.

More able
- Encourage children to read *The Spectre Bridegroom*, which contains more challenging vocabulary.

Beginnings

Objectives

NLS
T1: To analyse the features of a good opening and compare a number of story openings.
T11: To experiment with alternative ways of opening a story using, eg description, action or dialogue.
S5: To understand the difference between direct and reported speech.
S7: To understand how dialogue is set out, eg on separate lines for alternate speakers in narrative, and the positioning of commas before speech marks.

What you need

● Photocopiable pages 17 and 18
● box 1 from photocopiable page 18 with punctuation and line indents removed.

Differentiation

Less able
● Ask children to act out their own beginning to the story, and then begin writing it.

More able
● Ask them to write two different types of beginning to the story.

Shared text-level work

● Tell the children that they are going to compare a number of alternative story beginnings for *The Ghostly Wedding*.
● Display photocopiable page 18. Read the three beginnings and ask the children to match the beginnings to these headings: first person, description of a place, dialogue.
● Ask the children if they can think of other story openings. (Perhaps a scene of dramatic action, detailed description of a character, or an exciting scene from the middle of the plot, followed by a flashback.) Look at the class novel or another story the children are reading for examples.
● Return to the shared text and talk about the features of each type of beginning. Annotate as appropriate.
● Ask the children to work in pairs to discuss the three openings. Include the following questions, allowing about one minute for each:

● Which beginning tells us most about what Leonora is feeling?
● Which beginning sets the scene most effectively?
● Which beginning fits best with traditional story features?
● Which beginning to you like best and why?

Shared sentence-level work

● Using box 1 as an example, show how dialogue is set out, for example, on separate lines for alternate speakers, and the positioning of commas before speech marks.
● Then display the amended version and work with the children to add the correct punctuation and layout features.

Guided and independent work

● Play a simple game to help a group of children to understand indirect speech. Ask Child 1 to make a simple statement, such as *It's raining*. Child 2 then tells Child 3 what was said: *Sarah said that it's raining*. Pass several statements around and discuss how the sentences change. Turn any passage of direct speech from the story into indirect speech.
● Ask some of the children to work in pairs and cut out the three beginnings. Place each in turn at the beginning of the story, and read the story to see how it sounds. Ask them to discuss which beginning they prefer and why.
● Encourage the children to come to an agreed decision for discussion in the plenary. Building on their ideas, ask them to begin writing a first draft of their own beginning for this story.

Plenary

● Ask the children which beginning they chose and why they thought it was the most effective.
● Share the first drafts of their own ideas for beginnings.

UNIT 1 HOUR 3 ▄ **Narrative structure**

Endings

Objectives

NLS
T2: To compare the structure of different stories to, discover how they differ in pace, build-up, sequence, complication and resolution.

What you need
● Photocopiable page 19
● children's copies of photocopiable pages 17 from Hour 1 and 18 from Hour 2.

Shared text-level work
● Tell the children that now they are going to compare a number of different story endings for *The Ghostly Wedding*.
● Explain that many types of ending are possible and that they will focus on just three in this lesson. List the following types on the board and give a brief explanation:

● Humorous – the 'serious' problem turns out to be something trivial and funny.
● Explanation – a mystery is explained.
● Twist-in-the tale – an unexpected ending that makes the reader look back on the story in a different way.

● Read photocopiable page 19 and ask the children to match the texts to the three types of ending.
● Discuss the features of each type and annotate the texts as appropriate.
● Ask the children: Can you think of any other type of story ending? Jot down any good suggestions that they make, such as anti-climax, achieving a goal, back to normality, happy-ever-after, moral (like a fable or a fairy tale by Charles Perrault).

Shared sentence-level work
● Re-read box 2 and discuss the difference between direct and indirect speech. In indirect (or reported) speech, we report what was said but don't use the exact words of the speaker. Speech marks are not used, and typically, we change pronouns and tenses. It is often indicated by *said that*.
● Suggest that the best way to get it right is to imagine that you are explaining what someone else said.

Guided and independent work
● Organise the children into the same pairs as Hour 2. Ask them to cut out the three endings, place each in turn at the end of the story, and read the whole story to see how it sounds.
● Ask them to discuss and agree on which ending they prefer and why.
● Then ask the children to think of another explanation of why Henri disappeared and write a story ending (see the different types of ending above).
● If children are stuck for an idea, suggest they try an anti-climax ending in which Henri has gone out for a very ordinary reason.
● Encourage the children to try out some indirect speech in their endings.

Differentiation

Less able
● Support the children to speak clearly in sentences by elaborating their words or phrases and by modelling complete sentences.

More able
● Encourage the children to use a greater range of vocabulary.

Plenary
● Ask children which ending they chose and why they thought it was the most effective.
● Share some examples of their own endings.

Dramatic development

Shared text-level work

● Display photocopiable page 17 and re-read the complete story of *The Ghostly Wedding*, with a beginning and ending agreed on by the children. Discuss how well their choices fit.
● Explain to the children that they are now going to develop the story by bringing it to life with drama. One member of the group will take notes that can be used later when they convert their scenes into writing.

Guided and independent work

● Organise the children into groups of five, including a more able child in each group as the note-taker.
● Then meet with all the note-takers and explain that their task is to watch for true-to-life actions and dialogue and note down good examples. Emphasise that they should not try to note everything but concentrate on the best examples with the purpose of converting physical drama to written story.
● Allow the actors to have a couple of rehearsals (at which the note-taker can make comments) before the note-taker begins noting down.
● Ask the children to choose one part of the story: beginning, build-up, complication or resolution, and to develop it through drama. Explain that, they can invent minor characters and add more action and dialogue.
● Tell the groups to agree on a part for each group member. Where necessary, make up a new part, such as Leonora's maid, Henri's manservant, a jester, the priest, a tenant farmer and his wife.
● Let the children improvise the scene, making up movements and dialogue as they go along. Explain that, as there is no narrator, they will need to improvise more dialogue than is currently given in order to tell the story without gaps in the audience's understanding.
● Encourage the children to think themselves into their parts, speaking and behaving as the characters would.

Plenary

● Choose one group to act out each part of the story, and ask their note-taker to read out his/her notes, commenting on what could be effective in developing the written story.

A final version

Objectives

NLS
T2: To compare the structure of different stories.
T15: To write new scenes or characters into a story, in the manner of the writer, maintaining consistency of character and style, using paragraphs to organise and develop detail.
W10: To use adverbs to qualify verbs in writing dialogue.

What you need
● Photocopiable page 20
● the children's work from the previous hours.

Shared text-level work
● Explain to children that they are going to write their story with a more developed structure and more detailed narrative, description and dialogue.
● Display photocopiable page 20 and read through the story structure menu, using the questions at the end of each item to involve the children.
● Ask the children which device they find most interesting, and model how to include it in a box plan of the story: a series of boxes showing each section of the story (similar to photocopiable pages 17-19 but containing just a brief note about what happens). Arrows can be added to show features such as flashbacks.

Shared word- and sentence-level work
● Choose a box from the plan that requires dialogue and demonstrate how to write simple dialogue (using *said* only – no synonyms or adverbs).
● Ask the children how the dialogue could be made more interesting, for example, replacing *said* with a synonym such as *shouted*, or adding an adverb: *said angrily*. They can sometimes be combined for maximum effect: *shouted angrily*.
● Revise how the dialogue can be varied by changing direct speech to reported speech. For example, instead of *'Go away,' she said angrily* you could write *She told him angrily to go away*. Conclude that varied dialogue is interesting dialogue.

Guided and independent work
● Ask the children to plan their stories using the box method and their chosen structure.
● The next step is to begin writing the stories. Tell them to:

● Use any existing story boxes, for example, a beginning and ending that they liked or that they wrote in Hours 2 and 3.
● Write new story boxes based on their plan.
● Try to include realistic action, description and dialogue based on ideas from drama.
● Write interesting dialogue.

Differentiation

Less able
● Ask children to add one more problems to the story, or to write the story of Henri's journey using the quest device.

More able
● Encourage children to try complex plot types, such as Y-plot or timeshift (see photocopiable page 20).

Plenary
● Share the box plans and work completed so far, and encourage children to borrow ideas from each other.

The Ghostly Wedding

Many years ago, on one of the summits of the Odenwald, there stood the castle of Baron Landshort. When his daughter Leonora was still a child, the baron had arranged a marriage between her and Henri, the son of Count Altenburg of Bavaria. Soon after Leonora's 18th birthday, the preparations for the wedding began. She watched these preparations with dismay. She had never seen Henri and was afraid that he might be ugly or have an unpleasant personality – or both! But she needn't have worried. When Henri arrived, she saw to her relief that he was handsome and noble – and just as important, he seemed to like her too and told her that she was very beautiful.

Traditional opening

Traditional setting – a castle

Traditional characters – a baron, a count

Traditional situation – an arranged marriage

Not much description

Indirect speech

Henri and his followers, rested for a while, then they all set off in procession to Landshort Church for the wedding ceremony. Afterwards, a great feast was held in the castle. All the baron's relatives and invited guests sat at the high table, while the villagers were entertained at the tables below. Leonora had never felt so happy, but she noticed that Henri seemed sad. "What is wrong?" she whispered. "Are you sorry you married me?"

"I love you with all my heart – but there is a problem, though I cannot explain it just yet."

Indentation to mark new paragraph

Not much description of Henri

Longest passage of dialogue

A hint of the problem

The clock chimed midnight and the candles guttered in their sockets. Henri and Leonora climbed the spiral staircase to their new bedchamber. Henri looked sadder than ever, and without taking off his clothes, threw himself down on the bed. In a moment he was sound asleep. Leonora lay down beside him, trying to cheer herself up by remembering Henri's words of love. It had been a long and tiring day, and soon she too fell asleep.

When she awoke the next morning, the place beside her was empty. She called his name and sent the servants to search the castle and the grounds but they could not find him anywhere. Henri had mysteriously disappeared.

More hints about the problem

The problem is now serious – though we still don't know what it is

What has happened to Henri?

TERM 1

Beginnings

■ Match these beginnings to the following types: first person, description, dialogue.

"But, father, what if I don't like Henri?" said Leonora, who was sitting at the window seat.

"You used to like him when you were children," laughed the baron.

"That was ages ago. I can hardly remember him!"

"Only four years. That was when Henri's father and I arranged the marriage. It will be a good match. Henri's father, is one of the richest men in Bavaria."

"But...but...what if I don't like him," repeated Leonora with tears in her eyes.

Baron Landshort, seeing how upset she was, said, "You have my word, that if you don't like Henri, the marriage will be cancelled."

Dialogue

Leonora's words catch reader's attention

Reporting clause

New speaker, new indented line

No need for reporting clause – reader knows the order in which the characters are speaking

Descriptive phrase added to reporting clause

First-person point of view

'My' and 'I' establish the first person

Leonora's Diary

Today is my 18th birthday. It should have been a happy day, but it wasn't. My father told me that, now I am of age, I must marry. But how can I marry someone I don't know? Yes, I did meet him once when I was 14, but I can't remember what he looks like. Father tells me that it is my duty to marry Henri. He says it is a good match because Henri's father, is one of the richest men in Bavaria. Father says he won't force me to marry Henri if I don't like him, but – poor father – how can I let him down! Everything is ready: my bridal gown, the church and priest are booked, and the feast is being prepared. Everything is ready – except me!

Tell us about Leonora's thoughts and feelings

Necessary story information

More about how she feels

Description

Helps reader to imagine scene

Adjectives to describe scene

Nothing can be more picturesque or solitary than Baron Landshort's castle. It stands on a low hill in the forest. The old road passes in front of its drawbridge and crosses the stream on a steep stone bridge. The moat is stocked with perch and covered with water lilies and beautiful swans. The castle has many windows, towers and a gothic chapel. As I have said, this is a very lonely place. From the hall door towards the road, the forest extends fifteen miles to the right and twelve to the left. The nearest village, Landshort is about five miles away.

Vivid description built up by details

Describes the isolation – necessary element of the story

Endings

⬛ Match these endings to the following types: humour, explanation, twist-in-the-tale.

Henri was woken by the daylight shining in his eyes. It came from a hole in the roof where the tiles had fallen away. He sat up in bed and looked around. The bed was a rotting frame covered with rags, the walls of the room were weathered and covered with ivy. He got up and searched the castle – it had long been a ruin. Stumbling through the gatehouse he saw a cart passing on the old road. "The people who lived here – where are they?"

The carter looked at him with surprise. "All dead – years ago. Nothing there but ghosts now!"

So that was the explanation, thought Henri with a shudder. He had felt that something was wrong at the feast – and it was – he had married a ghost!

Twist-in-the-tale
Reader is surprised by this description – what has happened?

Dialogue

This is the twist – reader thought Henri was going to be the ghost

Explanation

At length she gave up the search and lay on her bed. Why had he left her? Had she done something wrong, did he not love her – or was it something to do with his secret problem? Suddenly, someone lifted her from her pillow and wiped away her tears – it was Henri. "Oh Henri – where have you been?" sobbed Leonora.
"My love, did you not get the message I left on your pillow?" replied Henri. "It explained that, just before the wedding, I heard the news that my father had died. It upset me, but I did not want to tell you and spoil your happiness. I left at daybreak to make the funeral arrangements."
"Oh Henri," sighed Leonora, "how foolish I have been!"

Problem of previous paragraph followed by shock – Henri is dead – and horror – Leonora thinks she has married a ghost

Explanation given in indirect speech
Switch back to direct speech

Humorous
After last paragraph reader expects a serious problem –groaning noise builds up suspense

Dialogue

Leonora threw herself on her bed and lay there sobbing, but even the most miserable of people must answer the call of nature. Leonora rose from the bed and made her way to the little closet at the top of the tower. As she approached the door she became aware of a groaning noise. At first she was frightened, but she plucked up her courage and said timidly: "Henri? Is that you?"

"Yes, my love, it is me," said Henri. "I have been here most of the night. I got indigestion at the feast but didn't want to tell you in case it spoilt your happiness, and now I've got a bad dose of diarrhoea."

Problem turns out to be nothing more than diarrhoea!

Story structure menu

Circular
Develop the story so it ends where it started. For example, Henri turns out to be an impostor who has kidnapped the real Henri. The impostor is found out and punished, and Henri is freed. The story ends where it began with Leonora waiting to meet the real Henri. What other circular plots can you think of?

Flashback
Begin the story at an exciting point in the middle and use a flashback to bring the reader up to date with earlier events. For example, at the wedding feast, Leonora could tell Henri about her feelings when she was waiting for him to arrive. Can you think of another example?

Quest
A quest is a series of adventures on a journey with an important goal. Tell the story from Henri's point of view and describe his adventures on the way to Landshort. Perhaps he gets lost in a forest or is attacked by robbers. What other adventures could he have?

Timeshift
Find a way of shifting between present and past. For example, a visitor to Landshort castle in the 21st century could find Leonora's diary. She, also, is waiting for her boyfriend to arrive. Develop the plot by shifting from one time to another. Is there a way to link them at the end?

Whodunnit?
Develop the story into a crime story. For example, Baron Landshort calls in an officer to investigate Henri's disappearance. The officer looks at evidence and questions suspects. Can you include a 'red herring' – something that draws the reader's attention away from the real villain?

Y-plot
In the first half of the story the narrative shifts between two people: Henri, who loves Leonara and wants to marry her, and Malcolm, who intends to stop Henri, and marry Leonora for her father's money. The story comes together when they meet. What will happen when they do?

SCHOLASTIC

UNIT 2

Plays

This unit explores a short playscript about an event in the lives of the Trubbs, a typical modern family with two children: Trevor, 10, and Trisha, 12. The text is used as the starting point for examining playscript conventions, experimenting with drama performances, consolidating understanding of direct and indirect speech, and giving children the opportunity to write their own playscripts. The daily activities build towards the collaborative writing of a Trubb family soap opera in Hour 5. Hours 1 and 2 link with Unit 36 in *Grammar for Writing*.

Hour	Shared text-level work	Shared word-/ sentence-level work	Guided reading/ writing	Independent work	Plenary
1 Trisha turns veggie	Reading playscript; revising playscript conventions.	Revising different ways to present dialogue.	Annotating script for performance.	Discussing and rehearsing performance.	Watching and evaluating performances.
2 Direct to indirect	Watching performance; improvising different scene, using indirect speech.		Further annotating and rehearsing performance.	Using role-play to write indirect speech.	Role-playing several situations; noting indirect speech.
3 Trouble at the Trubbs'	Considering problems for characters in script; introducing improvisation.	Revising adverbs, applying them to dialogue.	Developing improvisations.	Discussing scenes, allocating roles and improvising.	Watching and evaluating improvisations.
4 Writing a playscript	Examining layout conventions of playscripts.	Discussing uses of punctuation in scripts.	Writing script from improvisation in previous hour.	Writing script from improvisation in previous hour, including proper layout.	Reading children's scripts, checking layout; evaluating performances.
5 Trubb family soap opera	Discussing methods for adapting the play as a TV soap opera.		Putting scenes from the week into logical order.	Reworking scenes for TV adaptation.	Watching soap opera adaptations.

Key assessment opportunities
● Can the children annotate a playscript for performance?
● Can they improvise a dramatic scene?
● Can they collaborate on writing a playscript?
● Have they evaluated dramatic performances?

Trisha turns veggie

Objectives

NLS

T5: To understand dramatic conventions including: the conventions of scripting, how character can be communicated in words and gesture.

T19: To annotate a section of playscript as a preparation for performance, taking into account pace, movement, gesture and delivery of lines and the needs of the audience.

S7: To understand how dialogue is set out.

S&L

51 Drama: To perform a scripted scene making use of dramatic conventions.

What you need

● Photocopiable pages 27 and 28.

Shared text-level work

● Explain to the children that they are going to perform a playscript in groups, but the first step is to revise playscript and drama conventions.

● Display photocopiable pages 27 and 28 and pick out typical playscript features, for example, stage directions in the present tense and character names on the left-hand side of the page.

● Read the script through once. Next, go around the class to practise reading aloud, emphasising realistic intonation and expression as indicated by scene development, characterisation and stage directions.

● Briefly discuss the issues raised. Is vegetarianism a good thing? Do children have the right to make their own choices about whether they become vegetarians, or about other issues?

Shared sentence-level work

● To recap on ways of presenting dialogue in other text forms, demonstrate how the first seven lines of the script can be turned into story dialogue by turning stage directions into past tense descriptions, setting out the dialogue on separate indented lines for alternate speakers, and adding reporting clauses (he said and so on). For example:

> Trish rushed in from school, dumped her school bag and popped her head round the kitchen door. 'Hi, Mum, what's for tea?' she said breathlessly.
> 'Sausage and chips,' replied Mum.
> Trish pulled a face. 'But Mum! I'm a vegetarian!'
> 'I thought that was just a passing fad,' laughed Mum.

Guided and independent work

● Help a group to re-read the script and annotate it for performance. Ask questions like: How would the character say this line? What movements or gestures would the character make here? How can we annotate that?

● Organise the children into groups of four to act out the play. Tell them to begin with reading, discussing and annotating the playscript before trying to act it. Give the following advice:

> ● Remember the needs of the audience. Plan your moves so that the actors' faces can be seen most of the time.
> ● Give careful thought to the pace of speaking.
> ● Use movement and gestures suited to what you are saying.
> ● Deliver lines clearly and audibly. Whispers must be loud enough to be heard!

Differentiation

Less able

● Help the children with difficult vocabulary and idioms.

More able

● Encourage the children to try to learn their parts and perform as much as possible without the script.

Plenary

● Choose one or two groups to perform the play (other groups will get a chance later in the week).

● Ask the audience to evaluate the performance using the criteria outlined in the independent session.

Direct to indirect

Objectives

NLS
T15: To write new scenes or characters into a story.
S5: To understand the difference between direct and reported speech through: transforming direct into reported speech and vice versa, noting changes in punctuation and words that have to be changed or added.

What you need
● Children's annotated copies of photocopiable pages 27 and 28.

Shared text- and sentence-level work

● Ask another group of children to perform 'Trisha turns veggie' to the rest of the class.
● Intervene if necessary to give advice on performance and demonstrate how to use movement and gesture, appropriate intonation and so on.
● After the performance, highlight particularly good points to the rest of the class.
● Now ask the child who played Trisha to improvise, explaining to a school friend what happened at home the previous evening, for example, *I told Mum that I was a vegetarian and that I'd been a vegetarian for three days...*
● Write some good examples of the child's use of indirect speech on the board and revise the conventions from Unit 1, Hour 3.

Guided and independent work

● Encourage the children to experiment, rehearse and discuss their adaptations of the play.
● Focus on auditory learning by asking the children to choose one of the situations listed below.
● Tell the children first to role-play the situation.
● Ask the children to imagine that they are telling a person who wasn't there what happened (using indirect speech).
● Finally write down the indirect speech:

● Trisha tells a friend what happened at home the previous evening.
● Trevor tells a friend about the moment he decided to become a vegetarian.
● Mum tells a counsellor about the plan she explained to her husband.
● Dad tells another driver about the problems he is having with his kids.

Plenary

● Choose one or two pairs of children to repeat their role-play and give their report of indirect speech on each of the situations considered in independent work.

Differentiation

Less able
● Make sure children understand direct speech before moving on to indirect speech.
● Give extra time for preparatory role-play.

More able
● Ask children to write a story version of the situation which used direct and indirect speech.

UNIT 2 HOUR 3 📄 Plays

Objectives

NLS
T5: To understand dramatic conventions including: the conventions of scripting, how character can be communicated in words and gesture.
W10: To use adverbs to qualify verbs in writing dialogue.

S&L
42 Drama: To develop scripts based on improvisation.

What you need
● Photocopiable page 29, plus copies cut into cards.

Trouble at the Trubbs'

Shared text-level work
● Display photocopiable page 29 and explain to the children that they are going to use the cards as a basis for role-playing problems in the Trubb family.
● Read card 1 and ask the children what they think would happen. How would Dad react? How would Trisha explain herself? What could she suggest to improve the situation? Note some of the children's ideas on the board.
● Ask the children how they might convert their ideas into dialogue. Encourage them to suggest a few lines. Again, note these on the board.
● Explain or revise the term improvisation: making up dialogue and movement as you go along, interacting with other characters.
● Work with an able child or ask two more able children to demonstrate improvisation using card 1.
● Emphasise that improvisation is a performance and basic drama rules still apply (see Hour 1).

Shared word-level work
● Revise the term adverb by reminding the children of the definition: adverbs give extra meaning to a verb, an adjective, another adverb or a whole sentence.
● Reinforce the concept by asking children to think about how they are going to say their lines during their improvised conversation, for example, *timidly, gruffly, excitedly*.
● Ask the children to suggest more speech adverbs and list them on the board.

Guided and independent work
● Organise the children into groups of four and ask one child from each group to pick a card at random.
● Ask the group to work out an improvised play scene based on the information written on the card.
● Tell the children to discuss the situation as a group and consider what might happen and what might be said, before allocating roles and beginning the role-play.
● Encourage the children to stop as often as they like to talk through the action and perhaps change some lines.
● Ask them to begin developing the improvisation for more formal performance.

Differentiation

Less able
● Give children card 1 to work from as in the shared session.

More able
● Ask children to think of their own idea/problem as the basis of an improvised scene.

Plenary
● Choose one or two groups to perform their improvisations to the rest of the class.
● Encourage the children to improvise further as the performance flows.
● Ask the rest of the class to evaluate the performances on the drama criteria from Hour 1, and on the extent to which the scenes were true to life.

Writing a playscript

Shared text-level work
● Display photocopiable pages 27 and 28 and revise the key layout and text conventions of scripting.
● Model how a script should be written by copying out the first few lines onto the board. The following steps are recommended:

1. Rule a wide margin. Write characters' names in the margin in small caps followed by a colon, for example Dad:.
2. Write stage directions, in the present tense, in brackets with the dialogue.
3. Write dialogue with the usual punctuation but without speech marks.
4. Leave a whole blank line before and after general stage directions.

Shared sentence-level work
● Revise the punctuation that will be needed for the actors.
● Discuss the use of the different punctuation marks on photocopiable pages 27 and 28, in order of appearance, and how they should affect the way an actor says a line or how the actors interact together.
● Discuss less familiar marks, such as an ellipsis to show hesitation or interrupted speech.

Guided and independent work
● Ask the children to work in the same groups as Hour 3 and to work together to write their improvisation as a playscript.
● Give each group a large sheet of paper or OHT to write on which can be displayed in the plenary.
● Remind the children to recall and discuss details of their improvisation as a group. Allocate one scribe if necessary.
● Advise them to use layout conventions and punctuation carefully.

Plenary
● Choose one or two groups to display their scripts and ask the rest of the class to evaluate how well their scripts have been set out and punctuated.
● Ask groups to perform their scripts to the class while the rest of the children evaluate the performance on the criteria from Hour 1: pace, use of movement and gesture, clarity and audibility.
● Consider how realistic and effective are the dialogue and interaction of characters. Does the conversation work well in context with the rest of the play?

Trubb family soap opera

Objectives

NLS

T18: To write own playscript, applying conventions learned from reading; include production notes.

T20: To evaluate the script and the performance for their dramatic interest and impact.

S&L

51 Drama: To perform a scripted scene making use of dramatic conventions.

What you need

● The children's playscripts from Hour 4.

Shared text-level work

● Ask the children what a soap opera is. (An ongoing drama with a large cast of characters, often families; usually set in and around their homes and workplaces; lots of intrigue, gossip and gripping events.)

● Do the children watch any television soap operas? (Coronation Street, EastEnders, Neighbours, Emmerdale and so on.) Do they listen to any on the radio, such as The Archers or Silver Street? Spend a few minutes discussing recent storylines and favourite characters.

● Discuss the structure of a typical soap opera episode: several scenes strung together, sometimes at various settings and with various groups of characters, often with a cliffhanger ending.

● Explain to the children that they are going to adapt the ideas they have developed during the week as a Trubb family TV soap.

● Consider the setting, characters and events of 'Trisha turns veggie' and compare them to other soaps.

● Tell the children that for the adaptation they need to make a list of all the scenes written by members of their group, and decide on the best sequence of those scenes as an episode or part of an episode.

● Next, discuss some of the differences between writing a play for the theatre, and drama for television. For example, in the theatre, scenery changes are difficult, so there are fewer scenery changes, longer scenes and simple scenery. For television dramas, scene changes are easy and viewers are used to sequences of short scenes.

Guided and independent work

● Working in the same groups of four, ask the children to rework the playscripts produced earlier in the week so that they form a continuous soap opera containing at least four different scenes.

● Warn them that the all scenes will probably need some changes to make sure that they fit in to the sequence.

● Help the children to put their scenes into an effective sequence. Discuss the most logical order.

● Explain to the children that they can include any material from earlier in the week, as well as adding new material.

Plenary

● Choose one group to perform their soap opera episode to the class and ask the rest of the children to evaluate the performance.

● If possible, arrange for more performances, for example, in assembly.

Differentiation

Less able

● A group should combine two episodes from Trubb family life.

More able

● Ask the children to include brief production notes, including guidance on scenery, costumes, lighting and music.

Trisha turns veggie

The Trubbs are a 'typical' family. Dad is a long-distance lorry driver and Mum works part-time in a call centre, but their hardest job is coping with their terrible twosome: Trevor, 10, and Trisha, 12.

TRISH: (*rushing in from school*) Hi, Mum, what's for dinner?

MUM: Sausage and chips.

TRISH: But Mum! I'm a vegetarian!

MUM: I thought that was just a passing fad.

TRISH: No, it's not. I've been a vegetarian for three days now!

MUM: Well, what are you allowed to eat?

TRISH: Lots of things: nuts, seeds, vegetables, beans, fruit... er... nuts...

TREV: (*rushing in from school*) Nuts? I like nuts. Where are they?

TRISH: There're no nuts, stupid. I was just telling Mum that I don't want sausages 'cause I'm a vegetarian.

TREV: (*gobsmacked*) A vegetarian! Well, it's you that's nuts! Mum, can I have Trisha's sausages?

MUM: (*sighing*) I suppose so.

TRISH: What am I going to have?

MUM: Sausage and chips – without the sausage.

TRISH: What! I'll starve!

TREV: Serves you right!

TRISH: Shut up you! At least I'm trying to do something for the planet.

TREV: Like what?

TRISH: Like preserving animal life.

TREV: I didn't know that pigs and cows were dying out.

TRISH: They might if we keep eating them!

TREV: Well, if that's what you think, why are you wearing leather shoes?

TRISH: I'll wear trainers tomorrow.

TREV: Trainers are against school rules.

MUM: Stop arguing, you two. Trish, I'll do some beans as well – will that be OK?

TRISH: Thanks Mum.

Soon after, the family are sitting round the dining table.

TREV: (*eating his sausage with a disgusting noise in the hope of winding Trisha up*) Mmm, this sausage is delicious!

TRISH: (*winces, then thinks of a way to get her own back*) Do you know how

TERM 1

they make sausages? Only about half is meat, the rest is offal.

TREV: (*still munching exaggeratedly*) What's offal?

TRISH: Leftover bits, heart, lungs... (*Trev stops in mid munch*) ...eyeballs, intestines...

TREV: (*speaking through his half-munched sausage*) Is it true, Mum?

MUM: Yes, in a way, but...

TREV: (*spitting out his sausage*) I think I'll turn vegetarian as well.

MUM: Trish! Now look what you've done.

At that moment, DAD walks in.

DAD: Sorry I'm late, Love; contraflow on the M25... now, what's all this arguing about?

TRISH & TREV: (*together*) We've turned vegetarian.

DAD: Oh no you haven't! I'm not going to put up with any 'isms' in this house - especially vegetarianism!

TRISH & TREV: Why not?

DAD: Because it'll ruin your health.

MUM: Not to mention the fact that you'd have me running round to all sorts of special shops paying fancy prices for things like quorn and pulses and what-have-you.

TRISH: Dad, the point is that you can be a vegetarian and perfectly healthy.

DAD: No, the point is that, until you're 18, I'm responsible for you, and I want you eating a proper balanced diet.

TRISH: That's not fair – children have rights too.

DAD: Yes, the right to a good hiding!

TRISHA slams down her knife and fork and storms off to her bedroom. TREV, looking regretfully at his unfinished plate of chips, does the same.

MUM: Now look what you've done.

DAD: Well, somebody's got to put their foot down. They're growing kids. They need a mixed diet of meat and vegetables.

MUM: (*looking in an encyclopedia*) T... U...V...Vault...Vega...ah, here it is Vegetarianism (*reads quietly for a moment*). It says here that vitamin B12 deficiency can be a problem for vegetarian children.

DAD: Just as I thought. But don't worry, I'll soon knock some sense into them!

MUM: I've got a better plan. We'll go along with it, but I'll make them really boring meals, and make ours really varied and delicious. They'll soon come round...

Trouble at the Trubbs'

◼ Improvise what happens when:

1. Dad gets this bill in the post: 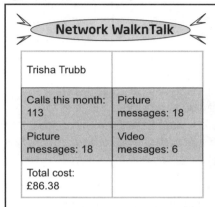	2. Trevor comes home with a bad school report. 
3. Trish is invited to a party and wants to stay out until midnight. 	4. Mum finds this under Trevor's bed. 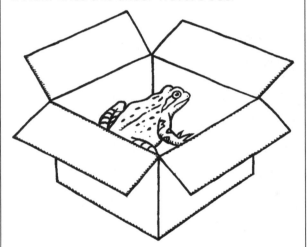
5. Mum decides to make everybody share the household chores. 	6. Dad reads this letter to the family. 

Aspects of narrative

This unit on aspects of narrative should follow the reading of a class novel outside the Literacy Hour, but however you organise it, try to ensure that these lessons are not done in isolation from the complete text. Ideally, all children should have their own copies of the novel. If this is not possible, there should be enough for one group and the week's activities can be organised on a rotational basis. The unit is based on *Kensuke's Kingdom* by Michael Morpurgo (Egmont), but all the teaching ideas and some of the photocopiable pages can be adapted for use with any book. The first five hours focus on reading and responding to the text and the following five on children writing their own 'island' stories. An ideal follow-up unit would use a similar approach, but be based on a related classic text, such as *Treasure Island*. Hours 5 and 9 link to *Grammar for Writing* Unit 35.

Hour	Shared text-level work	Shared word-/ sentence-level work	Guided reading/ writing	Independent work	Plenary
1 Story cards	Reading and modelling story summaries.	Editing the summary.	Writing summaries of chapter, character or setting.	Writing summaries of chapter, character or setting.	Grouping summaries and putting them in order.
2 Story response cards	Empathising with main character.	Looking at examples of different tenses.	Writing personal responses to summaries from Hour 1.	Writing personal responses to summaries from Hour 1.	Reading response cards; adding them to chart begun in Hour 1.
3 Scene in detail: character	Reading an extract to examine character presentation.	Looking at personal pronouns and point of view.	Reading another extract and exploring characterisation.	Reading another extract and exploring characterisation.	Sharing annotations and discussing different responses.
4 Another scene in detail	Recapping methods of annotation.	Focusing on synonyms; using thesauruses.	Reading an extract to investigate synonyms.	Annotating an extract to evaluate a text.	Presenting extracts to other groups; sharing synonyms found.
5 Creative responses	Considering different ways to develop creative responses to the story.	Revising dialogue conventions.	Writing further dialogue for the book.	Writing a creative response to the book.	Sharing creative responses and testing them out.

UNIT 3

Hour	Shared text-level work	Shared word-/ sentence-level work	Guided reading/ writing	Independent work	Plenary
6 The story island	Reading an extract focusing on setting, recalling details from throughout the book.	Picking out descriptive details.	Finding descriptive words and trying out synonyms.	Using descriptive details to draw a map of the setting.	Discussing different interpretations.
7 Own island	Brainstorming other places to add to the setting.	Re-reading for descriptive phrases; thinking of phrases for new places.	Finding descriptive words and trying out synonyms.	Adding to the maps and writing descriptive captions.	Focusing on descriptive synonyms.
8 Describing the island	Developing island notes to write a description.		Writing descriptions of their islands.	Writing descriptions of their islands and considering events that could happen.	Sharing descriptions, focusing on vivid descriptions and events.
9 Developing a story	Discussing possible story structures.	Considering audience.	Developing description for younger children or teens.	Compiling detailed plan of stories.	Evaluating plans.
10 Writing the story	Revising elements of story structure.	Revising story language.	Writing stories.	Writing stories, using a checklist.	Sharing and evaluating work in progress.

Key assessment opportunities
● Can the children analyse story structure and presentation of characters?
● Have they written a creative response to a story?
● Can they use interesting story structures and create strong characters and believable settings?
● Do they use standard English, spelling and punctuation correctly?

Story cards

Objectives

NLS
T10: To evaluate a book by referring to details and examples in the text.
S1: To investigate word order by examining how far the order of words in sentences can be changed.
S8: To revise and extend work on verbs, focusing on tenses.

What you need
- The class novel
- photocopiable page 42
- postcards or record/index cards
- sugar paper.

Shared text-level work

- Display the first card on photocopiable page 42, explaining that it is a chapter summary short enough to fit on a postcard.
- Read the text and discuss what has been included and what has been left out from the original novel.
- Ask the children what tense the summary is written in. (Story summaries are usually written in the present tense.) Do the same with card 2, explaining that it is a brief character description, and card 3, explaining that it is a brief description of a setting.
- Help the children to see how all three summary texts only include the most important points. For example, in the first text, details of Michael's everyday life are left out.
- Begin modelling the process of writing a chapter summary by asking the children to recall the next chapter of *Kensuke's Kingdom* or your class novel.
- Show the children how you select only the most important points from their suggestions.
- Draft the summary in complete sentences, but don't attempt to link the sentences into a coherent paragraph at this stage.

Shared sentence-level work

- Work with the children to edit the model summary by checking that nothing important is left out, nothing inessential is left in, every sentence makes sense, repetition is avoided by use of pronouns, and phrases and sentences are reordered to achieve a coherent paragraph.
- As a final check, ask one of the children to read the summary aloud while others listen to see if it is clear.

Guided and independent work

- Allocate to each pair of children a particular chapter, character or setting in the book.
- Ask them to make their summaries or brief descriptions first on paper, then, after discussion and redrafting, on cards.
- Explain to the children that the reasons for writing on cards are a) to ensure that the summaries are short, and b) so that the summaries can later be placed on a poster.
- In your allocation, try to ensure that all of the main events, characters and settings are covered.
- When the display is complete, arrange for the children to look at the display in groups.

Plenary

- Set up a large poster with these column headings: Story cards: characters and settings; Story cards: chapters; Story response cards.
- Help the children to sort the cards first so that characters and settings are in order of appearance, and chapters are in chronological sequence.
- Then ask all of the children to paste or pin their cards to the poster.

Differentiation

Less able
- Ask the children to tell you about the chapter in their own words before they begin writing.

More able
- Allocate cards for minor characters. These are more challenging as information usually has to be found in several places in the book.

Story response cards

Objectives

NLS
T13: To record their ideas, reflections and predictions about a book.
S1: To investigate word order by examining how fapPostcards or record/index cards.

What you need

● The class novel
● photocopiable page 42
● the children's story cards from Hour 1
● postcards or record/index cards.

Shared text-level work

● Display card 1 from photocopiable page 42, keeping the other cards covered at this stage.
● Read the chapter summary on card 1 and ask the children how they would feel if they were in that situation. Would they be excited? Do they think they would be scared at all? How would they feel about spending a long time on a small boat with only family, and a dog, for company?
● After this discussion, reveal and read card 4, which is an example of a personal response to the events summarised in card 1. Compare it with the children's thoughts.

Shared sentence-level work

● Ask the children which tenses are used in the story response card (a range of tenses are used: present, past and conditional). Point out examples, or ask the children to.
● Advise the children not to worry about tenses too much when writing their responses, but to concentrate on expressing what they think and feel. They can identify and discuss tenses afterwards.

Guided and independent work

● Organise the children into the same pairs as Hour 1 and ask them to write their story response cards responding to the chapters, characters or settings that they have already worked on and placed on the poster at the end of Hour 1.
● Remind them that their response is a personal one, and that they should refer to details in the story rather than describe it.
● Where appropriate, encourage the children to discuss responses in their pairs first, before writing their cards individually.

Plenary

● Encourage some of the children to read their responses – choose a variety of responses to maintain a broad coverage of different story elements.
● Compare any different responses to the same characters, events or settings.
● Finally, ask the children to paste their response cards on the class book chart (see Hour 1).

Differentiation

Less able
● Allocate the most exciting/eventful chapters to less able children as these are easier to respond to.

More able
● Encourage children to use the conditional tense, for example, *If I fell in the sea, I would swim to the nearest land.*

Scene in detail: character

Objectives

NLS
T3: To investigate how characters are presented, referring to the text.
S8: To revise and extend work on verbs focusing on person: 1st, 2nd, 3rd. Identify examples from reading.

What you need
● Photocopiable page 43 (if you are using a different book, choose a scene that introduces a major character)
● copies of a similar extract, for example, the description of a different aspect of Kensuke's character.

Shared text-level work
● Display photocopiable page 43. Read the extract to the children, and then, using the prompt as a guide, demonstrate how to pick out the techniques the author has used to present the character.
● Examine the way the character acts and the language he uses. Look at the adjectives and powerful verbs the author uses to describe him and what the character does.
● Work with the children to write annotations in the margins of the text and explain that they will be doing a similar exercise with another extract from the story.

Shared sentence-level work
● Explain that in grammar, a distinction is made between first, second and third person: we use the first person when referring to ourselves (I/we); the second person when addressing the listener or reader (you); and the third person when referring to somebody or something else (he/she/it/they/my friend/the book).
● Discuss how, in stories, the person can help to establish the point of view, that is, from whose perspective the story is told.
● Demonstrate this by asking the children to highlight some of the *I*'s and *he*'s in the extract. Then ask: Whose point of view are we seeing these events from? (Michael's.) Reinforce understanding by asking: How can we tell?
● Discuss which types of text is best suited to which grammatical person. (first person = autobiography, autobiographical novels, and novels which explore in detail the thoughts and feelings of the main character; second person = quite rare, but can be found in adventure game novels; third person = biography, most novels, especially those which are action-based or have a large number of characters.)

Guided and independent work
● Ask the children to work in pairs to read, analyse and annotate the second extract you have chosen in the way that was modelled in whole class work.
● Ask the children to look for features of character presentation.
● It may sometimes be helpful to give the children one or two questions to consider. For example, if they are annotating another extract about Kensuke, they could be asked: What new things do we learn about Kensuke in this extract? Why do you think he seems so different in the two extracts we have read?

Plenary
● Re-read the extract the children have been working on and discuss some of the annotations.
● If you gave any additional questions for the groups, ask them to the whole class and discuss different responses.
● Ask the children: Has anyone's opinion of the character changed after reading the second description?

Differentiation

Less able
● Ask children to concentrate on how characters are presented through dialogue, action and description and to highlight words revealing point of view.

More able
● Ask children to focus on sentence construction: the effect of long and short sentences, simple and complex sentences.

Another scene in detail

Objectives

NLS
T10: To evaluate a book by referring to details and examples in the text.
W7: To explain differences between synonyms.

What you need
● Annotated photocopiable page 43
● five to six key extracts from the novel (a different extract for each group; extracts could focus on characters, settings and/or action)
● thesauruses.

Shared text-level work
● Go through some of the annotations on photocopiable page 43 (or the extract from the class book) compiled in previous lessons, to remind the children of how an extract can be analysed.
● Explain to the children that, they are going to work in groups to analyse and annotate different aspects of the book, including other characters, settings and action scenes.

Shared word-level work
● Revise the term *synonym* with the children: a word that has a meaning similar to another word, such as *wet* and *damp*. Discuss how including well chosen synonyms avoids overuse of a word, adds variety and accuracy.
● Look at a chosen extract and encourage the children to pick out interesting words and then ask them to suggest plainer synonyms. For example, in *Kensuke's Kingdom*, the word *diminutive* has been used instead of *small*, *tattered* has been used instead of *torn* and *breeches* instead of *trousers*.
● Ask the children what effect these have. Why are these synonyms more effective than their simpler alternatives? For example, breeches sounds old fashioned, which is appropriate for Kensuke who's been out of touch with civilisation for so long; tattered is more descriptive and accurate and suggests that the garment has got that way over a period of time.
● Ask volunteers to look up some of the words in a thesaurus, and discuss alternative synonyms.
● Briefly suggest some plain words that might describe some of the children, for example, *tall*, *good*, *hardworking*, *naughty*. Ask the children to think of or look up suitable synonyms.

Guided and independent work
● Read a chosen extract with a group and ask the children to list synonyms of key words.
● Encourage the children to investigate the different synonyms further using a thesaurus.
● Ask the children to work in groups of four to six to annotate their extract for vivid descriptions, powerful words and phrases.
● Ask the children what appeals to them, what they find interesting and what elements that they may not like. Encourage them to note down their reasons.
● Tell the groups to prepare to present their analysis to another group.

Differentiation

Less able
● Give children an extract of exciting action. Ask them to focus on the adverbs.

More able
● Ask children to focus on the range of synonyms, sentence construction, use of powerful adjectives and adverbs.

Plenary
● Organise for each group of children to join another group and ask them to present their story extracts to each other, explaining the points they have annotated. Encourage any questions and comments.
● Note some of the synonyms found for key words in the extracts and check children's understanding of this vocabulary.

Creative responses

Objectives

NLS

T9: To develop an active attitude towards reading.
T15: To write new scenes or characters into a story, in the manner of the writer.
S4: To adapt writing for different readers and purposes.
S7: From reading, to understand how dialogue is set out.

What you need

● *Kensuke's Kingdom* or your class novel
● photocopiable pages 43 and 44
● dictionaries.

Differentiation

Less able
● Ask children to work in a group to use dictionaries to compile a glossary (response 6).

More able
● Allocate creative responses that require writing in the same style as the author.

Shared text-level work

● Read photocopiable page 44 and explain to the children that they will be writing one of the creative responses for the book they have been studying.
● Briefly discuss each item on the menu, asking for suggestions how each idea might be developed with reference to the book.
● Choose one item and, prompted by the children, demonstrate how to develop it into a piece of creative writing.
● Begin with the children's ideas, then make a plan and follow up by beginning a first draft.
● Explain for example, that the children could choose a different ending in which Michael decides to stay on the island, grows old, and becomes the new Kensuke.
● Discuss how this version could end. Perhaps Michael, as an old man, sees a small boy shipwrecked on the island – a 'circular' ending.

Shared sentence-level work

● Since many of the creative responses will require dialogue, this is a good time to revise the conventions of punctuating and the different ways of setting out dialogue.
● Display photocopiable page 43 and use it to demonstrate how speech marks and other punctuation are used together and that new paragraphs are started when the speaker changes.

Guided and independent work

● Work with a group of children to write their own short dialogues using photocopiable page 43 as a model.
● Suggest that the dialogues can be between any two characters in the book during an existing event or a new one of the children's imagination.
● Ask the children to independently write one of the creative responses on photoc opiable page 44.
● Encourage the children to make their own choice of creative response, but allocate them yourself if necessary, or the item can be picked randomly by thinking of a number from 1 to 8.
● Tell the children to use the extract they worked on in Hour 4 as a starting point.
● Encourage the children to write at least one side of A4.

Plenary

● Share some of the responses and explore how they have contributed to a deeper appreciation of the work.
● Display creative responses alongside the story cards chart.
● Where appropriate, try them out on the intended audience. For example, if the children have adapted a scene for younger listeners give them the chance to try it out on a younger year group.
● If the children have written questions for the author, send them to him if possible.

UNIT 3 HOUR 6 📖 Aspects of narrative

The story island

Objectives

NLS
T9: To develop an active attitude towards reading: seeking answers, anticipating events, empathising with characters and imagining events that are described.

What you need
● Photocopiable pages 42 and 45
● the map in *Kensuke's Kingdom*
● thesauruses.

Shared text-level work
● Read photocopiable page 45 and discuss with the class what the extract is about.
● Ask the children to talk about what language they find effective, what atmosphere is created, and how Michael's feelings begin to change during the extract.
● Explain that at the beginning, Michael seems desperate and frightened and his loneliness is emphasised; later he is comforted by the place's beauty and is elated to be alive.
● What else can the children remember about the how the island looked from their reading of the book? Write down some of these ideas on the board.
● Explain to the children that they are going to draw a map of the island using the information in the extract and the any points listed on the board.
● Ask the children: What are the key details you need to put on your map? Note down key points on the board.
● If appropriate, refer to card 3 on photocopiable page 42 for a summary description of the island.

Shared word- and sentence-level work
● Re-read the text, focusing on the techniques used to describe the island (adjectives, synonyms) and how the exploration of the island is narrated (powerful verbs, adverbs).

Guided and independent work
● Work with a different group of children in a guided reading activity to list key words used to describe the island in the extract, for example, *swathe, brilliant, hill, steep, thick.*
● Ask the children to look up the words in a thesaurus to find synonyms.
● Discuss which of those synonyms would fit best in the text.
● Focus on visual learning by organising the children into pairs to draw a map of the island. Tell the children to base their maps on the description provided on photocopiable page 42.
● Tell them that you would also like to see all of the features mentioned in the novel (covered in the extract plus the list of points on the board from other parts of the book).
● Make sure the children don't copy from the map of the island at the beginning of the book!

Differentiation

Less able
● Near the beginning of the extract, the overall shape of the island is described. Ask the children what the shape is and advise them to begin their map by sketching this shape.

More able
● Ask the children to add Michael's route around the island.

Plenary
● Display the children's maps and discuss the different ways that the information in the text has been interpreted.
● Show Michael Morpurgo's map of the island and discuss the similarities and differences with those drawn by the children.
● Which of the children's maps would be accurate enough to be used to move safely around the island?

Own island

Objectives

NLS
T15: To write new scenes or characters into a story, maintaining consistency of character and style, using paragraphs to organise and develop detail.
W7: To explain the difference between synonyms; collect, classify and order sets of words to identify shades of meaning.

What you need
- Photocopiable page 45
- thesauruses
- the children's maps from Hour 6.

Shared text-level work
- Explain to the children that they are going to develop the maps they began in the previous lesson by adding new places and things. Tell the children that their maps will then be used as a basis for their own stories.
- Explain that this story can include characters from *Kensuke's Kingdom* or be a completely new story with new characters, but in the same setting.
- Ask the children: What other places and things might you find on an island? List suitable suggestions on the board, for example, *a lake, a lost civilisation, a swamp, buried treasure, crocodiles, dinosaurs, indigenous people*, and so on.
- Discuss how these places and things could be used to build up a story. Who discovers them? What happens? How will this tie in with the story so far and affect the rest of the story?

Shared word-level work
- Re-read photocopiable page 45 and ask the children to look for models of vivid description in the extract, such as *brilliant white beach*.
- Ask the children to discuss in pairs for a few minutes and come up with brief descriptive phrases for the new places and things to put on the map.
- List the best suggestions, trying to cover each new item.
- Finally experiment with different ways of combining the phrases of description to make interesting sentences and paragraphs.

Guided and independent work
- Continue as Hour 6, with a different group.
- Ask the children to work in the same pairs as the previous hour to develop their maps by adding five new places or things and writing phrases or sentences to describe them.
- Ask the children to use their ideas to now write a short paragraph describing their islands.
- Encourage the children to think about and discuss where the best sites would be for their new places.
- Remind them to consider: How will the story be affected? What new characters might be introduced?
- Advise them to sketch on small pieces of paper and try out positions by placing them on the map and discussing them as a pair before drawing and writing on the map itself.

Differentiation

Less able
- Help children to identify dull words in their descriptions which could be looked up in a thesaurus. Ensure they understand the meaning of any synonyms they use.

More able
- Ask children to write a descriptive paragraph for each addition to the map.

Plenary
- Share ideas about new places and things and the phrases used to describe them.
- Give particular attention to well-chosen words. Ask the children how they found the word. Did they think of it themselves or did they find it in a thesaurus?
- Share examples of paragraphs of description.

Describing the island

Objectives

NLS

T2: To compare the structure of different stories, to discover how they differ in pace, build up and resolution.

T15: To write new scenes into a story, maintaining consistency of character and style, using paragraphs to organise and develop detail.

S1: To investigate word order by examining how far the order of words in sentences can be changed.

What you need
● Photocopiable page 45
● the children's maps.

Shared text- and sentence-level work
● Explain to children that they are going to develop their island setting further, into a descriptive scene for a story.
● Ask one pair to display their map and point out new places and things they have added. Read out their descriptive phrases.
● Demonstrate how these places and things can be collated to create a vivid description of the island. For example, *The island looked… It was shaped… I heard a strange noise… On the rocks in the distance… I looked for a place to sleep…*
● Read and discuss the text. Does it sound like part of a story? Is there potential for exciting things to happen?
● When re-reading the story, give particular emphasis to examining how far the order of words in sentences can be changed to achieve the most vivid description and the smoothest flow from one sentence to another.
● Discuss further possible events. The character could, for example:

> ● find something that will be important in the plot (a cave, a shipwreck and so on)
> ● come face to face with danger (a gorilla, a pirate, a skeleton, a trap)
> ● get completely lost.

● Work through one or two possible events, seeing how the island description affects them.
● Invite additional suggestions from the children for possible events and add good ones to the list.
● Conclude by emphasising that these suggestions are just starting points. Encourage the children to develop them freely.

Guided and independent work
● Ask the children, working in pairs, to write about half a page to a page of description of their islands and the events that happen the next day. Note the different paragraphs.
● Ask the children to try to build up the story events to an interesting conclusion.
● Guide them towards the most effective synonyms and word order for their descriptions.
● Encourage the children to share ideas and try out sentences by reading aloud, but to write their descriptions individually.

Differentiation

Less able
● Ask children to write directly onto a story scaffold (a series of prompts and/or sentence starters).

More able
● Encourage children to write freely and incorporate their paragraphs from Hour 7.

Plenary
● Share some of the island descriptions and ask the rest of the class to listen for the following:

> ● vivid description using appropriate adjectives and synonyms
> ● interesting and varied sentence construction
> ● series of events with a build-up to a climax
> ● effective resolution to the scene.

UNIT 3 HOUR 9 ▢ Aspects of narrative

Developing a story

What you need
● The children's stories from Hour 8
● photocopiable page 20 (from Unit 1).

Shared text-level work
● Discuss the following outline of the complete island story and ask the children for specific ideas to develop it.

1. Say how your character came to the island. Begin at an exciting point, such as a shipwreck. (How else?) Other background information could be filled in as a flashback. (How and where could you fit this in?) Build up your character through dialogue, action and description. (Suggest suitable characters.)
2. Incorporate the island description and exploration from the last lesson. You will need to redraft this to make it fit the rest of the story better. (What would you have to do to make it fit better?) The description should end with a complication (Any ideas?).
3. Narrate how the character solves the complication. (How could suggestions you have already made be solved?) If you wish, develop the story with more complications. (Any ideas?)
4. Bring the story to a satisfying ending (Perhaps the character gets off the island and returns safely home, or decides to stay on the island).

Shared sentence-level work
● Explain that the next step is to think carefully about who the story will be written for.
● Discuss how to adapt vocabulary, tone and sentence structures for different audiences. Give them the following examples:

Audience	How to adapt	Example
Very young	Simple words, short sentences, nothing too frightening.	Amanda was tired out after running away from the penguin. 'Help!' she shouted.
Teenage	More difficult words, more complex sentences, teen-speak, teen issues, more frightening situations.	Almost overwhelmed with exhaustion after fleeing from the pterodactyl, Amanda fumbled for her mobile. 'Pls hlp me!' she texted.

Differentiation

Less able
● Suggest to the children that they make up the story orally before attempting to write a plan.

More able
● Ask the children to use a sophisticated plot technique from photocopiable page 20.

Guided and independent work
● Help a group to adapt their island description from Hour 8 for one of the audiences above. Ask half the group to adapt their descriptions for the very young and half to adapt for teens.
● Compare and discuss the results.

Plenary
● Ask children to evaluate each other's plans. Does the plan work? Is it free from flaws in logic (the main character kills a wild pig with a knife, but earlier he arrived on the island with nothing)? Is it interesting? Are events thrilling? Will it have a satisfying ending?

Writing the story

Objectives

NLS
T15: To write new scenes or characters into a story.
S2: To understand the basic conventions of standard English and consider when and why standard English is used.
W3: To use independent spelling strategies.

What you need

● Photocopiable page 46
● the children's island descriptions from Hour 8 and the story plans from Hour 9.

Shared text-level work

● Keep this shared session short to allow the maximum possible time for individual and group writing.
● Explain to the children that they are going to spend most of this lesson writing the stories that they planned in the last lesson.
● Read through photocopiable page 46, and use it to remind the children of key story features: an interesting story structure with pace, build-up, logical sequence, complication and resolution; strong characters presented through dialogue, action and description; believable settings brought to life through vivid description.

Shared word- and sentence-level work

● Use the checklist on photocopiable page 46 to remind the children of the key word- and sentence-level skills that they will need to use when writing the story: correct use of standard English, appropriate language for the intended audience, correct punctuation, correct spelling.

Guided and independent work

● Ask the children to write their island stories, using the checklist to help them.
● Support the children in any particular aspects of the checklist that they may have found troublesome during earlier lessons, for example, presenting characters or writing dialogue.
● Remind them to keep their audience in mind when writing.
● In follow-up Literacy Hours, ask the children to check their first drafts in pairs by working through the checklist.
● Ask the children to produce final versions for display purposes, possibly in bound booklets with illustrations, including scaled-down versions of their island maps, using ICT to 'publish' where possible.

Differentiation

Less able
● Ask the children to concentrate on one section of the story, for example, the problem and resolution.

More able
● Challenge the children to produce an extended story in short chapters.

Plenary

● Ask the children to share their ongoing work while the rest of the class help to evaluate it using the story checklist. Encourage positive comments and suggestions for improvement.
● At the end of the whole writing process, the completed and published stories should be swapped around the class so that all of the children have a chance to enjoy them before putting on display.

Story cards

Chapter 1

When Michael is 11, he finds his mother crying because his father has gone to find another house down south. Later, his father tells them that he has bought a boat called the Peggy Sue in which he plans to sail round the world with his family. A man nicknamed Barnacle Bill gives them lessons in sailing and navigation, and on September 10, 1987, they set off on their voyage around the world.

Character – Kensuke

The reader's first impression is that he is old and possibly mad. However, he helps Michael to survive, and saves his life when he is almost killed by a jellyfish. As Michael recovers he makes friends with Kensuke and finds out that he is a superb painter and craftsman. Later we find out that Kensuke was a doctor in the Japanese navy. Kensuke heard about the bombing of Nagasaki and believed that his family had died. When he was shipwrecked on the island he decided to stay there.

Setting – the island

The island is two or three miles in length and shaped like an elongated peanut. There is a white beach on both sides of the island and a peak at each end. The rest of the island is covered with forest. Nobody lives on the island except Michael, Kensuke, a group of baboons and a group of gibbons. There are coconuts, many kinds of fruit, and lots of fish in the sea, but Michael finds life difficult at first and only survives with Kensuke's help.

Story response card – Chapter 1

If I were in Michael's situation, I would be excited at the thought of sailing round the world, but also frightened. I would worry about the dangers we would face - such as storms and sharks. I would be glad if my dog was coming and I think I would find Barnacle Bill interesting and really enjoy his lessons on sailing and navigation. On the whole, I think I would rather read about it than actually do it!

Characterisation

◀ Look for:

● point of view (first or third person, story, letter, diary form)
● how characters are presented through dialogue, action and description (direct and indirect speech, adjectives, adverbs)
● how settings are described (adjectives, synonyms)
● vocabulary and phrasing (powerful verbs, adverbs; difficult/unusual words
● sentence construction (long/short, simple/complex).

He was diminutive, no taller than me, and as old a man as I had ever seen. He wore nothing but a pair of tattered breeches bunched at the waist, and there was a large knife in his belt. He was thin, too. In places – under his arms, round his neck and his midriff – his copper brown skin lay in folds about him, almost as if he'd shrunk inside it. What little hair he had on his head and his chin was long and wispy and white.

I could see at once that he was very agitated, his chin trembling, his heavily hooded eyes accusing and angry. "*Dameda! Dameda!*" he screeched at me. His whole body was shaking with fury. I backed away as he scuttled up the beach towards me, gesticulating wildly with his stick, and haranguing me as he came. Ancient and skeletal he may have been, but he was moving fast, running almost. "*Dameda! Dameda!*" I had no idea what he was saying. It sounded Chinese or Japanese, maybe.

I was about to turn and run when Stella, who, strangely, had not barked at him at all, suddenly left my side and went bounding off towards him. Her hackles were not up. She was not growling. To my astonishment she greeted him like a long lost friend.

He was no more than a few feet away from me when he stopped. We stood looking at each other in silence for a few moments. He was leaning on his stick, trying to catch his breath. "Americajin? Americajin? American? *Eikokujin?* British?"

"Yes," I said, relieved to have understood something at last. "English, I'm English."

It seemed a struggle for him to get the words out. "No good. Fire, no good. You understand? No fire." He seemed less angry now.

Michael Morpurgo

Creative response menu

<table>
<tr>
<td>

Adapt a scene for younger readers
1. Simplify vocabulary.
2. Use shorter sentences.
3. Cut long scenes of description or narrative.
4. Try it out on your audience.

</td>
<td>

Write a scene in a different form
● Diary
● Log (see *Kensuke's Kingdom*, Chapter 3)
● Narrative poem
● Newspaper report
● Playscript

</td>
</tr>
<tr>
<td>

Write interview questions for the author about the book
1. General questions, such as: "Where do you get your ideas from?"
2. Specific questions about a book, such as "Why did you make Kensuke stay on the island?"
3. Ask a partner to answer the questions in role as the author.
4. Alternatively, put your questions in a letter and send it to the author.

</td>
<td>

Write a different ending to the book
● Consider different types of ending (see work on *The Ghostly Wedding*). For example, from *Kensuke's Kingdom*, Michael decides to stay on the island, or Kensuke decides to leave with him.
Rewrite a scene from a different point of view
● Change first person into third person or vice versa.
● Tell the story through the eyes of another character. For example, Kensuke could narrate the story beginning with the bombing of Nagasaki.

</td>
</tr>
<tr>
<td>

Compile a glossary of difficult words
1. List the difficult words.
2. Put them in alphabetical order.
3. Read definitions in a dictionary.
4. Adapt the definitions to fit the meaning of the word as it is used in the text.

</td>
<td>

Add a new character or scene
● Introduce a new character. In *Kensuke's Kingdom*, Michael could have a sister.
● Write a new scene. Michael could make a boat and try to leave the island alone.
Note: Try to match the style of the author.

</td>
</tr>
<tr>
<td>

Write a prequel or sequel
● Use ideas from the book. For example, you could write the story of what happened to Kensuke before he came to the island, or of Michael after he left the island.
NB: Try to match the style of the author.

</td>
<td>

Design a bookjacket
● Draw a picture for the cover
● Add Key information for example: title, author, publisher
● Write a 'blurb' for the back cover

</td>
</tr>
</table>

The island

The sun was blazing down. I had not really felt the burning heat of it until then. I scanned the horizon. If there was a sail somewhere out there in the haze, I could not see it. And then it came to me that even if I were to see a sail, what could I do? I couldn't light a fire. I had no matches. I knew about cavemen rubbing sticks together, but I had never tried it. I looked all round me now. Sea. Sea. Sea. Nothing but sea on all sides. I was on an island. I was alone.

The island looked perhaps two or three miles in length, no more. It was shaped a bit like an elongated peanut, but longer at one end than the other. There was a long swathe of brilliant white beach on both sides of the island, and at the far end another hill, the slopes steeper and more thickly wooded, but not so high as mine. With the exception of these twin peaks the entire island seemed to be covered with forest. So far as I could see there was no sign of human life. Even then, as I stood there, that first morning, filled with apprehension at the terrifying implications of my dreadful situation, I remember thinking how wonderful it was, a green jewel of an island framed in white, the sea all about it a silken shimmering blue. Strangely, perhaps comforted somehow by the extraordinary beauty of the place, I was not at all down-hearted. On the contrary I felt strangely elated. I was alive. Stella Artois was alive. We had survived.

I sat down in the shadow of a great rock. The gibbons set up a renewed chorus of howling and hooting in the forest, and a flock of raucous birds clattered up out of the canopy of the trees below us and flew off across the island to settle in the trees on the hillside opposite.

Michael Morpurgo

TERM 1

Story checklist

■ **This checklist can be used as a reminder when writing stories, and as a guide for redrafting. The first part can also be used as a tool for evaluating stories written by others.**

A good story should have:
An *interesting structure:* pace, build-up, sequence of events, complication and resolution
■ Plan the story carefully.
■ Consider using a more complex plot-type, for example, a flashback or a parallel plot.
■ Think carefully about the ending. Could you include a twist in the tale, an anticlimax?

Strong characters presented through dialogue, action and description
■ Don't present your characters completely straight away. Reveal them gradually by feeding in description a bit at a time and mixing it with dialogue and action.
■ Bring dialogue and action to life by using adverbs: "he spoke *angrily*", "he swam *powerfully*".

Believable settings brought to life through vivid description.
■ Improve description with adjectives, figures of speech, and well chosen synonyms: "The bleached sand looked like a sheet of snow but the *schooner's* sails were even whiter." Use sparingly for best effect!

■ *Proof read* the story for:
■ Correct use of standard English. Check agreement between nouns and verbs; consistency of tense and subject. Avoid double negatives. Avoid dialect, except where chosen for a specific purpose, such as dialogue.
■ Appropriate language for the intended audience. For example, simple vocabulary and short sentences for young children; a wide range of vocabulary and longer sentences for older readers.
■ Correct punctuation and paragraph layout, especially dialogue.
■ Correct spelling. Use a spellchecker or dictionary when in doubt. Keep a list of words you get wrong and keep learning them.

UNIT 4

Poetry

This unit is based on several very different poems that exemplify key aspects of the text-level objectives for this term: poetic forms, word play, feelings, similes and metaphors. The poems should provide inspiration for the children to experiment with writing their own poetry. All the different aspects of poetry covered throughout the week are brought together in Hour 5 to help children write a simple analysis of a poem.

Hour	Shared text-level work	Shared word-/ sentence-level work	Guided reading/ writing	Independent work	Plenary
1 Forms	Reading and identifying different poetic forms.	Juggling word order in a limerick.	Writing a limerick.	Trying out different forms.	Enjoying the poems.
2 Word play	Sharing 'Knock knock' jokes to examine word play; reading *Stately Verse*.	Brainstorming homophones for use in poems.	Adding more homophones.	Experimenting with word play poems.	Enjoying jokes and word play poems.
3 Feelings	Reading and discussing *Cold Morning*.	Building poems around 'emotions' words and phrases.	Trying out synonyms in own poems.	Writing free verse to express strong emotions.	Sharing and discussing powerful images in children's poems.
4 Simile and metaphor	Reading 'Nessie', noting similes and metaphors.	Examining uses of punctuation.	Finding similes and metaphors in the poem; writing metaphors from similes.	Writing a descriptive poem in couplets, using similes or metaphors.	Reading poems.
5 Analysing a poem	Revising forms and features, discussing favourite poems.	Identifying proofreading points.	Explaining and justifying personal tastes.	Analysing the poems; proofreading and editing their comments.	Presenting analyses to the class.

Key assessment opportunities
● Can the children recognise and use a range of poetic forms?
● Can they analyse poems and justify their responses?
● Do they recognise examples of word play, simile and metaphor?

Forms

Objectives

NLS
T7: To analyse and compare poetic style, use of forms and the themes of significant poets... to consider the impact of full rhymes, half rhymes, internal rhymes and other sound patterns.
S1: To investigate word order by examining how far the order of words in sentences can be changed.

What you need
● Photocopiable page 53.

Shared text-level work
● After reading the poems as suggested below, discuss responses.
● Begin by defining haiku. (A succinct, descriptive poem of three lines with a set number of syllables in each line.)
● Read the haiku and count the syllables in each line. (17 in total in the pattern 5, 7, 5.)
● Ask the children if they can see a link between the two haiku. (One is by Li Po, a Japanese poet of the classical period, and the second is by a modern poet, about Li Po's death.)
● Now define clerihew: a four-line comic verse with two rhyming couplets. Lines may be of any length. The first line is the name of the person or thing about which the rhyme is written.
● Read the clerihews. Explain that the form is named after its inventor, Edmund Clerihew Bentley. Explain who Bram Stoker was if necessary.
● Ask the children to count the syllables in each line – they should find that the lines are of unequal length.
● Now define limerick: a five-line comic verse form following the syllable pattern 8, 8, 6, 6, 8 (with slight variations) and a rhyme scheme of AABBA. The bouncy rhythm is also important.
● Read the two limericks and note the difference in their forms. (The second limerick rhymes the last line with the first.)
● Encourage the children to tell you any limericks they know.

Shared sentence-level work
● Explain to the children that, in writing their own poems, they will need to try different ways of saying things to get the right number of syllables or find rhymes. Demonstrate this by writing a limerick:

> A skeleton once in York. Is that the right number of syllables? No, and it lacks the "bouncy" rhythm. Let's try Sheffield. What rhyming words can you think of: shield, yield? These are difficult words to rhyme. Let's try Khartoum. Rhymes? Boom, doom, gloom, tomb, room – much better. Invited a ghost – where? – to his room...

(The rest of the limerick is: They spent the whole night/In the eeriest fight/As to who should be frightened of whom.)

Guided and independent work
● Work with a group of children to write a limerick following the process outlined above.
● Ask the children to independently try out the forms. Advise them to begin with a haiku or clerihew. Limericks are more difficult because the writer has to think of both syllables and rhyme, as well as creating the 'bouncy' (dactyllic) rhythm. Edward Lear's limerick form is slightly easier.

Plenary
● Share some of the poems. Discuss how well they fit the form and how interesting or funny they are.

Differentiation

Less able
● Ask the children to try one form only: haiku or clerihew.

More able
● Auditory learning: explain the term dactyllic: one stressed followed by two unstressed syllables. Show the children how to mark the stresses on one of the limericks.

Word play

Objectives

NLS
T8: To investigate different examples of word play, relating form to meaning.
Term 2 W6: To distinguish between homophones.

What you need
● Photocopiable page 54.

Shared text-level work
● Ask the children if they know any 'Knock, knock' jokes. You will, no doubt, get several offerings like this:

> Knock, knock,
> Who's there?
> Olive.
> Olive who?
> Olive here, so let me in!

● Ask the children why it is funny. (*Olive* means two things at once: it is the name of a person and it sounds like I live).
● Explain that this is an example of word play. This particular kind of word play is called *a pun*.
● Read the first stanza of 'Stately Verse' on photocopiable page 54 and explain that it is an example of a quatrain: a four-line stanza of 8, 6, 8, 6 syllables, rhymed abab.
● Write the syllable numbers and rhyme letters at the end of the lines.
● Now read the whole poem and ask the children to listen out for the word play. In each stanza, the name of a US state sounds the same as something else. The last two stanzas are more difficult (*Illinois* – 'ill of noise'; *Rhode Island* is a state).
● Finally, ask who can explain the word play in the title. (Stately means both about states and being dignified, which is used ironically!).

Shared word-level work
● Brainstorm a list of homophones (words that have the same sound as another but different meaning and spelling, for example, read/reed; pair/pear; right/write/rite; hair/hare; eight/ate).
● Explain to the children that some of these homophones will be useful when they come to write their own word play poems.

Guided and independent work
● Organise the children to work in groups to experiment with writing their own word play poems. Tell them to begin by trying out ideas orally.
● Encourage them to focus on word play by writing very simple forms, such as a four-line free verse, or a clerihew.
● Encourage them to use the homophone list for ideas.

Differentiation

Less able
● Ask the children to focus on word play only, by writing any 'Knock, knock' jokes they may know.

More able
● Encourage the children to write short word play poems in quatrains.

Plenary
● Share and enjoy 'Knock, knock' jokes and word play poems. Ask listeners to identify the word play.
● Occasionally, ask a volunteer to explain a particularly interesting example of word play in detail.

Feelings

Objectives

NLS
T7: To analyse poetic style, use of forms and themes; to respond to shades of meaning; to explain and justify personal tastes.
T16: To convey feelings, reflections or moods in a poem through the careful choice of words and phrases.

What you need
● Photocopiable page 55
● thesauruses
● box of tissues.

Shared text-level work
● Begin by explaining that the next poem is written in free verse: poetry that is not constrained by patterns of either rhyme or rhythm.
● Count the syllables in each line of the first verse with the children. Ask which lines have the most syllables. (The first and fifth.)
● Read the poem to the children, then ask them how the poem made them feel. This may be a general feeling of sadness, but encourage them to explain which particular parts of the poem or particular words and phrases created the images that generated those feelings.
● Highlight/underline appropriate suggestions, such as the repetition of galloped, the closeness and shared joy and then the expression of huge size and overwhelming emotion in avalanche – there are many simple but powerful images.
● Explore this use of understatement. Celia Warren describes the dream and feelings of loss very simply and with few words (note how short the poem is and some of the lines are). There is no attempt to play on or manipulate the reader's emotions, yet the effect is very powerful.

Shared word-level work
● Ask the children to brainstorm word lists for different emotions, such as, for happiness: bliss, cloud nine, delight, ecstasy, euphoria, rapture, thrill, and then begin to build poems around them. For example:

> I was on cloud nine
> When I got my console
> It was rapture
> To play that first game...

Guided and independent work
● Ask the children to write a short free-verse poem in which they express a strong feelingm, for example: sadness, happiness, anger, disappointment and so on.
● Encourage them to keep the lines short: no line should be longer than eight syllables. (Without this limitation, there is a danger that they would lapse into writing prose.)
● Let the children explore words for strong feelings in a thesaurus and to try out the synonyms they find in their own emotive poems.

Differentiation

Less able
● Ask the children to rewrite their ideas in prose sentences, then break up each sentence into lines of poetry. Advise them to make a line break when they want to emphasise something.

More able
● Encourage the children to aim for the same powerful understatement as Thompson achieves.

Plenary
● Ask some of the children to read out their poems.
● Ask the rest of the class how the poems made them feel and which words, phrases or images were particularly powerful.

Objectives

NLS
T17: To write metaphors from original ideas or from similes.
S6: To understand the need for punctuation as an aid to the reader.

What you need
● Photocopiable page 56.

Simile and metaphor

Shared text-level work
● Before reading, explain that the poem is written in couplets: two consecutive lines paired in length or rhyme.
● Read and enjoy the poem. Ensure that the children notice the rhyming couplets.
● Then read it again, asking the children to listen to the way Nessie is described, particularly lines that say what she is like.
● Explain that these descriptions are similes: an image made by comparing a subject to something else using the words *like* or *as*. There are also some metaphors where the poet describes something by saying it is something else.
● Annotate similes and metaphors identified by the children. For example, *It's shaped like a pop bottle* is a simile that describes Nessie's shape; *its hedge-clippers* is a metaphor that describes her mouth. (There is another teaching point not to be missed – the difference between it's and its!)
● Go through the poem again, asking children to look for examples of word play, particularly the way Ted Hughes has fun with the names of animals and dinosaurs, such as *hippopot* for hippopotamus.
● Then show the children how to write metaphors from similes by omitting *like* or *as* and changing the wording where necessary, for example:

> Simile: It's shaped like a pop bottle with two huge eyes in the stopper.
> Metaphor: It is a pop bottle with two huge eyes in the stopper.

Shared sentence-level work
● Examine the use of punctuation in the poem. Ask the children: What is the effect of the commas, full stops, and exclamation marks? What is the difference between a hyphen and a dash? What is the effect of the dashes?
● Write some couplets on the board (for instance, from *Mislaid by the ages* to *ten-foot smiles*) without punctuation and ask the children to read them and to comment on what is lost. (Commas and full stops – as in prose – help the reader to know when to pause and read with a falling intonation for the end of a sentence. The exclamation marks signal that the reader should indicate surprise. A hyphen joins compound words, but a dash indicates that whatever follows next is surprising or important.)

Differentiation

Less able
● Ask the children to write a short free-verse poem containing one simile.

More able
● Encourage the children to include humour and/or rhyme.

Guided and independent work
● Ask the children to write a short poem in couplets describing an animal or dinosaur.
● Ask them to include at least one simile or metaphor in their poem.
● Advise the children that the poem doesn't have to rhyme.

Plenary
● Ask some of the children to read out their poems while the rest of the class listen for metaphors, similes and word play.

Analysing a poem

Objectives

NLS
T7: To analyse and compare poetic style, use of forms and the themes of significant poets... to explain and justify personal tastes.
S3: To discuss, proof-read and edit their own writing for clarity and correctness.
W1: To identify mis-spelt words in own writing.

What you need
● Poems chosen for analysis (see Shared text-level work).

Shared text-level work
● 'Cold Morning' or 'Nessie' would be suitable for this activity, but it would be good to choose new poems too. Ensure that the poems are in one of the forms covered during the week and contain good examples of word play, powerful expression of feelings, similes and/or metaphors.
● Write the following terms on the board and recap work so far:

> **Form:** What forms have we read and written? Which was easiest/hardest? Which did you like best?
> **Word play:** What kind of word play did we look at?
> **Feelings:** What feelings did we read and write about? How did we express our feelings?
> **Metaphor and similes:** What is the difference? What metaphors and similes can you remember from Ted Hughes' poem? Which did you like best?

● Finally, ask the children which is their favourite poem overall and discuss why.
● Explain that they are going to put all these things together to write an analysis of a poem. Each heading will be one paragraph in their analysis (word play will not apply to every poem).
● Read and display the chosen poem and elicit annotations from the children according to the headings listed above. Then model developing the annotations into paragraphs.

Shared sentence- and word-level work
● Tell the children that they will be analysing the poem in a similar way and that you expect them to proofread and edit their analyses.
● Ask the children what they think you will be looking for. (An analysis of a poem written in three or four paragraphs, in standard English with correct spelling and punctuation.)

Guided and independent work
● Work with a group of children on explaining and justifying their personal tastes. Ask the children what they liked and disliked about the shared poem. Help them to think about specific aspects, for example: Did you like the verse form? Or Do you prefer rhyming verse? What did you think was the most vivid simile? How did it make you feel?
● Ask the children to work in pairs to analyse one of the poems. They should begin by annotating their poem. Next, ask them to write paragraphs for each heading above, as appropriate. Then ask the children to proofread and edit their work.

Differentiation

Less able
● Ask the children to write annotations and paragraphs on the poem used in the shared session.

More able
● Give the children two related poems, such as two describing the same animal, for analysis and comparison.

Plenary
● Ask pairs to present their analysis. They should enjoy doing it as a shared reading session: talking about it and writing their annotations 'live'.
● Try to find opportunities for all the pairs to present, perhaps as an ongoing plenary in a follow-up week of reading and writing poems.

Three simple forms

Haiku

Storm clouds gathering.
The forest sighs in the wind.
A screech from a crow.

Li Po

Li Po

Li Po saw the moon
Reflected in the river,
Reached for it and drowned.

Anon

Clerihew

The art of biography
Is different from geography
Geography is about maps,
Biography is about chaps.

Edmund Clerihew Bentley

Mr Bram Stoker
Was a bit of a joker;
Either that or he
Had bats in his belfry.

Charles Connell

There was an old man in a tree
Who was horribly stung by a bee;
When they said: "Does it buzz?"
He replied: "Yes , it does,
It's a regular brute of a bee!"

Edward Lear

Limerick

There was a young fellow from Leeds
Who ate a whole packet of seeds,
In less than an hour
His nose was a flower
And his head was a garden of weeds.

Anon

Stately Verse

If Mary goes far out to sea,
By wayward breezes fanned,
I'd like to know—can you tell me?
Just where would Maryland?

If Tenny went high up in air
And looked o'er land and lea,
Looked here and there and everywhere,
Pray what would Tennessee?

I looked out of the window and
Saw Orry on the lawn;
He's not there now, and who can tell
Just where has Oregon?

Two girls were quarrelling one day
With garden tools, and so
I said, 'My dears, let Mary rake
And just let Idaho.'

A friend of mine lived in a flat
With half a dozen boys;
When he fell ill I asked him why.
He said: 'I'm Illinois.'

An English lady had a steed.
She called him 'Ighland Bay.
She rode for exercise, and thus
Rhode Island every day.

Anon

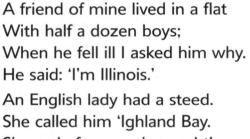

Cold Morning

Someone was sweeping a dusting of snow.

From the front door my dog appeared, suddenly,
her eyes fixed on mine, her tail a joyous flag
as she galloped and galloped to meet me.
I shrieked her name as she came
and held her gaze long enough to feel her soft coat;
rub my head against hers; sense her breath...
Then I woke.

Dreaming of snow's a good omen, they say.
And to dream of snow in autumn
foreshadows happiness...

I'd dream myself an avalanche
if it brought me back my dog.

Celia Warren

Nessie

No, it is not an elephant or any such grasshopper.
It's shaped like a pop bottle with two huge eyes in the stopper.

But vast as a gasometer, unmanageably vast,
With sing-things like a whale for flying underwater fast.

It's me, me, me, the Monster of the Loch!
Would God I were a proper kind, a hippopot or croc!

Mislaid by the ages, I gloom here in the dark,
When I should be ruling Scotland from a throne in Regent's Park!

Once I was nobility—Diplodocus ruled the Isles!
Polyptychod came courting with his stunning ten-foot smiles.

Macroplat swore he'd carry me off before I was much older.
All his buddy-boys were by, grinning over his shoulder—

Leptoclid, Cryptocleidus, Triclid and Ichthyosteg—
Upstart Sauropterygs! But I took him down a peg—

I had a long bath in the Loch and waiting till I'd finished
He yawned himself to a fossil and his gang likewise diminished.

But now I can't come up for air without a load of trippers
Yelling: 'Look at the neck on it, and look at its hedge-clippers!

Oh no, that's its mouth.' Then I can't decently dive
Without them sighing: 'Imagine! If *that* thing were alive!

Why, we'd simply have to decamp, to Canada, and at the double!
It was luckily only a log, or the Loch-bed having a bubble.

It was something it was nothing why whatever could it be
The ballooning hideosity we thought we seemed to see?'

Because I am so ugly that it's just incredible!
The biggest bag of haggis Scotland cannot swallow or sell!

Me, me, me, the Monster of the Loch!
Scotland's ugliest daughter, seven tons of poppycock!

Living here in my black mud bed the life of a snittery newty,
And never a zoologist a-swooning for my beauty!

O where's the bonnie laddie, so bold and so free,
Will drum me up to London and proclaim my pedigree!

Ted Hughes

UNIT 5

Note-taking and recount

This unit is based on one of Michael Morpurgo's reports during his role as the Children's Laureate, thus providing a link with the unit on *Kensuke's Kingdom*. Information about the role of the Children's Laureate and more reports can be found at www.child renslaureate.org. However, if another author was featured in Unit 3, it may be possible to find similar resources at www.mystworld.com/youngwriter/index.html. Children begin the unit by reading the report and identifying key features of recount texts, then they write a similar report about themselves, building it up a lesson at a time. Hour 1 ties in with Unit 37 in *Grammar for Writing*, and Hour 5 with Units 34 and 35.

Hour	Shared text-level work	Shared word-/ sentence-level work	Guided reading/ writing	Independent work	Plenary
1 The sixth report	Reading the report and discussing the author.	Re-reading to focus on tenses.	Investigating verb tenses.	Writing about the scene outside the classroom.	Discussing annotations; reading descriptions.
2 Own recount	Re-reading, focusing on structure.		Compiling a connectives poster.	Recounting a recent visit.	Discussing the use of connectives in the recounts; recapping key genre features.
3 Note-taking 💬	Demonstrating note-taking.		Giving oral recounts for partner to take notes; writing up notes.	Giving oral recounts for partner to take notes; writing up notes.	Reading back biographies to check accuracy.
4 Own news report	Re-reading, focusing on structure.	Revising tenses.	Compiling a present-tense connectives poster.	Writing extra sections to report.	Incorporating new sections; comparing with Morpurgo's report.
5 Redrafting	Noting formal and informal features.	Considering how to adapt writing for different audiences.	Completing and editing reports.	Completing and editing reports, incorporating additional text.	Sharing recounts; revising key genre features.

Key assessment opportunities
- Can the children recognise key features of recounts?
- How successfully did they write their own recounts?
- Are they able to take and use notes?
- Do they use tenses and level of formality appropriately?

The sixth report

Objectives

NLS

T21: To identify the features of recounted texts such as diaries.
S8: To revise and extend work on verbs, focusing on: tenses (past, present, future; investigating how different tenses are formed by using auxiliary verbs) and person (1st, 2nd, 3rd).

What you need

● Photocopiable pages 63 and 64.

Shared text-level work

● Explain that you are going to read a recount. Ask the children if they can give you any examples of this type of text (such as a description/ retelling of a visit, a news story, a biography).
● Tell the children that the recount is written by Michael Morpurgo. It is a chronological recount and shouldn't be confused with non-chronological reports that will be studied in Term 2.
● Ask the children what they know about Michael Morpurgo, his work, and about his position as Children's Laureate.
● Read photocopiable pages 63 and 64. How would the children summarise what it is about? (A news update on what Morpurgo has been up to recently and his future plans.). Spend some time talking about the people and places mentioned.

Shared sentence-level work

● Go through the report and ask the children to identify the tenses in the first two paragraphs.
Ask the children: Why has Morpurgo used the present tense for the first paragraph? (He is describing his garden at the time of writing.) Why does he use the past tense for most of the second paragraph? (He is recounting what happened.) He uses future at the end of the second paragraph to write about something he is looking forward to.
● Point out the auxiliary verbs used to form the future tense.

Guided and independent work

● Help the children to pick out present, past and future tense verbs from the text and investigate their structure by compiling a verb table:

Verb:	To be
Singular	
1st person	I am
2nd person	you are
3rd person	he/she/it is
Plural	
1st person	
2nd person	
3rd person	

● Ask the children to write a present tense description of the scene outside using postive vocabulary.

Differentiation

Less able
● Ask the children to complete the annotation of photocopiable page 63.

More able
● Ask the children to describe the outdoor scene in the previous season (if it is spring, they write about winter) using the past tense, or in the next season using the future tense.

Plenary

● Display photocopiable page 64 and ask the children to suggest annotations. Confirm that tenses have been correctly identified.
● Share some of the children's descriptions. Ask the class to listen out for present tense verbs, and phrases that describes the beauty of the scene.

UNIT 5 HOUR 2 ▢ Note-taking and recount

Own recount

Objectives

NLS
T21: To identify the features of recounted texts such as sports reports, diaries, including: introduction to orientate the reader; chronological sequence; use of connectives.
T24: To write recounts based on personal experiences, for example, an account of a field trip.

What you need
● Photocopiable pages 63 and 64, including annotated version from Hour 1.

Differentiation

Less able
● Ask the children to write five statements about their visit in the order in which they happened. Encourage them to try them out orally to a partner first. Then help them to join the statements.

More able
● Ask the children to include a section in which they look forward to the future.

Shared text-level work
● Re-read the text and discuss the structure: introduction; details of recent events, organised into paragraphs by event; the general round-up to finish off.
● Annotate the text as appropriate suggestions are made.
● Ask the children to think of a subheading for each event that Morpurgo recounts. Add the headings as children suggest them.
● Morpurgo writes very little about the Bath Festival. Invite the children to suggest what he might have done there and to say it in sentences that use the past tense.
● Now focus on how the paragraphs are linked together. Remind the children of the term connective: a word or phrase that links clauses or sentences. Recap that these can be conjunctions (but, when, because), connecting adverbs (however, moreover, therefore) or temporal connectives (first, next, later.)

Shared sentence-level work
● Ask the children which temporal connectives they can find in the text (as soon as, just before, sometimes, then). Which is used most often? (Then.) Add these to the annotations as the children suggest them. Notice how most of them come at the start of a paragraph in the sentence that introduces the subject of the paragraph.
● Introduce the term 'Topic Sentence'. The topic sentence is the sentence that introduces the subject or 'topic' of the paragraph. It is usually the first sentence, though sometimes the first sentence is a linking sentence and the topic sentence is the second sentence.

Guided and independent work
● Work with a group of children to brainstorm useful past-tense connectives for recounts, especially temporal connectives. Include, for example, after, before, finally, first, later, next, secondly, since, sometimes, then, thirdly.
● Work together to sort the connectives in chronological order (as far as possible). If they write the words on cards or use ICT, the children can have fun shuffling the order manually.
● Finally, ask the group to make a connectives poster to help the rest of the class.
● Ask the children to independently write a recount of a recent visit. Ideally, this should be a school visit, or other educational trip, but could be a recent holiday or outing.
● Remind them to use the past tense and link their sentences and paragraphs with appropriate connectives.

Plenary
● Share some of the recounts. Discuss how connectives have been used and how clear and interesting the recount is overall.
● Recap on the key features of recounts: a scene-setting introduction, chronological sequence, use of connectives.

Objectives

NLS
T26: To make notes for different purposes and to build on these notes in their own writing or speaking.

S&L
42 Listening: To listen to a speaker, make notes on the talk and use the notes.

What you need
● Photocopiable page 63.

Note-taking

Shared text-level work

● Explain to the children that they are going to write a biography of their partner. The first step is to take notes while their subject talks about his/her early life. Emphasise that they should not try to take down every word, just jot down key words or phrases and dates to help them to remember.

● Demonstrate how to take notes by asking a child to read (fairly slowly) the second paragraph of photocopiable page 63. Explain that you are concentrating on main points only and writing in a kind of 'shorthand'. Jot notes like these on the board:

Notes	Notes on the notes
Feb – Children's Laureate Scottish Tour – 16 days – 5000 children Edin, Glasg, Airdrie, Dumfries etc Kim Bergsagel went with him – runs a puppet theatre Back in June – Inverness, west coast islands 'most bitey midges'	common abbreviation abbreviations for well-known places – less well-known written in full; etc, indicates that the list of towns continues Bergsagel written carefully because unusual noted because it's funny and it's good to include some direct quotes

● Ask how the notes differ from ordinary writing. (They are written quickly (but legibly!), they are not in sentences, any non-crucial words and most punctuation is left out – dashes are used instead. Abbreviations are used.)

● Brainstorm a list of common abbreviations that might be useful, for example, m, cm, max, min, etc, eg, yrs, approx, days and months.

Guided and independent work

● Ask the children to take it in turns and give their partners an oral recount of a performance they have recently enjoyed; preferably a concert, sporting event, or a film. Advise the partners to take notes with the aim of writing them up as a mini biography.

● Encourage note-takers to ask questions if they missed anything or did not understand anything.

● Finally, ask the children to write up their notes as a short recount. Recommend this process:

1. Re-read the notes to remind yourself what they are about.
2. Group the notes into paragraphs representing different events, or important stages in the events.
3. Rewrite the notes in sentences using temporal connectives where necessary.
4. Add an introduction to orientate the reader and conclusion to round off.

Differentiation

Less able
● Play children a short pre-recorded recount that is simple and clear. Ask them to replay the recount to check their notes.

More able
● Challenge note-takers to note as much detail as possible.

Plenary
● Ask the pairs to read the biographies back to each other and discuss how accurate they are and how helpful the notes were.

Own news report

Objectives

NLS
T24: To write recounts based on personal experiences, eg an account of a field trip, a match, a historical event.
S9: To identify the past tense in recounts and use this awareness when writing for these purposes.

What you need
● Photocopiable pages 63 and 64 (with annotations)
● the children's written work done during the week.

Shared text-level work
● Display the text on photocopiable pages 63 and 64 and explain to the children that they are going to write a news report with a similar structure.
● Re-read the text, pausing after each paragraph to ask the children to pick out (from the annotations if appropriate) the subject/heading for each section.
● List these paragraph subjects on the board to form the left-hand column of a table:

Morpurgo's structure	Your structure
Introduction (present tense) The Children's Laureate Scottish tour The Bath Festival and trip to France Oxford Literary Festival Birmingham conference Watched Private Peaceful New books Farewell	Description of outside from Hour 1 or recount of a recent visit from Hour 2 Two paragraphs in the past tense to be written today about a field trip, match, historical event. Write up of oral recount of a performance from Hour 3 (either their own or their partner's oral recount) A conclusion with a 'farewell' to the reader to be written today

● Next, write in and explain each section of the structure suggested for the children's report (the second column above), relating it to Michael Morpurgo's.

Shared sentence-level work
● Remind the children that most of their additional sections will be in the past tense.
● Revise the simple past tense by completing a table like the one on page 58 [hour 1] for two or three regular verbs. Ask the children: What is the common pattern? (All the endings are -d or -ed.)

Guided and independent work
● Ask the children to write the extra sections for their news report as shown in the table above.

Plenary
● Tell the children to decide where to insert their new sections.
● Ask the children to read their first drafts to each other. Encourage suggestions for improvement.
● Then ask a volunteer to read his or her draft news report, and ask the class to compare it to the structure of Morpurgo's report.

Differentiation

Less able
● Ask the children to write one extra paragraph only.

More able
● Let the children experiment with different structures and refer to past, present and future events.

Redrafting

Shared text- and sentence-level work

● Display the checklist on photocopiable page 65 and explain to the children that they are going to use it as a guide to evaluate and redraft the news report they have been working on.

● As the structure of the report was established in Hour 4, focus on the second main point: formality. Explain the different levels of formality in the table, and encourage the children to suggest examples from each type.

● Ask the children which level of formality Michael Morpurgo used in his report. If the children need reminding, re-read part of the report. We can tell the report is informal because he uses contractions, some colloquial terms such as bitey and uses a warm, friendly tone. Draw attention to the farewell which is also an informal feature. Why is this tone appropriate? Who is his audience? (Children of their age, as well as younger and older children; parents and teachers; people who are already familiar with him and interested in him. The chatty tone suits the 'diary' format.)

● Tell the children to make sure that their own recounts are written in an informal tone. Advise them to imagine the audience as people they know of any age.

● Using a good example from the children's work so far, take them through at least the beginning of the editing and proofreading process.

Guided and independent work

● Ask the children to finish their recounts, by writing the oral recount they gave in Hour 3, and to use the checklist to prepare a final version.

● Encourage the children to choose their own audience, and discuss appropriate tone, vocabulary and so on.

Plenary

● Share the recounts of several children, including informal and formal versions, and use them to recap on the key features of recounts: a scene-setting introduction, chronological sequence, use of connectives.

● Ask where they might see formal and less formal recounts.

News from Michael Morpurgo

The daffodils here in Devon are definitely yellow, not golden. So my garden is a host of yellow daffodils. The yellow of primroses punctuate the hedgerows. The gorse grows thick and yellow. It is a season of yellow, and just outside my window the cherry tree is about to burst into blossom – but it will be white and wonderful.

But I've not had a lot of time looking out of the window at home just recently. In late February I went with Clare on the first leg of the Children's Laureate Scottish Tour, organised by Scottish Book Trust. It was a 16 day whirlwind tour during which I spoke to over 5000 children, sometimes in huge theatres and concert halls seating 800 people, sometimes in little village halls with 50 or 60 children who came from little village schools all around. We went to Edinburgh, Glasgow, Airdrie, Dumfries, Kilmarnock, Lochgoilhead, Aberdeen, Stracathro and back to Aberdeen. And we went in a yellow van, accompanied all the way by Kim Bergsagel, who with her husband runs a wonderful puppet theatre company (www.puppet-lab.com). She kept us happy all the way and was a marvellous support to us, as was everyone at Scottish Book Trust. We are due to go back for the second leg of the Children's Laureate Scottish Book Trust tour in June when we'll be going even further north to Inverness, then over to the West Coast and the islands. At one point I will be going to an island school with just 7 children. I'm really looking forward to it. I've never been to the Scottish Islands and everyone says they're very beautiful, but that you have to look out for midges. Scottish midges are the best, most bitey midges in the world they tell me. No problem. I'll tell them a story, put them to sleep.

As soon as I got back from Scotland I was off to the Bath Festival where I spoke to a room full of chandeliers, and lots of people too. Then it was off to France for ten days. I go to France 4 or 5 times a year to talk in French schools and colleges and libraries.

As soon as we got back it was off to Abingdon to talk to English children, thence to Derbyshire and afterwards to the Oxford Literary Festival, where I was part of a panel discussing 'cross over books' with Philip Pullman, Adèle Geras and Nicolette Jones. It was a lively discussion I can tell you!

The truth is that by now I had a sore throat and needed a bit of a rest. But I recovered in time to do a talk at The Federation of Children's Book Groups conference in Birmingham where I read a new story I'd written in France, called 'Meeting Cezanne'.

Then just before Easter we went off to Bristol, to the Bristol Old Vic to see the first night of 'Private Peaceful'. It was an extraordinary night. The actor Paul Checkers is on stage for nearly two hours – he's even on in the interval! It was a supremely moving performance. The director Simon Reade has adapted the book with great sensitivity. I shall be going again on April 22nd and with Simon will be doing a pre-performance talk about the book and the stage adaptation. Then it's going to Edinburgh, where it will play as part of the Edinburgh Literary Festival. We hope later it will be touring the country in different theatres.

It's been tidying up time too, putting the finishing touches to a few new books coming out later this year and next year. The first to look out for is Dolphin Boy, out in May, with glowing and glorious illustrations by Michael Foreman, my good friend and partner in crime, who's a very happy person because Chelsea are in the semi-finals of the European Cup. (See his love of Chelsea and how it influenced me in Billy the Kid and Cool).

That's all for now folks.

Michael Morpurgo

www.childrenslaureate.org

TERM 1

Checklist for recounts

◼ **This checklist can be used as a reminder when writing stories, and as a guide for redrafting. The first part can also be used as a tool for evaluating stories written by others.**

A good story should have:
An *interesting structure:* pace, build-up, sequence of events, complication and resolution
- Plan the story carefully.
- Consider using a more complex plot-type, for example a flashback or a parallel plot.
- Think carefully about the ending. Could you include a twist in the tale, an anti-climax?

Strong characters presented through dialogue, action and description
- Don't present your characters completely straight away. Reveal them gradually by feeding in description a bit at a time and mixing it with dialogue and action.
- Bring dialogue and action to life by using adverbs: "he spoke angrily", "he swam *powerfully*".

Believable settings brought to life through vivid description.
- Improve description with adjectives, figures of speech, and well chosen synonyms: "The bleached sand looked like a sheet of snow but the *schooner's* sails were even whiter." Use sparingly for best effect!

- *Proof read* the story for:
- Correct use of standard English. Check agreement between nouns and verbs; consistency of tense and subject. Avoid double negatives. Avoid dialect, except where chosen for a specific purpose, such as dialogue.
- Appropriate language for the intended audience. For example, simple vocabulary and short sentences for young children; a wide range of vocabulary and longer sentences for older readers.
- Correct punctuation and paragraph layout, especially dialogue.
- Correct spelling. Use a spellchecker or dictionary when in doubt. Keep a list of words you get wrong and keep learning them.

A good recount should have:

1. A clear structure, for example:
- a short introduction to orientate the reader (could be in the past or present tense – one paragraph)
- a chronological sequence beginning with the earliest events (mainly in the past tense – one or more paragraphs)
- an ending which may refer to current or future events (in the present or future tense – one paragraph).

2. An appropriate degree of formality – see the following table:

	Formal	Informal	Very informal
Audience	Unknown, could include politicians or critics	Known – in Morpurgo's case, his readers	Friends
Vocabulary	Some words that are usually used only in writing, for example, 'aquaintances'; no contractions – 'I am' instead of 'I'm'	Spoken language written down; contractions and colloquial terms, for example, 'pals' or 'mates'	Very chatty, may use text-message-type abbreviations, slang and dialect
Sentences	Complete sentences, some of which will be complex	Complete sentences though of simple structure	Part-sentence, part-note form
Tone	Serious	Warm, friendly	Chatty, very friendly

3. Appropriate connectives, for example:

For paragraphs in the past tense	after, as soon as, before, just after, just before, finally, first, later, next, secondly, since, sometimes, then, thirdly
For paragraphs in the present tense	at present, at the moment, at the same time, currently, just now, meanwhile, this time

■ Proof read the recount for:
- Correct use of standard English where appropriate (some informal texts may use non-standard English). Check agreement between nouns and verbs; consistency of tense and subject. Avoid double negatives. Avoid non-standard words, except where you are writing in an informal style.
- Correct spelling and punctuation.

UNIT 6 🗩

Instructions

This unit is based on a theme park management simulation. It provides opportunities for children to write a wide range of instructional texts. The simulation lends itself to being extended for another week or two to cover a range of different text types, such as explanations of how the different attractions work, recounts of imaginary visits to the park and stories about people who visit the park. Hour 2 can be used with page 43 of *Spelling Bank* and Hour 5 with Unit 34 in *Grammar for Writing*.

Hour	Shared text-level work	Shared word-/ sentence-level work	Guided reading/ writing	Independent work	Plenary
1 Theme park rules 🗩	Discussing instructions at theme parks; reading a list of rules.	Identifying positive and negative verbs.	Adding detail to rules.	Working collaboratively to prioritise rules.	Discussing chosen orders for rules.
2 Fantasmorgoria 🗩	Introducing problems at a fictional theme park.	Exploring prefixes.	Using prefixes to make up names for attractions.	Working as consultants to improve the park.	Evaluating presentations from consultancy teams.
3 Recipes	Reading a recipe and menu and noting typical features.	Picking out imperative verbs.	Discussing ethics of fast food to come up with a policy slogan.	Writing a menu and recipes for a food stall.	Choosing the most appealing menu.
4 Directions	Reading directions; giving directions orally.	Revising imperative verbs useful for directions.	Writing directions and giving directions orally.	Writing directions and giving directions orally.	Giving and trying to remember long sets of directions.
5 Making a presentation 🗩	Discussing preparations for presenting improvement ideas to the class.	Stressing the need for proofreading work.	Preparing a presentation using ICT.	Preparing presentations.	Giving and discussing the presentations.

Key assessment opportunities
● Can the children recognise key features of instructions?
● Can they write a range of instructions, rules and directions and evaluate those written by others?

Objectives

NLS
T22: To read and evaluate a range of instructional texts in terms of their: purposes; organisation; clarity and usefulness.
S9: To identify the imperative form in instructional writing.

S&L
50 Group discussion and interaction: To plan and manage a group task.

What you need
● Photocopiable page 72 (with annotations removed).

Theme park rules

Shared text-level work
● Tell the children that they are going to read some instructions in the context of theme parks.
● Explain that instructions are written to help readers to do things. For example, recipes and instructions for a new toy or electronic gadget.
● Before displaying the text, ask the children if they have been to a theme park, and what rules and instructions they had to follow. Where did they see the different instructions? (On signs, on notices at the entrances to rides and so on.)
● Read photocopiable page 72. Ask the children who they think the rules are for and if they think they are helpful.
● Go through the text again and annotate the key features of the text type: statement of purpose, subheadings, direct address to the reader (including imperative verbs).

Shared sentence-level work
● Revise the imperative form of verbs, which tells us to do something or not do something, for example, *Never give up. Don't move!*
● Ask the children to point out more imperative forms in the text. The easiest to find are at the start of sentences, but there are many preceded by clauses beginning with *If*.
● Note the rule expressed with *shouldn't* and explain that should/shouldn't and must/mustn't are other ways to write rules. Compare it with school/class rules such as *You must not run in the corridor*.

Guided and independent work
● Work with a group to add more details to the general rule *Stay cool*, and *Don't get burned*. These details could include advice about what to wear, drinking plenty of water, wearing sunscreen.
● Ask the children to work collaboratively in groups of four on these prioritisation exercises:

> 1. Pick out and agree on the three most important rules.
> 2. Put all the rules in order of importance (they are in alphabetical order in the text).

● Tell the children that you will be listening for group discussion and good reasons for decisions.

Plenary
● Discuss the choices of rule order and the reasons. (Robert Niles says that heat is the main cause of injury and illness. After that, any well-argued priority is acceptable.)

Differentiation

Less able
● Ask the children to cut up the rules (or use ICT) and physically shuffle them around.

More able
● In addition to prioritising, ask the children to sort the rules into general rules and rules which apply to specific people.

Fantasmagoria

Objectives

NLS
T25: To write instructional texts.
W6: To collect, and investigate the meanings and spellings of words using the following prefixes: auto, bi, trans, tele, circum.

S&L
39 Group discussion and interaction: To take different roles in groups and use language appropriate to them.

What you need
● Photocopiable page 73.

Shared text-level work
● Introduce the Fantasmagoria park. Read the introductory paragraph and ask the children how the problems would put people off.
● Look at the map and talk about the attractions and facilities. Ask: Which rides would you like to try? Do you think it looks like a good theme park? If they agree that it has potential, ask: How would you improve it? Explain that to fulfil the brief, they need to advise people what to do to increase the park's success.
● Read the instructions and rules and tell the children that they will be using them as a model for their own writing. Note the following features:

● bullet points
● list format
● imperative verbs.

Shared word-level work
● Briefly revise prefixes and ask the children to brainstorm in pairs, theme park words that begin with the prefixes auto, bi, trans, tele and circum, ensuring the children know what the prefixes mean. For example, automatic, bilingual (perhaps a bilingual attendant), transport, circumference (for a train that goes around the edge of the park). List the suggestions on the board, with brief definitions where necessary.

Guided and independent work
● Help the children to make up names for new park attractions by attaching the prefixes to roots taken from theme park words, for example, *autocar* - a self-driven car that takes you round the park or *circumcine* - a cinema screen that goes all around you.

Drawing a table like this may help:

Prefix	Meaning	Root (add to any prefix)
auto	by itself	bar, car, cine, coaster, golf,
circum	around	guide, information, swing,
tele	over a distance	refreshments, roundabout,
trans	across	toilet and so on.

● Ask the children to work in groups of four as teams of consultants brought in to rejuvenate the park. Ask them to write at least two sets of instructions for staff and two sets of rules for customers. Tell them the team with the best ideas will be chosen to develop the park.

Differentiation

Less able
● Help the children to write rules and instructions that follow the models closely.

More able
● Ask the children to consider the different purposes of instructions for staff and rules for customers: the instructions need to be fairly detailed, whereas the rules need to be clear and short.

Plenary
● Ask at least one of the teams to present their ideas to the rest of the board in practice for Hour 5. Ask the rest of the class, as the board, to evaluate their presentation.

Recipes

Objectives

NLS
T25: To write instructional texts.
S9: To identify the imperative form in instructional writing.

What you need
• Photocopiable page 74.

Shared text-level work

• Display photocopiable page 74, which shows a variety of texts that might be useful at the theme park. Look at the first text and ask the children what it is. (A recipe for a snack.) Read it and note the following features:

> • list of ingredients
> • chronological order of steps to follow
> • imperative verbs.

• Read the fast food bar menu. Ask the children what other menu items would be suitable for each stall and write suitable suggestions in the blank spaces.

• Consider how one of the items could be prepared. Select appropriate suggestions and model the writing of a recipe, referring to the shared text as appropriate. Ask the children: What do we need to know first? (Ingredients and quantities.) Note that these are written as a list. Then move on to the method. Involve the children in writing these instructions, and show them that words like *a* and *the* can be left out.

• Ask the children to read through the steps to check that they are in the correct order.

• Now discuss the ethics of the fast food bar. Is it right to sell unhealthy food in the theme park, or do the management have to provide what customers want, whatever that is, or what is profitable for the park?

• Conclude by discussing, agreeing and writing a sentence/slogan stating a food policy for the park, for example, *Fantasmagoria believes that you need to be healthy to have fun, therefore we do not sell any junk food.*

Shared sentence-level work

• Ask the children to identify the imperative verbs in the marshmallow crispies recipe. Advise them to look carefully so that they do not miss the imperative verbs in the middle of sentences (though they may notice that these longer sentences could be split into two).

Guided and independent work

• Ask the children to work in the same groups of four as in the last lesson. Ask them to imagine that they are in charge of one of the food stalls (check that both stalls are covered).

• Tell the children to begin by agreeing the four most important menu items (they may include any of their own ideas if they like). Ask them to write recipes for each item.

Plenary

• Choose one fast food group and one wholefood group to present their menu and recipes and ask the class which has the most customer appeal and why?

Differentiation

Less able
• Suggest simple recipes, such as salad sandwich, so children can concentrate on correct use of the imperative.

More able
• Challenge children to devise a really exciting menu and recipes for the wholefood bar.

UNIT 6 HOUR 4 ▭ **Instructions**

Directions

Objectives

NLS
T22: To read and evaluate a range of instructional texts in terms of their: purposes; organisation; clarity and usefulness.
T25: To write instructional texts, and test them out.
S9: To identify the imperative form in instructional writing.

What you need
● Photocopiable pages 73 and 74.

Shared text-level work
● Talk about the importance of directions, both orally and in writing. Ask the children if they have ever had the experience of receiving or giving directions? What happened? When giving directions, were they able to give them clearly? When receiving directions, did they remember everything they were told?
● Read the directions towards the bottom of photocopiable page 74. Ask the children: What is the difference in language and style between the written and oral directions?

● Written directions are more formal and precise, and as succinct as possible so they are easy to follow and remember. Note how the sentences are short and leave out unimportant words.
● Oral directions are informal and imprecise, for example, this street (not sure of street name), go for about (not sure of distance) and benefit from body language (pointing and so on).

● Ask the children to practise giving oral directions. Ask, for example, How would you direct someone to the hall/headteacher's office?
● Then model writing the directions on the board and see the contrast. Number the written instructions and compare them to the oral ones.

Shared sentence-level work
● Ask the children to identify the imperative verbs, and list any more verbs that might be useful in giving/writing directions.

Guided and independent work
● Organise the class so that the children can alternate between these two activities using the theme park map:

1. Ask the children, working in groups of four, to write at least four sets of directions to important places in the theme park.
Tell the children that all directions should be from the Visitors' centre.
Ask other children to 'walk' the map with their fingers according to the directions. Do the directions work?1.

2. Ask the children to work in pairs.
Child 1 tells Child 2 where s/he is: I am outside the Corkscrew-coaster, and where s/he wants to go: I want to go to the fast food bar.
Child 2 then gives verbal directions.
Child 1 traces the directions with a finger or pencil to check that they are correct.

Differentiation

Less able
● Suggest starting points for verbal directions to ensure that there are no more than four steps.

More able
● Encourage children to set difficult tasks for verbal directions involving many steps. Can they remember directions with more than four steps?

Plenary
● Have fun challenging pairs of children to give and remember long verbal directions.
● Pull the lesson together by asking the children to describe the features of good written and oral directions.

Making a presentation

Objectives

NLS
T22: To evaluate a range of instructional texts in terms of their: purposes; organisation and layout; clarity and usefulness
S3: To discuss, proof-read and edit their own writing for clarity and correctness.

S&L
55 Speaking: To present a spoken argument, sequencing points logically and making use of persuasive language.

What you need

● All the children's work from the week.

Shared text-level work

● Keep this session short to allow as much time as possible for group work and presentations.
● Tell the children that the last part of the Fantasmagoria simulation is for each team to present a formal and detailed proposal of its ideas for improving the theme park.
● Say that the winning team will get the job (and free entry passes), so stress the need to be as persuasive as possible.
● Explain that their presentation should last for three minutes and include one example of each of the following:

● a set of instructions for staff
● a set of rules for customers
● a recipe
● a statement of food policy for the theme park
● directions to one of the attractions from the visitor centre.

Shared sentence-level work

● Emphasise the importance of proof-reading and editing their work for clarity and correctness as errors at this level would seriously disadvantage a business presentation!

Guided and independent work

● Ask the children to divide the tasks among members of the group and to plan the use of visual aids. These could take the form of OHTs or sketches on large sheets of paper.
● Encourage one group to prepare a computer-based presentation. Ideally this should be viewed via a data projector, but it could also be viewed on a computer monitor.
● Suggest to the children that they might want to use large, coloured fonts; insert graphics (perhaps including an amended scan of the map) and add sound clips.
● Tell the children to prepare their presentations by selecting their best texts and then proof-reading and editing them.
● Ask the children to compile their texts for display as part of their presentation. This could either be done on large sheets of paper or OHTs.
● Provide the children with rehearsal time if possible.

Differentiation

Less able
● Give help with proof-reading and editing. Encourage their full involvement with speaking to the class.

More able
● Encourage them to give some thought to the visual appearance of the different texts and to simulate this where possible.

Plenary

● Ask the groups to give their three-minute presentations. The rest of the class act as the park developers to evaluate the proposals by discussing and voting for the one they think is most likely to improve the park.
● If you have time, discuss the decision the children reached. How well did the winning team meet the brief? Why was their presentation persuasive?

TERM 1

For your safety

Welcome to Fantasmagoria.
We want you to have a successful
and SAFE visit. Please take a
moment to read the advice in this leaflet.

Safety harness
Please ensure that seat belts, safety harnesses and lap bars are
properly fastened. Many lap bars lock automatically. If a lap bar
seems loose, call the Attendant. Make sure that loose objects are
secured, for example, coins, cameras, purses and bags.

Height and age restrictions
Some rides have restrictions based on height, age or health (such
as, people with heart conditions and pregnant women). Do not
be tempted to ignore these rules. A child who is too short will
not be held firmly by the safety harness, and may be thrown out
of his seat. A person with a heart condition may suffer a heart
attack because of the high G-forces of a sudden turn or stop.

Empty your mouth
Do not get onto a high-speed ride with food or gum in your
mouth, or if you have an unsettled stomach. A sudden turn or
bump could cause you to choke or vomit.

Follow instructions
Follow the instructions given by the Park Attendants. All our
attendants have been fully trained in the safe operation of the
rides and health and safety matters. If you are not sure about
anything, ASK.

Read the signs
Every attraction has a sign at the queue entry point which tells
you all you need to know. Please read these signs and obey
them.

Keep cool
The main cause of illness at theme parks is heat, which leads to a
range of problems such as dehydration, heat exhaustion and
sunstroke. So pace yourself. Take regular breaks, drink plenty of
fluids, and alternate outside rides with indoor attractions. If you
do feel unwell, go to the First Aid Post.

Legal Notice
Fantasmagoria Parks Ltd will not be liable for loss or injury arising from the
neglect of these rules, signs around the park or instruction given by Park
Attendants. This disclaimer does not affect your statutory rights.

*Introduction stating the
purpose of the rules*

*The following
paragraphs were in
order of importance, but
have been jumbled up*

*Negative form of the
imperative*

Reasons for the rule

*The imperative at the
very beginning of this
rule gives it added force*

*Imperative is used in the
conditional ('if') sentence*

*An explanation begins
this rule.*

Another explanation

*The small print. What is
its purpose?*

Fantasmagoria: the brief

Fantasmagoria fun park has almost gone out of business because there have been too many accidents caused by careless operation of rides and a lack of rules for customers. The food is poor, toilets are smelly, and visitors keep getting lost.

Your team has the task of making the park a success. To do this, you will need to write: instructions for the staff, rules for customers, menu ideas or recipes for the chefs and directions to the main attractions.

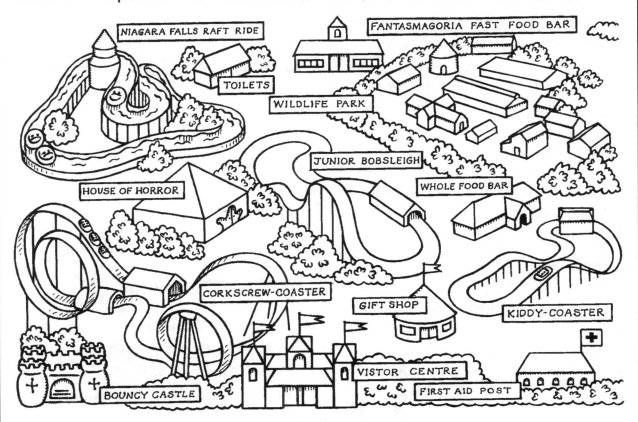

Sample staff instructions
Toilets
Mop floor twice a day.
Clean toilets twice a day and replace toilet paper.
Clean washbasins twice a day
Spray with air freshener twice a day.
Check regularly for more frequent cleaning as necessary.

Sample customer rules
Niagara Falls raft ride
Leave bags, umbrellas and any loose objects at the turnstile.
Wear the life-jacket provided. Put it on before boarding the raft.
Keep your arms inside the raft.
Wait until the raft has been tied to the landing stage before getting out.

Fantasmagoria odds and ends

Marshmallow crispies (6)

6 cups puffed rice cereal
1 6 pack of white marshmallows
3 tablespoons butter or margarine
No-stick cooking spray

Melt margarine in a non-stick pan and add the entire bag of marshmallows. Stir over medium heat until marshmallows have completely melted. Add puffed rice and mix well. Pour mixture into a 9" × 13" pan that has been greased or sprayed with no-stick cooking spray. Use a spatula to spread and flatten mixture. Leave to cool. Remove and cut into squares.

Menus

Fantasmagoria fast food bar
Cheeseburger
Double cheeseburger
Triple-decker cheeseburger
Bacon burger
Mega bacon and cheeseburger
Fries (small, medium, large)
Wholefood bar

Written directions

Corkscrew-coaster
Go straight down High Street
Turn left at Cine 360
Turn right at Barracuda Super-swing
Go straight ahead for 120 yards
Corkscrew-coaster is directly ahead.

Oral directions

You are outside the House of Horror and a visitor has asked how to get to the First Aid Post.
Keep going along this path and turn left at the end.
You'll see the fast food bar. Turn right there, and keep going straight for about 100 metres.
First Aid's on your left.

UNIT 1

Traditional stories and fables

This unit examines the genre features of traditional tales and fables, and looks at updating them through a sci-fi version of *Sleeping Beauty*, urban legends and modern phenomena/mysteries such as Big Foot. The children begin their genre analysis with a folk tale from India, and then retell stories through drama and puppetry before writing their own modern fairy tale. Speaking and listening and quick creativity are particularly encouraged in the exploration and invention of urban myths, also linking to work in Units 3 and 5.

Hour	Shared text-level work	Shared word-/sentence-level work	Guided reading/writing	Independent work	Plenary
1 A traditional tale	Reading the traditional tale *Amul and The Drum*, relating it to folk and fairy tales; identifying typical features.	Finding *ough* words and thinking of others with same string.	Converting a traditional tale into a playscript.	Annotating genre features of a fairy tale; noting *ough* words.	Identifying key genre features and finding them in another story.
2 Plot cards	Using plot cards to map the plot of *Amul and The Drum*.	Finding *ight, ear, ie* and *our* words in the story, and thinking of others.	Analysing and separating complex sentences.	Finding *ight, ear, ie* and *our* words; mapping the story with plot cards.	Checking the plot card sequences, seeing common patterns across genre.
3 Folk-tale theatre	Retelling *Amul and The Drum* with generic puppet figures.	Adapting a story to be suitable for dramatic retelling.	Reading their chosen story, adapting it and practising puppet retelling.	Reading their chosen story, adapting it and practising puppet retelling.	Watching the puppet shows; discussing their effectiveness.
4 Scientific Sleeping Beauty	Reading modern version of *Sleeping Beauty*; comparing genre features; predicting what happens next.	Exploring complex sentences.	Identifying modern style points of the story; highlighting complex sentences.	Identifying modern style points of the story; highlighting complex sentences.	Comparing genre features; changing ending of story.
5 Own version	Recapping genre features; suggesting how to update/change them.	Discussing modern idioms and figures of speech.	Making a poster of modern metaphorical expressions.	Starting their own 'traditional tale'.	Comparing old and new versions of traditional tales.

UNIT 1

Hour	Shared text-level work	Shared word-/ sentence-level work	Guided reading/ writing	Independent work	Plenary
6 The frogs and the well	Reading a fable; discussing typical features.	Revising dialogue conventions.	Adding dialogue to a fable.	Matching fables and morals.	Identifying morals and features.
7 The two boastful boys	Re-reading a modern fable; suggesting the moral and another story with same moral.	Exploring proverbs as a source of fable morals.	Researching and classifying proverbs; writing own fables.	Researching and classifying proverbs; writing own fables.	Guessing morals for stories read out; identifying traditional and modern.
8 Earwig in her ear	Discussing and reading urban legends.	Noting features of orally told tales.	Annotating further legends.	Swapping legends.	Recapping features; noting how stories vary with retellings.
9 Fried brains	Using prompt cards to make up an urban legend.	Identifying features of spoken language.	Using prompt cards to make up urban legends.	Using prompt cards to make up urban legends.	Comparing stories.
10 Bigfoot	Discussing modern myths/stories about modern phenomena.	Brainstorming specialist vocabulary.	Researching modern mythical phenomena for use in a story.	Researching modern mythical phenomena for use in a story.	Reading the stories; revising what they have learned about myths and legends.

Key assessment opportunities
● Can the children understand and recognise key features of traditional tales, fables, urban legends and modern myths?
● Do they understand that many features are common across countries and cultures?
● Can they write or update a traditional tale?
● Can they write their own fables and urban legends?
● Do they understand that myth-making still takes place?

A traditional tale

Objectives

NLS
T1: To identify and classify the features of myths, legends and fables and traditional tales (as required in the medium-term plans)
W5: To investigate words which have common letter strings but different pronunciations, eg rough, cough, bough; boot, foot.

What you need
● Photocopiable pages 87 and 88 (with annotations removed)
● at least one other similar traditional fairy tale.

Shared text-level work
● Explain to the children that you are going to read a traditional tale from India. Tell them that traditional tales are sometimes called folk tales or fairy tales.
● Display photocopiable pages 87 and 88 and read the story aloud to the children.
● Ask the children if they enjoyed it and why.
● Go through the story again to identify features of traditional tales. Use the annotations in the original as a starting point.
● Ask the children if they can think of any other key features of traditional tales not included in this short example, such as a *Once upon a time* opening and a *happy ever after* ending.
● Finally, summarise key features by writing a list like the following on the board:
Common opening phrases (not used in this example, but might include *Once upon a time, A long time ago, In a land far away*)
Stock characters (explain the term as typical character types, where characters are so similar it's as though they come from the stockroom of a character factory)
Common story patterns (in this example, a little boy leaves home, and is rewarded for helping someone, and this is repeated five times until he gets what he wants)
Traditional setting (a rural past with peasants, princes, palaces and castles. No cars, mobile phones or any other modern technology; a world based on magic instead of science).

Shared word-level work
● Ask the children to find words in the text with letter strings *ough* and *oo (enough, bought, brought, poor, wood, soon, looked)*.
● Then brainstorm other words with these letter strings.
● Finally, sort them into groups of common pronunciation.

Guided and independent work
● Work with one group of children to change a traditional story into a playscript. For example, discuss and decide what can be presented as dialogue and what must be said by a narrator.
● Remind the children of playscript conventions.
● Allocate a fairy tale to pairs of children and ask them to read it together, and then annotate the distinctive features that mark the text as a traditional tale.
● Remind the children to also look for the letter strings *ough* and *oo*.

Differentiation

Less able
● Ask the children to read and annotate *Amul and The Drum*, as in the shared session.

More able
● Ask the children to notice cultural differences between their tale and *Amul and The Drum*.

Plenary
● Ask the children to say which key features they were able to find in their fairy tales.
● Scribe the childrens' examples on the board.
● Read through the list and see if the children can identify the features in another traditional tale.

UNIT 1 HOUR 2 Traditional stories and fables

Plot cards

Objectives

NLS

T2: To investigate different versions of the same story; recognise how stories change over time and differences of culture and place that are expressed in stories.
W3: To use independent spelling strategies, including using common letter strings
W5: To investigate words which have common letter strings but different pronunciations.

What you need
● Photocopiable pages 87 and 88
● photocopiable page 89 (intact for shared work, cut into cards for activities)
● selection of traditional tales, including different versions of the same story.

Shared text-level work
● Display photocopiable page 89 and explain that it is a set of cards that can be used to map the plot of a traditional story, and later on, to plan one. Read the cards with the children.
● Demonstrate how to use the cards by re-reading *Amul and The Drum* and, at the appropriate point in the story, indicating the card that shows the plot (this should also help them to fully understand the vocabulary on the cards):

> B. Lack
> E. Departure
> G. Help (×5)
> K. Solution
> L. Reward.

● Explain to the children that they are going to do the same with a different traditional story. Warn them that the cards will not fit every story so neatly, but they should make them fit as best they can.

Shared word-level work
● Remind the children about the work done on letter strings on the previous day, and explain that the work will be continued in this lesson with a focus on letter strings *ight, ear, ie, our*. Write these on the board and ask the children to find examples in *Amul and The Drum* (there are several of each). Ask the children to brainstorm more examples.

Guided and independent work
● Help a group of children to work on the analysis of complex sentences by taking a section of a traditional story and highlighting all sentences that contain more than one statement – complex sentences.
● The next step is to ask the children to rewrite the section in a series of simple sentences.
● Give each pair of children a story. Ask them to read it carefully together, and then re-read it to look for letter strings *ight, ear, ie, our*. Then ask them to try to pick out some plot cards that match the plot.
● Encourage the children to discuss their ideas in their pairs and to come to an agreement on each card.
● Suggest that they take each card in turn and 'discard' any that don't fit. Ask them to review their selection and check through the story again.

Differentiation

Less able
● Give the children short stories that are easy to match to the cards.

More able
● Give the children more complex and challenging stories that need more interpretation.

Plenary
● Share the card sequences. Whose story was a good fit? A bad fit? How many stories resulted in similar card sequences?
● The results should demonstrate common patterns in traditional tales from different countries and cultures. See if the children can tell you where their stories are set.

Folk-tale theatre

Objectives

NLS
T3: To explore similarities and differences between oral and written storytelling.
S6: To be aware of the differences between spoken and written language.

What you need
● Photocopiable pages 87 and 88
● generic character cut-out figures: boy, helper, hero, heroine, king, peasant, stepmother, villain, witch
● the stories used in Hour 2 (but see note below)
● theatre props (see below).

Shared text-level work
● This could be a 'slow down' moment. If you decide to allow extra time for this activity, allocate a different story from Hour 1 or 2 for each pair of children.
● Ask the children to make their own resources (using your character figures as a starting point) and choose their own type of theatre (depending on resources). However, if you wish to complete the activity in one lesson, ask the children to use their story from Hour 2 (to save reading time), and give them ready-made resources.
● Using *Amul and The Drum*, demonstrate how to retell a folk tale using the character figures. Several methods are possible:

> **Shoebox theatre** - mount the figures on card and add a support to make them stand up; draw background scenery and use a cardboard box as a theatre; narrate the story as you move the characters.
>
> **OHP theatre** - transfer each character to the middle of a strip of acetate so that it can be moved from side to side; characters can be laid over another OHT showing a suitable background scene, and projected by OHP; narrate the story as you move the characters.
>
> **Computer theatre** - scan the characters and use them as clip art; combine them with fairy tale settings and create a slide sequence in a presentation package; narrate the story as the slides are shown (this is particularly effective if a data projector is available).

● Tell the children that they will need to find or create suitable backgrounds and that they can make new characters, animals and fabulous beasts as required.

Shared sentence-level work
● Explain to the children that they must not merely read out the folk tale they are presenting. They need to adapt it for the folk-tale theatre. Discuss how to do this most effectively, for example, a narrator says what happens; other group members speak the dialogue of the characters. Help them to make up extra dialogue as necessary.

Guided and independent work
● Ask the children to work in groups of three and to begin by reading their story.
● They should then plan how to adapt the story for the medium they have chosen or been allocated (see specific suggestions given in shared work).
● Ask the groups to practise performing their adaptations with the appropriate props.

Plenary
● Watch one or two theatrical presentations and discuss how effectively the written story has been changed into a form suitable for theatrical presentation.

Differentiation

Less able
● Ask the children to work on *Amul and The Drum*.

More able
● Ask the children to work on a more complex story.

Scientific Sleeping Beauty

Objectives

NLS
T2: To investigate different versions of the same story in print or on film, identifying similarities and differences; recognise how stories change over time and differences of culture and place that are expressed in stories;
S5: To use punctuation effectively to signpost meaning in longer and more complex sentences.

What you need
● Photocopiable page 90 (with annotations removed).

Shared text-level work
● Remind the children that traditional tales exist in many versions, including modern reworkings. Consider how many versions they know (both books and films) of, for example, *Little Red Riding Hood* and *Cinderella*.
● Tell them that they are going to read a version of *Sleeping Beauty* written in 2004, and recap on the traditional version.
● Begin reading photocopiable page 90 to the children, asking them to listen carefully for anything that makes it different from the traditional version.
● Conceal the ending and reveal it in two parts: 1. when we find out that the astronaut wants the drug not the girl, and 2. when we find out how she reacts. Before revealing each stage, ask the children what they think happens next.
● Go through the story again and ask the children to suggest annotations noting differences between traditional and modern versions. Use the original resource as a guide if necessary (ignore notes on complex sentences, brackets and commas for now).

Shared sentence-level work
● Help the children to understand the concept of additional information in sentences.
● Explain that this story contains many complex sentences and that these sentences contain a main point plus extra information often marked off by commas or brackets.
● Ask the children to find examples of complex sentences and annotate the examples they find. (Tell the children to use the annotations to help pick these out.)

Guided and independent work
● Ask the children to work in pairs to find and annotate in 'Scientific Sleeping Beauty' the vocabulary, concepts and style points that signify it as a modern version.
● Then ask them to highlight sentences where extra information is marked off by commas or brackets.

Plenary
● Pull the lesson together by asking the children to make suggestions for a table like this:

Sleeping Beauty	Scientific Sleeping Beauty
Traditional opening Traditional setting and characters – king, queen, castle...	Traditional opening followed by a surprise twist Non-traditional setting (which planet?)

● Encourage the children to think of and justify a different ending to 'Scientific Sleeping Beauty'.

Differentiation

Less able
● Ask the children to annotate the modern features only.

More able
● Ask the children to take the sentence analysis further by experimenting with the transposition of clauses marked off by commas.

Own version

Shared text-level work

● Remind the children of traditional *Sleeping Beauty* and modern 'Scientific Sleeping Beauty' and explain to them that they are going to write their own story that uses the style points, character types and plot lines of traditional tales or a new version of a traditional story.
● Recap typical features of traditional stories from Hour 1.
● Brainstorm ideas for their stories and jot down good ones on the board, for example:
Add or change to a non-traditional character (a tough princess, a rastafarian prince, a timid giant)
Change cultures (a Caribbean version of *Rapunzel*)
Create a non-traditional setting (a city, the future, the wild west)
Pick 'n' mix (Cinderella meets Ali Baba and his forty theives!)
Write a completely new traditional story (with traditional or modern characters and settings; use the plot cards to help to plan it).

Shared word-level work

● Explain to the children that they could use some common metaphorical expressions and figures of speech from everyday life in their stories, to give it a personal, contemporary touch. Give the children the following examples and see if they can explain them and where they would hear/say them:

> ● A bolt from the blue (in paragraph 2 of 'Scientific Sleeping Beauty')
> ● Get out of the wrong side of the bed
> ● Let sleeping dogs lie
> ● Let the cat out of the bag
> ● Take a back seat
> ● Throw the baby out with the bath water.

● Then ask the children to brainstorm in pairs for a few minutes and suggest more. Ask them to bear them in mind when planning their characters and story events.

Guided and independent work

● Work with a group to brainstorm more metaphorical expressions and figures of speech from everyday life. Use reference books or the internet to help.
● Ask the children to make a poster for the rest of the class to use.
● Ask other children to make a start on their own 'traditional tale' or updated version of an existing traditional tale. Encourage them to include figures of speech and modern expressions where appropriate.

Plenary

● Arrange for one traditional story and one non-traditional version of a story to be read out. Use the stories to pull together the learning so far: the features of traditional stories, their universality, the creativity of modern versions.

UNIT 1 HOUR 6 📖 Traditional stories and fables

The frogs and the well

Objectives

NLS
T1: To identify and classify the features of myths, legends and fables, eg the moral in a fable.
Term 1 S7: From reading, to understand how dialogue is set out, eg, on separate lines for alternate speakers in narrative, and the positioning of commas before speech marks.

What you need

● Photocopiable page 91, including copies cut into cards
● other fables from around the world (without stated morals)
● internet access (optional).

Differentiation

Less able
● Ask the children to do the matching exercise using photocopiable page 91 only.

More able
● Give the children fables with unusual morals (Chinese fables at www.chinavista.com/experience/fable/fable.html are recommended).

Shared text-level work

● Tell the children that they are going to read an example of a fable. Ask if anyone knows what a fable is and can give an example. Say that a fable is a short story that conveys a useful moral lesson. Talk about Aesop as the most famous writer of fables, but point out that other countries have fables of their own.
● Elicit the key features of fables from the children and write a list like the following on the board:

> ● traditional, 'everywhere' setting (forest, lake, palace, marsh and so on)
> ● traditional, generic, 'symbolic' characters (fisherman, woodcutter; animals often used to represent certain characteristics/failings of humans)
> ● a moral that gives the reader advice on how to live based on the story.

● Explain to the children that the moral is not always explicitly stated, but is clear from interpreting the story.
● Read the first fable on photocopiable page 91 and ask the children which typical features they identified. Ask them what the moral is. Point out events/choices and consequences in the story to prompt the answer (look before you leap).

Shared sentence level work

● Read the second fable, 'The two boastful boys', and use it to revise the layout and punctuation of dialogue.
● Remind the children of the rule: 'New speakers begin new paragraphs', and tell them to remember five things (use five fingers as a mnemonic) for each speech:
1. Speech marks
2. Capital letter
3. Comma, exclamation mark or question mark
4. Speech marks
5. Full stop at end of sentence
(Note: the above refers to the most common 'pattern' of dialogue: speech + reporting clause).

Guided and independent work

● Most fables are short and include little or no dialogue. Ask the children to choose a fable and extend it by adding dialogue. Emphasise that the dialogue must be correctly punctuated and set out and revise how to do this if necessary.
● Ask the children to match the fables to the morals at the bottom of the page. Kinaesthetic learners may find it helpful to cut out and physically match fable and moral. To make this activity more challenging, ask the children to investigate more fables.

Plenary

● Briefly go over the answers to the matching exercise, then choose one or two of the additional fables and discuss possible morals.

The two boastful boys

Objectives

NLS
T11: To write own versions of legends, myths and fables, using structures and themes identified in reading.
Term 1 W9: To collect and classify a range of idiomatic phrases, clichés and expressions.

What you need
- Photocopiable page 91
- internet access (optional).

Shared text-level work
- Re-read 'The two boastful boys' on photocopiable page 91.
- Explain that this is a modern fable that illustrates the same moral as Aesop's *The vixen and the lioness*. If time allows, the children should read this fable too and then compare the two versions.
- Ask the children to notice similarities and differences between this modern fable and traditional fables.
- Explain that the main differences are that the characters and settings are modern but everything else is the same.
- Now ask the children if they can think of the following:

- another moral for this fable
- another existing modern story that illustrates the same moral
- a little story of their own that illustrates the moral.

Shared word-level work
- Explain to the children that they are going to write similar modern fables and that the best way to do this is to think of a moral and then to write a story to illustrate it.
- A good source of morals for stories can be found in proverbs. Brainstorm some examples:

- A bird in the hand is worth two in the bush.
- Don't put off until tomorrow what you can do today.
- Necessity is the mother of invention.
- Too many cooks spoil the broth.
- Many hands make light work

- Ask the children to suggest a suitable story to illustrate one of the proverbs. Give them a few minutes to explore ideas in pairs before offering their ideas.

Differentiation

Less able
- Ask the children to write new stories for the morals in fables they have read, for example, 'Don't count your chickens until the eggs have hatched.'

More able
- Give the children unusual and thought-provoking morals to base their story on. Chinese proverbs would make an interesting starting point (for example, Have a mouth as sharp as a dagger but a heart as soft as tofu, from www.kn.pacbell.com/wired/China/proverb.html).

Guided and independent work
- Ask one group of children to research proverbs in the school library or on the internet.
- Help them to classify the proverbs they find, for instance, proverbs based on animals, people, or from other cultures.
- Ask pairs of children to write their own fables, similar to the model in the shared session. Let them start from the morals brainstormed earlier if necessary.

Plenary
- Ask several pairs of children to present their fables to the class, leaving out the morals.
- Encourage the rest of the class to guess the morals of the story.
- Identify which features of the fables are traditional and which are modern.

Earwig in her ear

Objectives

NLS
T1: To identify and classify the features of myths, legends and fables.
S6: To be aware of the differences between spoken and written language.

S&L
42 Listening: To listen to a speaker, make notes on the talk.

What you need
● Photocopiable page 95
● internet access (optional).

Differentiation

Less able
● Ask the children to re-read and annotate the two urban legends that were the focus of the shared session.

More able
● Ask the children to use annotations from independent work to retell a story orally. Challenge them to change/exaggerate certain details.

Shared text-level work
● Explain that you are going to read an urban legend and ask if anyone knows what the term means. Urban legends (also referred to as urban myths) are modern legends passed off as actually happening even though they are untrue or at least unverifiable. They are called 'urban' because they are a relatively modern form and deal with the issues of contemporary modern life. They tend to have the same simple structure as traditional fables but people really believe them. Urban legends often express peoples' fears or lack of understanding about technology.
● Write key features of urban legends on the board:

> ● told orally
> ● people believe they are true
> ● the story never happened to the teller, always somebody else (a friend of a friend...)
> ● modern settings and characters
> ● about things that affect people in the modern world.

● Read and enjoy the first fable on photocopiable page 92. Then identify typical features.
● Ask the children: Has anyone else heard a story about an earwig getting into anyone's ear, or a similar story?

Shared sentence-level work
● Explain that urban legends are primarily an oral form, often changing along the way. Read the second example on photocopiable page 92 and identify language features typical of the oral form. Jot down a list like the following and annotate examples as children identify them:

> ● looser sentence structure (see the first sentence)
> ● colloquial expressions usually used only in speech (...there was this...; well...)
> ● mixing of tenses.

Guided and independent work
● Ask pairs of children to read the next two urban legends on photocopiable page 93, and to annotate (perhaps in two colours) typical features of urban legends, and the features of spoken language.
● Ask other children to exchange orally similar urban legends they have heard for the listeners to write them down. Encourage them to use note-taking skills practised earlier.

Plenary
● Ask the children to report their annotations and use their ideas to sum up key features of urban legends and the differences between spoken and written language.
● Share a few more urban legends as taken down in notes and compare them with the original version to see how they change with repeated tellings by different people.

Fried brains

Objectives

NLS
T11: To write own versions of legends, myths and fables, using structures and themes identified in reading.
S6: To be aware of the differences between spoken and written language.

S&L
44 Speaking: To tell stories using voice effectively.

What you need
● Photocopiable page 93, including copies cut into cards
● internet access (optional).

Shared text-level work
● Show the children photocopiable page 93 and explain that it is a set of cards that can be used to make up urban legends. Model this creativity by making up your own urban legend by using one card from each column, or using this example based on A5, B4, C5, D7:

> A teacher who used to teach in this school went on a school trip to London. She missed her husband very much, so she spent ages talking to him on her mobile phone. Well, the radio waves from the phone must have fried her brain because when she got back she couldn't even add up 2 and 2!

● Explain that, though you just made it up, stories like it are often told, and reflect or make fun of a real concern about the dangers of excessive mobile phone use.

Shared sentence-level work
● Ask the children which features of urban legends and spoken language they can identify in your story.

Guided and independent work
● Ask the children to use the cards to plan their own urban legends in their pairs.
● Emphasise that the cards are a starting point only and that they are free to include their own ideas. Try the following:

> **Urban legend card sharps**
> 1. Place the cards face down in four shuffled packs A, B, C and D in the middle of the table.
> 2. Each child chooses one card from each pack.
> 3. S/he then has to make up an urban legend entirely orally and tell it to his/her partner.
> 4. After trying several urban legends, each child should choose one and improve it with his/her partner's help.
>
> **Urban legend circle time**
> 1. Divide the class in half, each half made of one of each pair of children.
> 2. Ask them to make two concentric circles.
> 3. Ask each child to tell a legend to the partner on his/her right, and to pass it on.
> 4. When the tale gets back to the original teller, ask him/her to note down how it has changed.

Differentiation

Less able
● Less able children and kinaesthetic learners will find it helpful to keep hold of the cards for their best urban legend as a reminder of the story.

More able
● Ask one group to select two cards from each pack and to combine the ideas more flexibly (leaving out anything that doesn't fit, but using the rest to compose a more complex story).

Plenary
● Ask several pairs of children to retell their urban legends.
● See if any other pairs had the same combination of cards but a different story.
● Discuss how the urban legends changed in the urban legend circle time.

Bigfoot

Objectives

NLS
T1: To identify and classify the features of myths, legends and fables.
T16: To prepare for reading by identifying what they already know and what they need to find out.
T17: To locate information confidently and efficiently.
W9: To search for, collect, define and spell technical words derived from work in other subjects.

What you need

● Access to school library and the internet.

Shared text-level work

● Recap that, in this unit, the children have studied a range of myths and legends from ancient times to the present day, and that you are going to finish off by researching and writing about modern myths/phenomena.

● Write 'Bigfoot' on the board and ask the children what they have heard about it. (Bigfoot is said to be a giant ape-man similar to the Yeti/abominable snowman. Footprints have been found and one Bigfoot was allegedly caught on film in 1967 in northern California.)

● First, explain what makes it a modern myth, such as continuous speculation; an enduring mystery; public fascination with things that are weird but possible; one way to answer something strange. Explain that there are similar stories in different countries (Bigfoot/Yeti; Nessie/Champ); and that though there is alleged evidence, modern myths are ultimately unprovable one way or the other.

● Brainstorm other modern myths with the children, for example:

> **aliens/flying saucers** (many people believe that intelligent aliens exist and have 'visited' Earth, but there is no convincing evidence)
> **Crop circles** (allegedly created by aliens but probably another hoax)
> **The Bermuda Triangle** (a collection of related myths around a natural phenomenon, most of which have natural, albeit very unusual, explanations)
> **The Loch Ness Monster** (plesiosaur or hoax?)
> **Global warming** (Is the problem really as bad as some people make out? If so, why do we still have freezing winters?).

Shared word-level work

● Tell the children they are going to research the topic and you will expect them to take special care to find out about and spell correctly any specialist vocabulary. Exemplify this by asking children to brainstorm any specialist words that might come up in the Bigfoot topic: Abominable Snowman, apelike, Himalaya, prehistoric, Sasquatch, Yeti and so on.

Guided and independent work

● Take the children to the library, or provide a range of reference books in the classroom. (Any good, up-to-date encyclopedias, including multimedia, should provide enough information for the task.)

● Ask the children, working in pairs but then writing individually, to choose a modern myth, research it and use the information as the basis for a story. For example, the children might meet Bigfoot, be abducted by aliens, go for a cruise in the Bermuda triangle or stumble across a mysterious crop circle.

Plenary

● Ask some of the children to read their stories.
● Pull the whole section of work together by asking the children what they have learned about different kinds of myths and legends.

Differentiation

Less able
● Ensure that the children have access to texts at an appropriate level.

More able
● Encourage the children to investigate one of the more arcane modern myths such as the Bible Code.

Amul and The Drum

Ever since he could remember, Amul had wanted a drum. As soon as his arms and hands grew strong enough, he would tap out rhythms on anything he could find. His Mother would say, " Amul! Amul! No more! You are turning my head into a drum!" Although she worked hard baking bread and cleaning the houses of the wealthy people in the town, she was poor. They only gave her grain in return for her work. Every week she would go to the market to sell the grain she had left so that she could buy food for the table and put clothes on Amul's back. Every time Amul's Mother went to the market, she would say to Amul, "is there anything I can bring you?" Amul would always reply, " Yes please Mother. A drum! A drum!" His Mother would smile and say, " I'll do my best." Amul knew she would, but he knew that she would never have enough money to buy a drum.

 One day, when Amul's Mother went to the market, she found that the price of grain had risen. She sold all the grain she had and when she had bought all she needed for Amul and herself, she found that she had money left over. There was enough to buy a drum! She set off quickly to the market stall, which sold musical instruments of all kinds. But, as she came round the corner of the street she came across a woman with four children. They were all crying. The woman begged her to help them. She had fallen on hard times and her children were hungry. Amul's Mother felt her heart fill with sorrow. She could not bear to see them go hungry so she gave them the money she had saved for Amul's drum. The woman was overcome with gratitude. " I have nothing I can give you in return," she said, "except these drum sticks. They belonged to my husband, but both he and the drum are long gone. What use are drumsticks without a drum?." Amul's Mother took them, thinking to herself, " well, if I couldn't get him a drum, I have got him the next best thing."

 Amul was delighted. He took his drumsticks with him, everywhere he went, tapping out rhythms on anything he found. As he was playing one day, he heard an old woman crying. She could not light her fire and she was making bread for a wedding party that very day. Amul could not bear to see her so upset. He loved his drumsticks but his heart filled with sorrow and he gave her his sticks to make a fire. She was so grateful that she gave him a piece of wedding bread. Amul was disappointed to have given away his drumsticks but did not let it show. He thanked her and went on his way.

 As Amul walked slowly home by the river, he heard the sound of raised voices. It was a washerman. He and his wife were arguing about which one of them should go home and fetch food for their hungry baby, who was wailing like a cat with a thorn in its paw. " You go!" Shouted the husband, " because I have to wash these clothes for the wedding party

Stock character – a poor woman

Common plot starter – lack of something

Not much description or dialogue

Letter string 'ough'

Letter string 'oo'

Repeated pattern begins here

Another stock character – a helper. By giving the boy a reward, the helper helps him towards his goal.

The pattern is repeated. The character is different but fills the same role – helper

this evening and it was you who forgot the food for the baby. Amul ran over to them and his heart was filled with sorrow when he heard the cries of the baby. He gave the child the piece of bread the old woman had given him. The washerman and his wife were delighted with Amul and gave him a fine coat, good enough for a wedding party.

As dusk fell, Amul strutted across the bridge that led to his house, wearing his fine new coat. Then he saw a man shivering with cold. He had no shirt to his back. " I was attacked by robbers!" said the man. "They took everything except my horse! They even took the shirt from my back. I was going to a wedding, but now I have nothing to wear, so I cannot go. What use is a horse, when I have no suitable clothes?" Again Amul's heart was filled with sorrow. He gave the man his fine new coat saying, " here, take this, for I have no need of a fine coat. I have no wedding to go to." The man was so pleased that he gave Amul his horse. " I have no need of my horse,"he said. " The wedding is but a short distance from here and you have shown me great kindness."

Amul climbed up on the horse's back thinking how proud his Mother would be when she saw him ride home and heard his tale. As he rounded a bend in the road he ran into a wedding party with musicians. They were sitting under a tree with faces as long as a lizard's tongue. Amul asked them why they looked so glum when they were going to a wedding. The bridegroom said, " The man who promised a horse for me has not arrived and so there can be no wedding procession. I cannot walk and besides it is getting late and I will miss the auspicious hour for the wedding." Yet again Amul's heart was filled with sorrow. " Here! Take my horse! I cannot see you all look so sad." The bridegroom was so overjoyed that he said to Amul, " You have saved my marriage! What can I give you in return?" Amul did not hesitate. " A drum! A drum! Please!" The musician gladly gave his drum to Amil when the bride groom told him that he would pay him well enough so that he could buy another one.

Amul rushed home to tell his Mother the whole story, beating his drum as he went. She heard him coming long before he came in through the door and smiled.

Campbell Perry

*Cultural feature –
an auspicious hour*

*This time, helper
gives him what he
wants – a drum*

Plot cards

A. Harm The villain harms a member of the family – by kidnapping, theft, casting a spell, switching a child, forcing a marriage… 	**B. Lack** A member of the family lacks something or desires something, eg, food, money, a magical potion… 	**C. Ban** The hero(ine) is told *not* to do something, eg, "Don't go there", "Don't do this", but the ban is disobeyed. 
D. Trick The villain tries to trick the hero(ine). The villain may be disguised or pretending to offer help. 	**E. Departure** The hero(ine) leaves home to try to solve a problem. S/he is sometimes the third family member to try. 	**F. Test** A difficult task proposed to the hero(ine), eg, trial by ordeal, riddles, test of strength or other tasks. 
G. Help A helper (wizard, fairy godmother, another character…) gives advice, a gift, or help. Sometimes the help is magical. 	**H. Magic** The hero(ine) gets a magical object – this can be found, given, bought, or appear magically. 	**I. Combat** The hero(ine) and villain join in direct combat. 
J. Victory The villain is overcome – killed in combat, defeated in a contest, killed while asleep, banished… 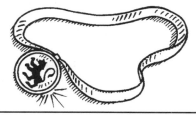	**K. Solution** The main problem is solved, eg, food or money is provided, the object of the search is found, the spell broken… 	**L. Reward** The hero(ine) is rewarded, eg, is married and ascends the throne, is given money, land, honour, fame… 

Scientific Sleeping Beauty

Long ago, in the year 2050, on the fourth planet of a yellow star, Bella was choosing her subjects for her Z-Levels (like A-levels, but 26 times harder). "I want to do maths, physics and chemistry," she said.

Traditional opening, followed by surprise

This was a bolt from the blue to her father. "I'm a scientist," he said, "and I know how tough it can be. I think you should choose childcare, cookery and beauty therapy."

Non-traditional setting

Beauty therapy was a mistake. There are chemicals in beauty therapy, and Bella's sharp mind wanted to find out all about them. Soon, she was carrying out experiments to invent what every scientist hoped would make him (or her) famous – SAD (the Suspended Animation Drug). This would allow astronauts to sleep for hundreds of years while their spaceships travelled to other star-systems.

Complex sentences

Political ideas – is her father sexist?
No – he has a reason

Extra information enclosed in brackets

Then it happened. The hypodermic needle, which should have gone into the furry bottom of a white rat, pricked her finger. Bella went into suspended animation.

Common figure of speech

In 2150, a young, handsome astronaut landed on the deserted fourth planet. He was taking a big risk, for it was a dangerous place, but he had heard rumours that a great prize was to be found among the ruins.

Commas separate items in a list

Non-traditional female character

He searched for hours until at last he came to a large dome. Over the door, a faded sign said, 'Beauty Products Laboratory'. He went in, and fast asleep in the middle of the room, was the most beautiful girl he had ever seen.

Extra information in clauses marked out by commas

He pressed his lips on hers and she opened her eyes with a start. "My astronaut!" sighed Bella, "You have come to awaken me with a kiss and claim my hand in marriage!"

Reminder of original version

"Unfortunately not," said the astronaut, "Marriage was abolished in 2149 by decree of the Chief Scientist."

Complex sentences

"Oh, well, why are you here then?"

"I've come for a great prize."

Non-traditional setting, but traditional description – young and handsome

"Me?"

"SAD."

"Well, I am now, but I wasn't when I..."

Change from the original version

"No, I mean the Suspended Animation Drug..."

After a hundred years he is still sleeping. He dreams about how she leapt up and stabbed him with the hypodermic needle; about how beautiful she looked; and about how much he wished that marriage had not been abolished in 2149.

Her reaction is told in his dream – a technique that would never be used in a traditional tale

Match the moral

The monkey and the mirror

A monkey somehow got hold of a mirror and went around showing it to the other animals in the jungle. The baboon looked into it and said he was very sorry he looked so old. The tiger said he didn't like his stripes. The snake said he didn't like his yellow eyes. In fact, every animal wished it had a different face. The monkey then took the mirror to a wise old elephant who had been watching what had happened. "No," said the elephant, "I don't want to look into it, for I am sure that knowledge is a source of pain."

"You are right," agreed the animals, and broke the mirror into a thousand pieces.

Traditional Indian

The two boastful boys

Two boys were boasting to each other about their family's possessions.

"We've got four tellies in our house," said the first boy.

"Four!" said the second boy, "What are they like?"

"Well, we've got a 24-inch in the lounge with five channels. Me and my sister have little portables, and my mum has an old one in the kitchen."

The second boy scoffed. "We might only have one TV in our house, but it's a plasma screen with 800 satellite channels and Dolby 5.1 surround sound."

Modern

The milkmaid and her pail

A farmer's daughter had been out to milk the cows and was returning to the dairy carrying her pail of milk upon her head. As she walked, she daydreamed about the future: "This milk will give me cream that I can sell at the market. I will buy some eggs, and these will produce chickens. By and by I shall have a large poultry-yard. Then I shall sell some of my chickens and buy a new gown. I shall wear it when I go to the fair, and all the boys will admire me – but I shall toss my head and have nothing to say to them." Forgetting all about the pail, she tossed her head. The milk was spilt, and all her dreams went with it.

by Aesop

The frogs and the well

Two frogs lived in a marsh. One hot summer the marsh dried up, and the frogs left to look for another place to live. By and by they came to a deep well. One of the frogs looked down into it and said, "This looks like a nice cool place. Let us jump in and settle here." But the other, who was wiser, replied, "Not so fast, my friend. Supposing this well dried up like the marsh, how should we get out again?"

by Aesop

Morals

Do not count your chickens before they are hatched.
Look before you leap.
Quality is better than quantity.
Ignorance is bliss.

Four urban legends

Earwig in her ear

Someone told me about this friend who got an earwig in her ear. A few days later, she had earache and went to the doctor. The doctor told her that the earache was probably caused by the earwig, but it had crawled in too far to reach it.

"What shall I do?" said the girl.

"You'll just have to wait until it crawls out," replied the doctor. "In the meantime, I'll give you a painkiller to stop the earache."

Well, next morning, the girl found an earwig on her pillow, so she took it to the doctor. Guess what he said. He told her that it was the earwig that had caused the headache – but it was a female and had laid eggs!

(It is a common belief that earwigs crawl into human ears – but don't worry, it's not true!)

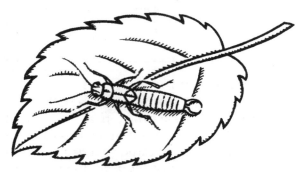

A fine bird

Have you heard the story about the son who sent his mother a cockateel as a present? Well, he had it trained to sing 'Amazing Grace' – cost him a bomb it did. He was ever so excited when he went to visit her because he wanted to ask her how much she liked her present. "Hi, Mum," he says, looking round for the birdcage. "What did you think of my present?"

"Delicious!" she says. "Much tastier than supermarket chickens."

(How can you mix up a cockateel and a chicken? And anyway, who sends live birds by post?)

Year 6 test cheat

In a school in the north – near Carlisle, I think – a Year 6 boy was sent to the headteacher. Well, he knocks at the headteacher's door, but there's no answer, so he pops his head round the door. There was nobody there, but he sees a pile of test papers on the desk. So he grabs one of the test papers, pushes it up his jumper, and goes back to his classroom.

Anyway, just before the test, the headteacher counted the papers and noticed that one was missing. She knew that if there was any cheating, she could lose her job. Then she had this brilliant idea. She guillotined a centimetre off the bottom of all the tests. She caught the thief dead easy – he handed in the longest test paper!

(The pressure caused by Year 6 tests has led to lots of stories about cheating. Some of them are true – but this one has all the characteristics of an urban legend.)

Alligators in the sewers

A girl who used to go to our school had pet newts – well, that's what she thought they were. One day, she put them in the sink so she could clean out their tank, but she accidentally pulled out the plug and they went down the plug hole. They ended up in the drains and grew and grew until they were six feet long, and now they're breeding in the sewers.

(This is one of hundreds of different versions of a common urban legend – there is even a film about it called Alligator.)

Urban legend cards

A. WHO it happened to	B. WHERE or when it happened	C. WHAT happened	D. HOW it turned out in the end
A1 ...a DIY enthusiast in the next street...	**B1** ...cleaning out his/her pet...	**C1** ...ate (or drank) it...	**D1** ...abducted by aliens...
A2 ...a friend of a friend of mine...	**B2** ...digging the garden...	**C2** ...found a lump of rusty metal...	**D2** ...came out in boils. When they burst, hundreds of grubs crawled out...
A3 ...a girl/boy who used to go to our school...	**B3** ...going home at night...	**C3** ...picked up the wrong suitcase...	**D3** ...crawled his/her other ear but the doctor said it had laid eggs inside...
A4 ...a girl/boy who used to go to our school...	**B4** ...on a school trip...	**C4** ...put it in the microwave to dry it...	**D4** ...ended up without shoes in the middle of the street...
A5 ...a teacher who used to teach in this school...	**B5** ...in a restaurant...	**C5** ...talking for ages on his/her mobile phone...	**D5** ...found £1 million in his/her suitcase...
A6 ...an old woman my mum knows...	**B6** ...on holiday in Florida...	**C6** ...stung by an insect...	**D6** ...hair turned white overnight...
A7 ...my grandad told me this story about when he was in the war...	**B7** ...sheltering in a ruined house...	**C7** ...the pet escaped...	**D7** ...is in hospital because it fried his/her brains...
A8 ...somebody who works with my dad...	**B8** ...surfing the internet...	**C8** ...wanted suntan lotion but picked up the wrong bottle...	**D8** ...are breeding in the sewers...

UNIT 2

Poetry

This unit is based on a narrative poem written in a fun, adventure-game format, called 'The Mystery of Sir Roger's Tomb'. Children later apply what they have learned from reading and studying this poem to poems they have chosen themselves for a class anthology. It is important that children are told in Hour 1 that they should each find at least one poem that tells a story, as this will be needed later in the week. Hour 2 links to Unit 39 in *Grammar for Writing*.

Hour	Shared text-level work	Shared word-/ sentence-level work	Guided reading/ writing	Independent work	Plenary
1 A poetry adventure	Reading and discussing Part 1 of *The Mystery of Sir Roger's Tomb*.	Identifying homophones.	Making a table of homophones from the poem.	Reading the poem in groups, solving puzzles and making decisions.	Finding solutions to the poem puzzles.
2 Own story	Considering how to turn Part 1 into prose.	Identifying pronouns and personal pronouns.	Finding pronouns and relating them to nouns.	Writing a story based on the poem.	Sharing stories; discussing differences between first and third person versions.
3 Extra section	Analysing the ballad form of *Sir Roger's Tomb*.	Discussing antonyms using examples from the poem.	Writing an extra puzzle/ section for the poem.	Writing an extra puzzle/section for the poem.	Discussing extra sections; noting rhythm and rhyme.
4 Anthology	Matching different poetic forms.	Noting onomatopoeia in poem extracts.	Holding group meetings to select poems for an anthology.	Holding group meetings to select poems for an anthology.	Presenting the case for their poems.
5 Choral presentation	Discussing how to present a poem chorally.	Using punctuation as a guide to intonation, pauses and gesture.	Preparing a choral presentation of a poem.	Preparing a choral presentation of a poem.	Choral readings of poems; evaluating the readings.

Key assessment opportunities
● Analyse different patterns of rhythm and rhyme.
● Recognise similes and metaphors.
● Recognise onomatopoeia.
● Write own poems experimenting with a similar range of techniques.

A poetry adventure

Objectives

NLS
T4: To read a range of narrative poems.
W3: To use dictionaries.
W6: To distinguish between homophones.

S&L
53 Group discussion and interaction: To understand and use the processes and language of decision making.

What you need
● Photocopiable pages 100–102 (ideally cut into parts and mounted on card)
● dictionaries.

Shared text-level work
● Display Part 1 of 'The Mystery of Sir Roger's Tomb'.
● Read the poem aloud with the class and talk about its unusual features. (It is a puzzle/adventure poem in which the reader is the hero and can affect the outcome of the adventure.)
● Ask the children if they know what kind of puzzle they have to solve (an anagram).
● Ask the children to work in pairs quickly to solve the puzzle and put their hands up if they think they have the answer.
● Stress that they must not shout it out, or even whisper it, as all the answers will be shared at the end of the lesson.
● Read the rest of the poem and spend a little time discussing the setting and how the poet creates atmosphere, for instance, through descriptions of the cold, damp, dank, dark air.

Shared word-level work
● Revise the term homophones (words that have the same sound as each other but different meaning and/or spelling: read/reed and so on).
● See if the children can find at least two examples in Part 1. (The best examples are: where/wear, which/witch, tax/tacks, there/their and through/threw.)

Guided and independent work
● Give out copies of the full poem. Make a homophone table on A3 paper (see the example below) and help children to find homophones in the poem and write them in the table.
● Encourage the children to use dictionaries when they think a word may have a homophone 'partner' but aren't sure what it is or are unsure of its meaning.

Word	Meaning	Homophone	Meaning
tax	challenge/payment	tacks	small nails

Differentiation

Less able
● Complete the first column of the homophones table with stair, hair, there, through, heard, bare, meet, write, prey, buy. Ask the children to find the words in the poem, then try to complete the other columns.

More able
● Ask the children to make up jokes (puns) using homophones, for example, Is a vicar's budgie a bird of pray?

● Give out a copy of the poem (preferably in card sets) to each group.
● Explain that they should take it in turns to read the parts of the poem, discuss each puzzle or choice and agree on what to do, considering consequences and solutions. This should be conducted as an independent activity.

Plenary
● Share ideas about the solutions and decisions in the poem by 'playing' the poem with the whole class.
● Begin by displaying Part 1 and asking a group to read it and suggest a solution.
● Try to involve all the groups as you work through the poem. (Answers: Press the eyes, Go on to Part 3, Bat, Go on to Part 5, Open grave 2).

Own story

Objectives

NLS
T12: To use the structures of poems read to write extensions based on these, eg additional verses, or substituting own words and ideas.
S4: To revise from Y4: the function of pronouns.
S10: To ensure that, in using pronouns, it is clear to what or to whom they refer.

What you need
● Photocopiable page 100
● picture story sheets of Parts 1 to 5 and 8 (prepared by cutting out the artwork for each part of the poem and pasting it at the top of an A4 sheet).

Shared text-level work
● Explain to the children that they are going to write a story version of 'The Mystery of Sir Roger's Tomb'.
● Display Part 1, read it, then ask the children what they would need to do to change it into a story.
● Explain that the most important changes would be the following:

> ● Write in prose (continuous sentences and paragraphs without rhythm or rhyme).
> ● Change the point of view from second person (you) to first person (I), or third person (he/she).

● Briefly revise the terms *point of view* and *person*.
● Model the process by asking for suggestions for the opening paragraph a sentence at a time.
● Take the best suggestions and begin writing them as a paragraph on the board.

Shared sentence-level work
● Revise the term pronouns (pronouns often replace nouns or noun phrases and enable us to avoid repetition).
● Ask the children to find at least two examples in Part 1 (*it, you*) and to explain which nouns they refer to.
● Show the following table of personal pronouns. Explain that personal pronouns are used to refer to yourself and other people or named things and that they establish the point of view of a story.

	Singular	Plural
1st person	I	we
2nd person	you	you
3rd person	he/she/it	they

Differentiation

Less able
● Give the children the picture story sheets and ask them to use the picture to help them write the story.

More able
● Give the children a list of possessive pronouns and ask them to write an extra scene in which two characters argue about who owns Sir Roger's gold.

Guided and independent work
● Ask the children to highlight all the uses of pronouns in the poem and draw an arrow to the nouns that they are standing in place of.
● When they have completed this, re-read the poem using the nouns rather than the pronouns and notice the effect.
● Ask the children to independently write a story version of 'The Mystery of Sir Roger's Tomb' in the first or third person.
● Encourage the children to refer to their experience of playing the game. For example, if they found a puzzle difficult to solve, they should include this in the story.

Plenary
● Ask some of the children to read out their stories to the rest of the class. If possible, share one written in the first person and one in the third person, and discuss the differences in effect.

Objectives

NLS
T6: To understand terms which describe different kinds of poems, eg ballad, narrative poem, and to identify typical features.
T12: To use the structures of poems read to write extensions based on these, eg additional verses.
W10: To investigate antonyms.

What you need
● Photocopiable page 100.

Differentiation

Less able
● Provide the children with subject matter to allow them to concentrate on writing the verse.
● Advise those who get rhyme difficult to write unrhymed verse.

More able
● Encourage the children to include internal rhyme in their extra section.

Extra section

Shared text-level work
● Display Part 1 of 'The Mystery of Sir Roger's Tomb'.
● Show the children how to note a rhyme scheme using letters of the alphabet, a new letter for each new rhyme. The rhyme scheme of the first verse is abcb (second and fourth lines rhyme).
● Next, show the children how to recognise the stressed syllables. Read the verses with additional emphasis so that the stressed syllables can be easily heard. Mark stressed syllables with a diagonal stroke.
● Explain that this pattern of poetic rhyme and rhythm is called ballad-form because it is commonly used in ballads – verses that tell stories about a person or place. In addition, this poem uses internal rhyme in the third line of most stanzas. Can the children find the internal rhymes in Part 1 (such as tomb/room)?

Shared word-level work
● Teach or revise the term antonyms (opposites) and ask the children for antonyms of the following words from the poem: ancient (modern), below (above).

Guided and independent work
● Ask the children to work in pairs to write an extra section to the poem to go between Part 3 and Part 4. Explain that they will need to plan what happens before they write the verse. For example, the door at the end of Part 3 could lead to a labyrinth or a giant spider's lair. The new part should end with another choice, one of which could lead on to the old Part 4.
● Next they will need to devise a puzzle for the reader to solve. Once they're happy with their puzzle, ask the children to write the section in verse(s), trying to use the same rhyme, rhythm and vocabulary style as the original poem.
● Suggest that the children challenge another pair to solve their puzzle.

Plenary
● Share and discuss the additional sections.
● Take the opportunity to reinforce understanding of verse forms by commenting on rhythm and rhyme.

Anthology

Objectives

NLS

T6: To understand terms which describe different kinds of poems, eg ballad, sonnet, rap, elegy, narrative poem, and to identify typical features.
T7: To compile a class anthology of favourite poems with commentaries which illuminate the choice.
W11: To explore onomatopoeia.

S&L

53 Group discussion and interaction: To understand and use the processes and language and decision making.

What you need

● Photocopiable page 103
● poems the children have chosen themselves (and 'spare' poems in case the children's choices are unsuitable).

Differentiation

Less able
● Ensure that the children are working with poems that they can understand.

More able
● Ask the children to select some poems with onomatopoeic words. Tell them to look for poems to do with breaking glass, fire, metal, water and wind. Ask the children to practise reading them aloud in a way that brings out the effect of the onomatopoeic words.

Shared text-level work

● Display the list of verse forms at the top of photocopiable page 103, keeping the poem extracts covered at this stage.
● Explain that the table shows some of the most popular forms for narrative poems.
● Ask the children to suggest a simple definition and/or example for each one:

● ballad – see Hour 3
● rhyming couplets – pairs of lines that rhyme
● blank verse – a rhythm of five stressed syllables per line, but no rhyme
● free verse – no rhythm or rhyme
● rap – strong rhythm and rhyme (usually couplets).

● Reveal the whole of photocopiable page 103 and enjoy reading the extracts.
● Ask the children to match the extracts to the forms, and to explain how they can tell. (The missing word in extract 4 is rap and the title is 'Write-A-Rap Rap'. The forms, from top to bottom, are: blank verse, free verse, ballad form, rap, couplets).

Shared word-level work

● Teach or revise the term onomatopoeia (words that sound like their meaning, like *clang, hiss, crash, cuckoo*).
● Read the last extract again and ask the children if they can hear any onomatopoeia.

Guided and independent work

● Explain to the children that they are going to put together an anthology of narrative poems for the class library.
● Organise the children to work in their groups. Ask each child to read their chosen poem to the group and then discuss as a group which one should be included in the class anthology.
● Say that you will be listening to how well they give reasons, listen to what others say, and justify their comments (make sure these are fair!).
● Tell the class to be prepared to accept other children's poems as the group choice.
● Ask each group to choose a spokesperson, and then help him or her to prepare a short presentation.
● Ask the spokesperson to explain why the poem was chosen for inclusion in the class anthology.

Plenary

● Ask each group to present its poem and the reasons for choosing it.
● Afterwards, discuss the choices as a class and see if there is a class favourite. Why do the children like this poem best?
● Allow some time later for writing or typing the poems and making the class anthology.

Objectives

NLS
T4: To read a range of narrative poems.
T5: To perform poems in a variety of ways.
S6: To be aware of the differences between spoken and written language, including: conventions to guide the reader; the use of punctuation to replace intonation, pauses, gestures.

S&L
57 Drama: To use and recognise the impact of theatrical effects in drama.

What you need
● Photocopiable page 103
● poems chosen for the class anthology
● sound effects CDs
● audio or video recorder.

Choral presentation

Shared text- and sentence-level work
● Display photocopiable page 103 and discuss with the children how each of the extracts could be prepared for a choral performance – reading aloud in groups.
● Suggest the following example, where you might say something like this about the extract from 'The Prelude':

> There are two sentences in this extract, but notice that the second sentence is very long. How would you read that? Where would you pause? Look at the commas. How would they affect the way you would speak? Yes, you would make a slight pause. The poem describes a frightening scene, so do you think it should be read in slow, solemn voices? What sound effects could you play in the background...?

● Help the children to practise reading the extract aloud in light of the discussion.
● Then go on to discuss how the other extracts could be performed. Use the following questions as starting points:

> ● What is the poem about?
> ● Do you think it should be fast or slow, loud or soft?
> ● Which lines can be read by one child, which lines by two or more children?
> ● How would the punctuation affect your reading?
> ● How could sound effects be used?
> ● How could gestures or actions be used?

Guided and independent work
● Organise the children to work in their groups to discuss and prepare their chosen poems for choral presentation.
● Ensure that each child has a role in the presentation.
● If necessary, subdivide larger groups to ensure that each child is fully involved and feels able to contribute.
● Remind the children to make use of the punctuation in the poems to help their oral reading.
● Encourage them to learn verses by heart where possible as this will free up their performances.

Differentiation

Less able
● Help the children working on the performance with the pronunciation of difficult words.

More able
● Ask the children to memorise their parts.

Plenary
● Listen to each group of children as they present their poem. Recording the performances on tape can heighten the sense of occasion and help with self-evaluation later.
● Note any distinct differences between different forms.
● Ask the class to evaluate the performances, and stress that these comments should be positive and constructive.
● Ask questions along the lines of *What did you like best about this performance? What changes could be made to make the performance even better?*

TERM 2

The Mystery of Sir Roger's Tomb

Part 1
In St Boniface Church is an ancient grave
Where Sir Roger De Flambeaux lies
And below the tomb is a vaulted room
Which is hidden from human eyes.

For in that room is Sir Roger's gold –
So much, it would fill a hearse,
But none is so bold as to seek the gold
Which is guarded by a curse,

And a puzzle to tax the sharpest minds:
No door leads to that room,
But there is a clue to let you through
Which is written upon the tomb:

serps eth yees

■ Can you solve the clue that will open the tomb? If you can, go on to Part 2.

Part 2
You _____ on the statue's face
And a doorway opens wide
To damp and gloom - and perhaps your doom!
With a prayer you step inside.

You grope your way down a winding stair,
With a borrowed church candle for light.
Dangling cobwebs brush your hair
And shadows confuse your sight.

The cold dank air and the sense of despair
Make you think of Sir Roger's curse.
Is it a vampire, a ghost or a ghoul
Or something that's even worse?

The time has come to make up your mind:
To go on, and to do your best,
Or give up and go back and close the tomb
And leave Sir Roger to rest.

IF YOU DECIDE TO GO ON, READ PART 3
IF YOU DECIDE TO GIVE UP, READ PART 6

Part 3
At the foot of the stair is a studded door
Which is locked, and there is no key
Instead is a row of buttons of brass
Which are lettered from A to T.

You must punch in a code to open the door
And to help you there is a clue:
You must solve the riddle that is written below
And the answer will let you through.

The world is upside down for me.
Night is my day.
I see through my ears
But I find my way.
I can even fly.
What am I?

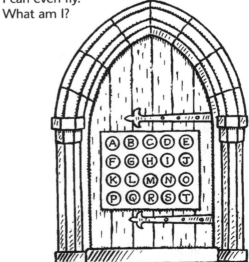

▪ SCHOLASTIC

⬛ Can you solve the clue that will open the door? If you can, go on to Part 4.

Part 4
You punch the word _____ in the buttons of brass
And the studded door opens wide.
You take a deep breath (though the air smells of death)
And gulp, and step inside.

You are in the room you had heard about -
The room with the vaults of stone.
But there's no sign of gold and its freezing cold
And you hear a ghostly groan.

You are tempted to run and save your life
After all, the room is bare.
The legends told of a hearse full of gold
But only a ghost is there.

⬛ If you decide to run, read Part 6.

⬛ If you decide to stay for a closer look, read Part 5.

Part 5
But it's only the sound of the studded door
As it creaks in its rotting frame.
You mutter "Good grief!" and sigh with relief,
And continue your searching again.

The walls are bare, and there's nothing up there
Where the pillars and ceiling vaults meet,
But the flickering light reveals a strange sight -
Two gravestones right under your feet!

But both are inscribed in an ancient tongue
That none now can read or write.
You must try to decipher them both if you can;
Then choose - I pray you choose right!

⬛ Try to decipher the message on the gravestones, then choose.

BENE
ATHTH ISST
ONE
AV AM PIRE LIE
SY OUW
I
ILLL
EAV EH IM
HERE
I
FY O UAR
E WISE

THE
RE IS NOT
FARTOG
OYO
URT
REA SU REL
I
ESBE LOW

⬛ If you chose to open 1, read Part 7.

⬛ If you chose to open 2, read Part 8.

Part 6

You sit by your fire with a cup of tea
Feeling cosy and safe in your room
But you're filled with doubt 'cause
    you'll never find out
The secret of Sir Roger's tomb.

Part 7

You didn't decipher the tombs - you guessed!
And sadly, your guess wasn't right.
With a harrowing shout a vampire leaps out
And drags you to endless night!!!

Poem over

Part 8

You deciphered well - or you guessed it right
For, just as the legend told,
There is buried a box the size of a hearse
And it's crammed to the brim with gold!

You buy yourself a big new house
And generously share out the rest.
And sometimes at night, when the moon is
    bright
You retell the tale of your quest!

Poem over

◗ SCHOLASTIC

Find the form

▦ **Read these extracts from narrative poems. Then, at the side of each poem, write the name of the form it is written in. Choose the names of the forms from this list:**

> ballad   rhyming couplets   blank verse   free verse   rap

1. Sleep seized me, and I passed into a dream.
   I saw before me stretched a boundless plain
   Of sandy wilderness all black and void,
   And as I looked around, distress and fear
   Came creeping over me...

from 'The Prelude' by William Wordsworth

2. There was a wicked woman called Malady Festing
   Who lived with her son-in-law, Hark Boley,
   And her daughter Angel,
   In a house on the high moorlands
   Of the West Riding of Yorkshire
   In the middle of the last century.

from 'Angel Boley' by Stevie Smith

3. There lived a wife at Usher's Well
   And a wealthy wife was she;
   She had three stout and stalwart sons
   And sent them o'er the sea.

from 'The Wife of Usher's Well', Anon

4. The rhyme keeps coming in the very same place
   so don't fall behind and try not to race.
   The rhythm keeps the tap on a regular beat
   and the rhyme helps to wrap up your ___* up neat.

Tony Mitton

5. Thwack! My boot bashed at the ball
   But didn't score a goal at all;
   Instead, with clatter, crunch and crash,
   It hit a window; smashed the glass.

anon

Myths and legends

The first part of this unit is based on Homer's *The Odyssey*, the epic narrative poem that includes many of the well-known myths of Ancient Greece. The activities are most effective when used with a good children's retelling such as *The Wanderings of Odysseus* by Rosemary Sutcliff (Frances Lincoln). However, the photocopiable pages are complete (though necessarily limited) by themselves. In the second part of the unit, children investigate how a legendary hero can develop from historical character by exploring the legend of King Arthur. This unit includes one complete episode (in different versions) from the Arthurian legend, but if time allows, it would be a good idea to read the full story. *Arthur, High King of Britain* by Michael Morpurgo (Egmont) is one of the best versions for children of this age, though more able children should try *King Arthur and His Knights of the Round Table* by Roger Lancelyn Green (Puffin). Hours 3 and 8 link to Unit 35 in *Grammar for Writing*.

WEEK 1

Hour	Shared text-level work	Shared word-/ sentence-level work	Guided reading/ writing	Independent work	Plenary
1 The Odyssey	Reading the beginning of *The Odyssey*.	Focusing on spellings of **shun** sound.	Exploring online versions of the myth.	Annotating the text for typical myth features.	Sharing ideas to reinforce understanding of myths and legends.
2 The Odyssey game	Examining text for genre features and epic style.	Revising possessive pronouns.	Researching Greek gods and goddesses.	Playing game to retell story.	Discussing the game and the story.
3 The Wanderings of Odysseus	Comparing different versions of the myth.	Comparing different versions of the myth.	Adding to the game by adding to the story.	Adding to the game by adding to the story.	Comparing different versions and relating them to the enduring nature of myths.
4 New adventures	Considering new adventures for Odysseus.	Exploring uses of pronouns and personal pronouns.	Writing new adventure for Odysseus to add to game.	Writing new adventure for Odysseus to add to game.	Seeing if new stories fit existing versions.
5 21st-century Homer	Talking about Homer; making notes for oral poetry adaptation.		Working collaboratively to prepare performance.	Working collaboratively to prepare performance.	Performing; noting differences in performances.

UNIT 3

Hour	Shared text level work	Shared word/ sentence level work	Guided reading/ writing	Independent work	Plenary
6 The Arthurian legend	Establishing existing knowledge of King Arthur.	Examining styles of book blurbs.	Exploring the legend on websites.	Writing blurbs for an Arthur story.	Recapping events and characters in the legend and its enduring quality.
7 The historical Arthur	Identifying features of a legend.	Revising spelling rules for double *l* and soft *c*.	Researching the legend online.	Preparing a talk about the historical figure.	Giving the talks and discussing differences between legendary and historical figures.
8 Two classic versions	Reading extracts from the most popular classic English poems of the legend.	Examining verse form; converting to prose.	Modernising the texts.	Modernising the texts.	Sharing adaptations and discussing preferences.
9 A present-day version	Reading extract from contemporary Arthur story; discussing narrator, point of view and descriptive style.		Redrafting adaptations to accommodate new ending.	Redrafting adaptations to accommodate new ending.	Evaluating adaptations.
10 Own version	Recapping differences between history and legend; creating new episode for the legend.		Playing a storytelling game for new episodes.	Playing a storytelling game for new episodes.	Telling the new stories.

Key assessment opportunities
● Can the children recognise key features of myths and legends?
● Can they tell stories about Odysseus and Arthur?
● Can they investigate the history behind a legend?
● Can they use notes to support oral storytelling?

UNIT 3 HOUR 1 ▢ Myths and legends

The Odyssey

Objectives

NLS
T1: To identify and classify the features of myths, legends and fables.
W8: To recognise and spell the suffix: -cian, etc.

What you need
● Photocopiable page 116.

Shared text-level work
● Read photocopiable page 116 to the children.
● Check the children's understanding of new or difficult vocabulary, such as *muse*, *sacked* and *nymph*.
● Re-read the first two paragraphs, then ask: If Homer was illiterate, how was he able to compose two very long poems?
● Talk about how it is possible to make up stories in one's head and remember them, and that, before writing was common, this was a very important skill.
● Point to the phrase: *poems based on the legends of the Trojan War*.
● Ask the children if they can explain the term, legend (a traditional story about heroic characters, such as King Arthur, that may be based on truth, but has been embellished over the years).
● Read the next two paragraphs, then ask the children: Who is deciding what happens to Odysseus? (The gods.)
● With the children's help, highlight all the names of the gods in the text and ask the children if they know what each god was responsible for. (Hyperion - the sun, Poseidon - the sea, Zeus - chief god, Athene - goddess of wisdom, Hermes - the messenger, Atlas - holds up the heavens.)
● Now discuss the term, myth (an ancient traditional story of gods or heroes that addresses a problem or concern of human existence, often including an explanation of some fact or phenomenon).
● Summarise this part of the analysis by explaining that *The Odyssey* has elements of both myth and legend but is generally categorised as a myth because of all the supernatural, theological and universal elements.

Shared word-level work
● Draw attention to *inspiration* (line 1) and *magician* (paragraph 3). Ask the children how the endings are pronounced ('*shun*').
● Point out that these are alternative ways of spelling two different suffixes with the same sound.
● Ask the children for any other *shun* words they can think of (they will all be nouns).

Guided work and independent work
● Ask the children to explore the illustrated online version of *The Odyssey* at www.mythweb.com/odyssey/index.html.
● Ask the children to independently work in pairs to annotate the text for features that mark it out as a myth or legend.
● Then ask them to write a short paragraph in answer to the following question: What are the elements of myth in *The Odyssey*?

Differentiation

Less able
● Help a group to act out the story as an aid to comprehension.

More able
● Ask the children to write about the elements of myth and legend in their paragraph.

Plenary
● Share some of the annotations and paragraphs that the children come up with. Use the ideas to consolidate understanding of the terms myth and legend.

The Odyssey game

Objectives

NLS
T1: To identify and classify the features of myths, legends and fables.
W7: To learn the correct use and spelling of possessive pronouns, linked to work on grammar.

What you need
● Photocopiable page 118
● a game set for each group: photocopiable page 117 (enlarged to A3), photocopiable page 118 and DD cut into cards, a dice or spinner and four coloured counters

Shared text-level work
● Display photocopiable page 118 and explain that it is part of a game based on *The Odyssey*. It gives some of the stories of *The Odyssey* in more detail, and from Odysseus' point of view.
● Go through the texts and ask the children to point out key features of myths and legends and Homer's style. Annotate these features, explaining names of gods and difficult vocabulary as necessary:

● ancient setting
● epithets (such as *green-eyed* Athene, *swift-footed* Hermes)
● fantastic beasts
● gods and goddesses
● unnatural/supernatural events
● heroes
● values such as courage, honour, perseverance.

● In addition, explain the names of gods and difficult vocabulary.

Shared word-level work
● Revise or teach the children about possessive pronouns. Brainstorm a long list and ask the children to find examples in the texts.
● Ask the children how each pronoun refers to the named person. For example, in the sentence, *John picked up his bag, his* refers to *John*. As the children point out the links, mark them in the text with arrows.

Guided and independent work
● Work with a group to research the names and roles of the main Greek gods and goddesses.
● Organise the children to play The Odyssey game in mixed-ability groups of four using photocopiable page 117 (enlarged to A3), plastic counters and dice:

1. Spread out the six cards from photocopiable pages 118 and 119 face up beside the game board.
2. Players take it in turn to roll the dice and move their counters.
3. When a player lands on a numbered square, he or she must pick up the card of the same number, read the card to the group, and follow the instructions.
4. The winner is the first to get to Ithaca.

Differentiation

Less able
● Ask the children to illustrate and caption some of the main gods and goddesses for display.

More able
● Encourage the children who have researched other gods and myths to write their own game cards.

Plenary
● Ask the children to talk about their experiences of the game. Ask what problems they encountered and what happened as a result. (Their problems will be similar to Odysseus', but not necessarily in the same order or with the same outcome, depending on the chances of play.)
● Finally, ask them what they have learned about the story of Odysseus. (They will have learned about many of the adventures that Odysseus had on his journey home, as well as something about Greek mythology: fantastic beasts, the gods, Hades and so on.)

UNIT 3 HOUR 3 □ Myths and legends

The Wanderings of Odysseus

Objectives

NLS
T2: To investigate different versions of the same story in print or on film, identifying similarities and differences.
S3: To understand how writing can be adapted for different audiences and purposes, eg by changing vocabulary and sentence structures.

What you need
● Photocopiable page DD
● game sets (see Hour 2)
● different retellings of *The Odyssey* (The *Wanderings of Odysseus* by Rosemary Sutcliff is particularly recommended)
● internet access
● video or DVD version (*The Odyssey* starring Armand Assante is excellent, but is a 12 certificate so select scenes with care)
● audio version if possible, such as *The Adventures of Odysseus* (Naxos)

Differentiation

Less able
● Ask the children to play a fun game of *The Odyssey* at www.users.glo balnet.co.uk/~loxias/ odchoice.htm.

More able
● Challenge the children to read relevant chapters of this 19th century children's version by Charles Lamb: www.online-literature.com/ lamb/adventures_ulysses.

Shared text- and sentence-level work

● Display photocopiable page 119. Remind the children that they have been using it in The Odyssey game but explain that now they are going to look at the stories in more detail and compare them with other versions of *The Odyssey*.
● Read the texts, and then ask the children to look for the key features of myths and legends and Homer's epic style as in Hour 2.
● Ask the children which of the episodes they liked best, and to explain why. Come to a general agreement on a favourite and then read and/or view that episode in other versions.
● Ask the children to notice differences in language, style and presentation between the forms. For example, there will be complex language in 'literal' translations of *The Odyssey* for adult readers; dramatised versions that include narrator, dialogue and sound effects in audio versions; emphasis on visual presentation in film versions.
● Afterwards, further compare two different versions by using questions like the following:

● Which version did they like best and why?
● Which contained the most detail?
● What was the purpose and audience of each of the versions, for example an accurate translation for study purposes, a simple story version for young children?

Guided and independent work

● Ask the children to work in groups to extend the game by adding another adventure from Homer's story. This can be done by reading another of Odysseus' adventures and working together to shorten and rewrite the story to fit an A5 card.
● Ask the children to decide what instruction to add (Miss a turn and so on), depending on the events of the story.

Plenary

● Choose three or four groups to report back on their comparisons.
● Pull the lesson together by noting how many different versions there are and explaining that myths and legends have an enduring nature and are kept alive by being retold in many different ways throughout the centuries and across the world.

New adventures

Shared text-level work
● Recap with the children the episodes of *The Odyssey* they have read. Which are their favourites? Why? What else do they think could happen to Odysseus before he reaches home?
● Explain that they are going to write new adventures for Odysseus. Read this example and discuss how it might end:

> Odysseus saw a strange ship on the horizon. It had a big square sail like his own ship, but a prow with a dragon's head. As they got nearer, he saw that all the men wore horned helmets, except the captain, who wore a winged helmet. 'Where are you bound?' he shouted.
>
> 'I am lost,' he said.
>
> 'Come aboard,' he said, 'and I will help you to find your way.'
>
> He told him that he had a magic stone called lodestone that always pointed north. He dangled the stone from a string and after swinging around a few times, it settled down in one position.
>
> He asked him which way he wanted to go, and when he was told 'West,' Horsa pointed in that direction.

Shared sentence level work
● Revise the term 'pronoun' and ask the children to point out the pronouns (specifically, personal pronouns: I, you, he). Ask: Who shouted *Where are you bound?* (It is not clear – either of the two men could have asked the question, either of the two ships could have been lost.)
● Explore similar ambiguities in the passage, such as who has the magic stone? Discuss how the text could be made clearer, by replacing some of the personal pronouns with proper nouns.

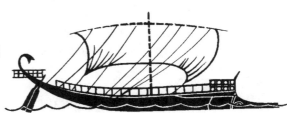

Guided and independent work
● Ask the children to write a new adventure for Odysseus. This should be about 150 words long and, after reading, discussion and redrafting, should be written onto cards to be used for an extended version of The Odyssey game and as a basis for oral presentation in Hour 5.

Plenary
● Ask some the children to read out their new adventures while the rest of the class evaluate them on how exciting their stories are and how well they fit in with what we know about Odysseus and the myths of *The Odyssey*.

21st-century Homer

Objectives

NLS

T3: To explore similarities and differences between oral and written storytelling.
T14: To make notes of story outline as preparation for oral storytelling.

S&L
48 Speaking: To tell a story using notes designed to cue techniques.

What you need
● A version of *The Odyssey*
● story cards from photocopiable pages 118 and 119 plus those written by the children.

Shared text-level work
● Ask the children what they can remember about Homer from Hour 1. (He was blind, illiterate and did not have the benefit of the NLS at school, yet he composed two great epic poems, *The Iliad* and *The Odyssey*.)
● Explain that scholars think that Homer, and poets like him, recited their poems partly from memory (using stories they had already heard elsewhere) and partly from making up new episodes as they went along. They would often use stock phrases to help them do this. One type of stock phrase is the epithet. See if the children can remember some of the epithets they have read. (Hopefully, this should demonstrate that they are memorable!)
● Tell the children that they are going to perform their poems just like Homer did. Model a short oral presentation by retelling one of Odysseus' adventures, such as the story of Scylla and Charybdis.
● Begin this by demonstrating how to make notes to support storytelling by writing and displaying notes for the story you are planning to tell. The key message is to keep notes brief, using the minimum number of words that will prompt recall, for example key events and characters and key features of the characters, making sure events are noted in chronological order.

Guided and independent work
● Ask groups of four to work collaboratively to prepare an oral performance of *The Odyssey*. This should include two adventures from Homer's version and two new adventures that they have made up in previous lessons.
● Ask the children to discuss which to include, then write brief notes to support their performance.
● Remind them to be prepared to elaborate on their notes imaginatively as they perform.
● Allow some time for rehearsal.

Plenary
● Organise for each group of four to perform their oral presentations to another group of four.
● Ask the children to notice any differences between the performances and the texts they are based on.
● Remind the children that they have been telling their stories in the same way that Homer did 2700 years ago.

Differentiation

Less able
● Some of the children may have a real talent for oral performance. Encourage and maximise this.

More able
● Encourage the children to incorporate epithets (including their own if appropriate) into their notes and oral performances.

The Arthurian legend

Objectives

NLS
T1: To identify and classify the features of myths, legends and fables, eg the moral in a fable, fantastical beasts in legends.
S3: To understand how writing can be adapted for different audiences and purposes, eg by changing vocabulary and sentence structures.

What you need

● Arthurian legend character cards (see Shared text-level work)
● good example of a book blurb
● computer access.

Shared text-level work

● Tell the children that they are going to share what they know about the legend of King Arthur.
● A good way to focus discussion would be to use cards showing the nine main characters (Arthur, Guinevere, Merlin, Sir Lancelot, Sir Galahad, Sir Gawain, Sir Mordred, The Black Knight, Morgana le Fay). The cards will be used again in Hour 10 and can be made by pasting images onto postcards. Suitable images can be found at www.kingarthursknights.com.
● Give the children the following summary of the Arthurian legend using the picure cards to illustrate it as appropriate:

> Early in the 5th century, the Romans left Britain to defend what was left of their empire. Without the legions to defend it, Britain was at the mercy of invaders, mainly the Saxons. However, the Britons organised a resistance which held the Saxons off for a generation. This much is historical fact; legend tells us that the leader of the resistance was King Arthur.
>
> The legend goes that, under the watchful eye of the wizard, Merlin, Arthur was born, and when a young man, drew a sword from a stone which proved he was King of all Britain. His wife was called Queen Guinevere, and his best knight was Sir Lancelot. Sir Lancelot and Queen Guinevere fell in love and betrayed the king. King Arthur's adventures include when Sir Gawain fought the Green Knight in a beheading contest, and the quest for the Holy Grail which led to the death of many knights but was achieved by Sir Galahad. King Arthur's round table was broken up by a civil war with a traitor called Sir Mordred. Sir Mordred was killed in the battle and Arthur was badly wounded. He was taken to the Isle of Avalon where, legend says, he waits for a time when he will be needed to help save Britain again.

Shared sentence level work

● Display the blurb on the back cover of a book, ideally one fairly familiar to the children. Revise that it is a short account of a story written in an exciting and enticing way so that the reader will want to know what happens and buy the book.
● Ask the children how the vocabulary and sentence structure of the blurb has been adapted to make it sound exciting.

Guided and independent work

● Work with a group to explore the Arthurian legend online. Encourage the children to identify typical features of legends.
● Tell the children to imagine they are the publishers of a story book that tells the legend of King Arthur.
● Ask them to use the information from the shared session to write a blurb for the book independently.

Plenary

● Share some of the blurbs and use them as a way of recapping on the main stories and characters in the Arthurian legend.

Differentiation

Less able
● Ask the children to base their blurb on one or more of the stories discussed in shared work.

More able
● Ask the children to refer to a wider range of stories, and issues such as the clash between good and evil, sorcery and religion.

Objectives

NLS
T1: To identify and classify the features of myths, legends and fables, eg the moral in a fable, fantastical beasts in legends.
W4: To explore spelling patterns of consonants and formulate rules: *-ll* in *full* becomes *l* when used as a suffix; *c* is usually soft when followed by *i*.

What you need

● Photocopiable page 120.

The historical Arthur

Shared text-level work

● Tell the children that they are going to confirm the definition of a legend by investigating how the story of a Dark Ages warrior developed into the legend of King Arthur.

● Read Text 1 and Text 2 on photocopiable page 120, then discuss and write on the board the following questions:

> ● What information does Text 1 give us? (The resistance to the Saxons was led by a Roman named Ambrosius. He defeated them at the battle of Mount Badon.)
> ● What new information does Text 2 give us? (The Saxon leader Hengest was succeeded by his son, Octa. Arthur is named and is described as 'a military commander'.)
> ● What information do the texts agree on? (The Saxons were defeated at the battle of Mount Badon.)
> ● What do the texts disagree on? (Text 1 says that the leader of the resistance is Ambrosius, Text 2, that it is Arthur.)
> ● Which of the texts is most likely to be accurate? (Text 1, because the events took place in the lifetime of the writer.)
> ● Is it possible to put the information together without any contradictions? (Several historians suggest that Ambrosius was the overall leader (like a king, or Roman governor) and that Arthur was his best general.)

● Finally, read the archaeological evidence, and ask the children how it fits in. (It proves that there was organised resistance to the Saxon invasion at about the time Arthur is supposed to have lived.)

Shared word-level work

● Use the examples in the text as an opportunity to revise the two consonant spelling rules for double *l* and soft *c*. For example, *thoughtful* in Text 1, *full* in Text 2, and *ancient* in the archaeological evidence.

Guided and independent work

● Help another group of children to research the historical Arthur online, for example, at www.historymedren.about.com/od/historicalarthur.
● Ask the children to independently work in pairs to prepare a talk for a history society. The talk should be entitled 'The historical Arthur'.
● Display the questions used in the shared session and ask the children to use them as a framework for their talk and to focus on texts 1 and 2 only of photocopiable page 120.
● Advise the children to write notes to help them with their talk, and tell them that they can use photocopiable page 120 as a visual aid.

Plenary

● Ask three different groups (a less able, an average and a more able group) to give their talks.
● Then ask the class to discuss the differences between the historical Arthur and the Arthur of legend.

Differentiation

Less able
● Ask the children to prepare a simple description of the historical Arthur.

More able
● Ask the children to talk about how evidence from the different sources can be used to build up a picture of the historical Arthur.

Two classic versions

Objectives

NLS
T2: To investigate different versions of the same story in print or on film, identifying similarities and differences; recognise how stories change over time and differences of culture and place that are expressed in stories.
S3: To understand how writing can be adapted for different audiences and purposes, eg by changing vocabulary and sentence structures.

What you need
● Photocopiable page 121.

Shared text-level work
● Display the top text on photocopiable page 121.
● Explain that Malory's *Morte D'Arthur*, written in 1470, is the classic version of the Arthurian legend, and the one on which almost all modern retellings are based.
● Read the extract to the children, explaining difficult vocabulary and phraseology where necessary.
● Examine how Malory's language and style differs from a modern story or narrative poem (vocabulary such as *thou seest*; strange word order as in the first sentence; unfamiliar idioms like *come again* instead of *come back*; repeating nouns instead of using pronouns, such as *sword* in the first sentence).
● Annotate the text as examples are discussed.
● Discuss the effect of the language and style on the story. (It gives the story a medieval flavour that suits the subject matter.)

Shared sentence level work
● Display and read the extract from Tennyson's poem, explaining that his 'Idylls of the King' is the second most popular classic version of the Arthurian legend.
● Explain that it is written in blank verse (unrhymed lines with five rhythmic stresses).
● Tell the children that they are going to adapt this into a modern story version for children of their own age.
● Demonstrate how to do this by changing the vocabulary and sentence structure of the first few lines:

> Sir Bedivere went for the second time over the hill and down to the lake. He was lost in thought, counting the wet pebbles under his feet. But then he noticed again how beautifully decorated the sword was. He clapped his hands and shouted out loud, 'If I do throw this sword away...'

Guided and independent work
● Organise the children to work in pairs to adapt the extracts into a modern story version.
● Advise the children to change the vocabulary and sentence structure of Tennyson's poem as demonstrated, and complete the episode by writing about what happens when Sir Bedivere reports back to Arthur, by adapting the second part of Malory's version in the same way.
● Encourage the children to read their first drafts aloud to each other and to change anything that sounds old fashioned.

Plenary
● Hear examples of the two different adaptations (as a modern story, and in the style of Malory).
● Then ask the children to express their own opinions about the impact that the different versions (Malory's, Tennyson's, the modern version) have on the reader drawing on evidence from the texts.

Differentiation

Less able
● Pair less confident readers with more able ones.

More able
● Ask the children to adapt Tennyson's version in the style of Malory and to complete the episode by making slight variations, for example Sir Bedivere says that he saw different things.

A present-day version

Objectives

NLS
T2: To investigate different versions of the same story in print or on film, identifying similarities and differences; recognise how stories change over time and differences of culture and place that are expressed in stories.
T8: To distinguish between the author and the narrator, investigating narrative viewpoint and the treatment of different characters, eg minor characters, heroes, villains, and perspectives on the action from different characters.

What you need
● Photocopiable page 122.

Shared text-level work
● Tell the children that they are going to read the end of the Sir Bedivere episode in a present-day version by Michael Morpurgo, taken from *Arthur, High King of Britain*.
● Display and read photocopiable page 122. Ask them to notice the spelling of Bedevere (written *Bedivere* on photocopiable page 121). Discuss how this could happen (details of legends change, like Chinese Whispers, as they are passed on).
● Explore the difference between author and narrator, and narrative viewpoint by discussing the following questions:

● Which person is the extract written in? Refer to work on person and point of view in Unit 2 if appropriate. (It is written in the first person.)
● Who is it that is speaking in the first person? (King Arthur. Arthur is the *narrator* of this story. He is telling his story to a boy from the future, and, through him, to the reader.)
● Why does the author tell the story through the narrator King Arthur rather than telling it himself? (Because this enables him to make the story much more personal and explore how Arthur feels about the events in his life.)

● Ask the children to pick out the words and phrases that bring the story to life. Tell them to look for descriptive details, such as *an arm in a white silken sleeve* and words describing feelings, for example, *a swirling blackness dragging me down*.
● Conclude this part of the lesson by pointing out that bringing a story to life is one of the key qualities of the modern novel.

Guided and independent work
● Ask the children to redraft their retellings of the first two parts of the Sir Bedevere episode to match the style of Michael Morpurgo. Suggest that to do this they will need to include:

● more descriptive details
● more descriptions of the way people feel
● more modern, informal dialogue

● Summarise by telling the children that the aim is to achieve a 'seamless' blend between their versions of the first two parts of the episode with Morpurgo's ending.
● Alternatively, give different groups of children different extracts from Malory's text to modernise. Morpurgo's text is still the model, but the subject matterwill be fifferent. Choose well-known scenes, for example, when Arthur pulls the sword from the stone.

Differentiation

Less able
● Ask the children to redraft the first episode only.

More able
● Ask the children to conclude their Malory-style version by changing Morpurgo's version into the style of Malory.
● Some of the children might like to try to write the whole episode in the style of Tennyson.

Plenary
● Ask some of the children to read out their full versions, and consider how 'seamless' they are. Can they hear the joins?
● If time allows, read Morpurgo's full version of the episode.

Own version

Objectives

NLS
T11: To write own versions of legends, myths and fables, using structures and themes identified in reading.

S&L
48 Speaking: To tell a story using notes.

What you need
● Arthurian legend cards from Hour 6 (one pack per group of four)

Shared text-level work
● Recap on the differences between the historical King Arthur and the legend by asking the children questions such as, how has the legend of King Arthur developed from what we know of the historical figure?
● Explain that almost everything in the legend of Arthur has been made up, for instance Excalibur, Camelot, the names of the Knights, Merlin, the Holy Grail. Much of what is historical fact has been lost: there is no mention in the legend of the Saxons, the Battle of Mount Badon, or the Hill Fort at Cadbury Castle.
● Tell the children that they are going to make up new adventures for King Arthur and his knights.
● Emphasise that the children need not worry about the authenticity of their new adventures, because most of the existing adventures were made up at some time in the past.
● Demonstrate (either yourself, or by asking a volunteer) how to use the legend cards as a starting point for stories.
● Explain that the pack of nine (made earlier in Hour 6) has three main characters, three knights, and three evil characters. Sort the pack into these groups, shuffle them and lay them face down on the table.
● Ask the children to select one card from each pack and make up an oral story based on the characters.

Guided and independent work
● Organise the children into mixed-ability groups of four to play the storytelling game.
● Emphasise that after each child has taken a turn, all the cards need to be replaced in their groups and reshuffled.
● Tell the children that, when every child has had a turn, they should discuss their stories as a group and choose one (or make up a new one) to tell to the rest of the class.
● Encourage the children to use their imaginations to make up the stories. The only limitation is that the new ideas must fit into the Arthurian 'world', so: dinosaurs, no; dragons, yes; aliens, no; goblins, yes; science, no; sorcery, yes.
● Tell the children to make brief notes to support their oral storytelling but emphasise that the notes are only a reminder, they must not write down everything.

Differentiation

Less able
● Ensure less confident children are allowed to fully participate.

More able
● Expect the children's episodes/notes to reflect styles of texts they have read.

Plenary
● Ask each group to tell its story to the class. The story can be illustrated by one of the children displaying a sequence of Arthurian legend cards.
● If more hours can be allocated to this unit, the children could go on to write a new version of the Arthurian legend by agreeing an order for their tales and fitting them in between the traditional beginning with the sword in the stone and the ending they wrote in Hour 9.

TERM 2

The Odyssey

Give me inspiration, Muse, to sing of that hero who travelled far and wide after he had sacked the famous city of Troy.

With these words (in ancient Greek, of course) the blind poet Homer begins his story about Odysseus. About 2700 years ago, Homer composed two epic poems based on the legends of the Trojan war (not bad for somebody who couldn't read or write!). The first of these, The Iliad, *describes the Greek siege of Troy, and the second,* The Odyssey, *tells of the wanderings of Odysseus as he tried to find his way home when the war was over. But let the poet continue…*

Odysseus had a terrible time trying to bring his men home. They got lost, fought fantastical beasts and faced untold dangers. They had almost reached home, when his men, weak with hunger, ate some of the cattle which belonged to the Sun-god, Hyperion. Zeus punished Odysseus by sinking his ship with a lightning bolt and sending him as a castaway to the island of Ogygia.

But there came a time when the gods decided that Odysseus should be allowed to go back to Ithaca. Only

Poseidon disagreed because he was still angry with Odysseus. But as soon as he was out of the way, visiting the Ethiopians, the other gods met in the house of Olympian Zeus to discuss what they should do.

The goddess, grey-eyed Athene, said: "My heart bleeds for Odysseus when I think of his sufferings. He is on a remote island covered with forest where the nymph Calypso, the daughter of the god and magician Atlas, lives. She wants Odysseus to marry her and is keeping him a prisoner in a cave until he agrees. You, Father Zeus, have done nothing to help him even though he made many sacrifices to you when he was fighting at Troy."

Zeus, the cloud-gatherer, answered, "I have not forgotten Odysseus, bear in mind that Poseidon is still angry with him for blinding Polyphemus, king of the Cyclopes. Let's put our heads together and see if we can help him to return."

Then the goddess, grey-eyed Athene said, "Father Zeus, I think we should first send swift-footed Hermes to Ogygia to tell Calypso that we have made up our minds to allow Odysseus to return home. In the meantime I will go to Ithaca to put heart into Odysseus' son Telemachus.

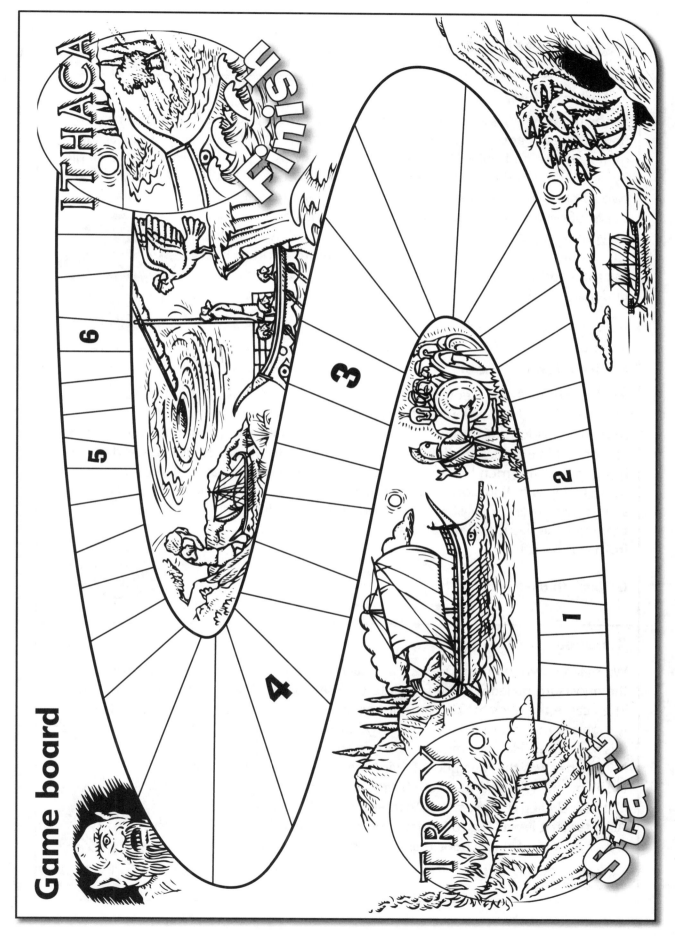

Game board

ITHACA

Finish

TROY

Start

1 2 3 4 5 6

Odyssey game cards (1)

1. The Cyclops

It was night when we arrived at the country of the Cyclopes. As soon as rosy-fingered dawn appeared, we explored the island. We found a cave full of lambs, goats, cheese and milk. The owner of the cave was a giant of a man with a single eye in the middle of the forehead. I tried to talk to him, but he got angry and ate two of my men. Then he started drinking. When he was drunk, I heated a beam of olive wood in the fire and thrust it into his eye. Blind Polyphemus, screaming with pain, ran to the doorway of the cave and sat there to catch anyone who tried to get out. But my men and I managed to pass him by clinging to the underside of the sheep.

Take an extra turn

2. The island of Aeoli

We landed on Aeoli. Aeolus and I talked much about Troy. A month later, when I said I must go, he made me an ox-hide sack to hold the roaring winds (Zeus had made Aeolus lord of the winds). Only the west wind was allowed to blow to take us home. Nine days and nights we sailed. On the tenth day Ithaca showed on the horizon. But the men had grown suspicious of the ox-hide sack. They thought I was hiding gold and silver from Troy that I should have shared with them. Foolishly, they opened the sack. Immediately, the winds flew out and raised a storm that blew us far away from our Ithaca.

Go back to the beginning

3. Hades

We sailed down the river Oceanus and sacrificed two sheep as Circe had advised. Then the ghosts from Hades came to talk to us. The first was that of my comrade Elpenor. Then came the ghost of Theban Teiresias with his golden sceptre in his hand. He recognised me and said, Odysseus, why have you left the light of day and come to visit this sad place? He gave me helpful warnings about my journey home. My mother was the next ghost to visit me. She told me about the problems my wife and son were having at home. I saw many other ghosts including the ghosts of Agamemnon and Achilles. I asked Achilles what it was like to be dead. He replied sadly, "I would rather be a servant in a poor man's house than a king in Hades."

Take an extra turn

Odyssey game cards (2)

4. The Sirens

All of a sudden the ship was becalmed, so the men took down the sails and started rowing. I guessed that we were near the island of the Sirens. Circe had warned us that the Sirens lure men to their deaths with their beautiful music. So I took some wax, softened it with the help of the sun-god, Hyperion, and made my men put it in their ears so they couldn't hear the singing. I did not put any in mine because I was curious to hear them. I had myself bound to the mast instead. Soon we were within earshot of the island and the Sirens began their alluring song: "Come here, Odysseus," they sang, "and listen to our beautiful music." I was so enchanted that I tried to ask my men to untie me, but fortunately, they just rowed all the faster until we had reached safety.

Take an extra turn

5. Scylla and Charybdis

We entered a narrow strait between two towering cliffs. On one side was Scylla – a dreadful monster with six heads on six necks long enough to reach passing ships. On the other side was Charybdis – a fearsome whirlpool all black with sand and mud. I took my spears and stood in the prow of the ship, while shouting instructions to my men to help them steer safely around Charybdis. While we were occupied with this, Scylla suddenly snatched up my six best men. In a moment I saw their limbs high above me, struggling as Scylla carried them to her den. They screamed to me in mortal agony, but I was unable to help them. This was the most sickening sight that I saw on all my voyages.

Miss a turn

6. The island of Hyperion

We came to the island of the sun-god, Hyperion. The men wanted to land to rest and eat. I agreed, but made them swear not to harm a single creature on the sacred island. A storm blew up which prevented us from leaving for many days. Soon the food from the ship ran out and the men, crazed with hunger, killed and roasted some cows. At last the storm abated, and we set off over the wine-dark sea. We had not gone far, when a terrific squall hit us – Zeus was punishing us for eating Hyperion's sheep. The ship went round and round, and caught fire as a bolt of lightning struck it. All the men drowned except me. I lashed myself to the broken mast and was carried to the island of Ogygia where I was held captive by the nymph Calypso.

Go back to the start

The historical Arthur

Text 1

The Britons took arms under the leadership of Ambrosius Aurelianus, a modest and thoughtful man, who was the only Roman leader left alive. After this, there were many battles until the year of the battle of Mount Badon when our cruel foes were slaughtered. This was, I am sure, forty-four years and one month after the landing of the Saxons, and also the time of my own birth.

Written by Gildas (a monk) in about 540

Text 2

At that time, Britain seemed to be full of Saxons, and they were growing stronger all the time. When their leader, Hengest, died, his son, Octa, came from the northern part of Britain and became king of Kent. All the kings of Kent are descended from him. Then Arthur, along with the kings of Britain, fought against them in those days. Arthur was the military commander. He fought many battles against the Saxons. His twelfth battle was on Mount Badon in which 960 men were killed by one charge from Arthur.

Written by Nennius (a monk) in the mid 900s

Archaeological evidence

Cadbury Castle in Somerset is a huge hill fort probably built by the ancient Britons many centuries before the time of King Arthur. However, an archaeological dig led by Leslie Alcock in 1970 revealed that the old fort had been repaired and strengthened between about 460 and 500 – at about the time that Arthur was believed to have been leading the resistance against the Saxon invasion.

The passing of Arthur

Said Arthur unto Sir Bedivere, "Take Excalibur, my good sword, and throw my sword in the water, and come again and tell me what thou seest."

"My lord," said Bedivere, "your command shall be done, and I will bring you word again."

So Sir Bedivere departed, but when he beheld that noble sword, that the pommel and the hilt was all of precious stones; he said to himself, "If I throw this rich sword in the water, what a loss it will be!"

And then Sir Bedivere hid Excalibur under a tree. And came again unto the king, and said he had been at the water, and had thrown the sword in the water.

"What saw thou there?" said the king.

"Sir, he said, I saw nothing but waves and winds."

"That is untruly said!" said the king, "therefore go thou lightly again, and spare not, but throw it in!"

Then Sir Bedivere returned again, and took the sword in his hand...

from 'Morte d'Arthur' by Thomas Malory

you see

saw

decorated ball at the end of the hilt

you

do not hesitate

◼ The story is continued in Alfred Lord Tennyson's version, 'Idylls of the King' (1842).

Then went Sir Bedivere the second time
Across the ridge, and paced beside the mere,
Counting the dewy pebbles, fixed in thought;
But when he saw the wonder of the hilt,
How curiously and strangely chased, he smote
His palms together, and he cried aloud:
'And if indeed I cast the brand away,
Surely a precious thing, one worthy note,
Should thus be lost for ever from the earth,
Which might have pleased the eyes of many men.
What good should follow this, if this were done?...
... What harm, undone? Deep harm to disobey.
The King is sick, and knows not what he does...'

lake

decorated hilt

sword

worth being famous

in this way

TERM 2

The last days of Camelot

■ The story of the passing of Arthur is finished in this version by Michael Morpurgo from his book *Arthur, High King of Britain*.

"My lord," he said, falling to his knees. "Do not make me do this, I beg you."

"Do you love your king, Bedevere?" I could barely speak now.

"You know I do, my lord."

"Then in God's name, do it." And I fell back, a swirling blackness dragging me down.

When I woke, Bedevere was cradling me in his arms and weeping. "I did it! I did it!"

"And what did you see?" I asked him.

"A hand, my lord, and an arm in a white silken sleeve. The hand reached up and caught Excalibur and drew it down into the lake. And the water never moved, my lord, not even a ripple."

"Good," I whispered. I looked up at the sky for the last time, and saw a white screecher-owl floating past on silent wings. I remember nothing more, until I heard the sound of waves lapping about me. I found myself lying on a boat, the Lady Nemue leaning over me. And around me stood five other ladies, all in black. Beyond them, Bercelet was standing on the bow of the boat and looking out over the sea, I could just make out Bedevere, alone on the shore. I wanted to wave, but was too weak now even to raise my hand.

"I said I would see you at Camlan," said the Lady Nemue; and I remembered then where I had heard that name before. "Oh Arthur, this is the saddest day there ever was. But you will live, and you will come back. The tree may have withered and died, but you are the acorn and your time will come again."

"Where are we going?" I asked her.

"To Lyonesse," she said. "To a place where we can look after you, a place you can rest, a place were no one will ever find you."

UNIT 4

Note-taking and explanation

This unit focuses on reading, understanding, researching and writing explanation texts. The lessons teach one particular method of research and note-making that is designed to help children retrieve information easily and make use of it without merely copying it out. This focus on one particular technique provides a sound basis for the development of more open-ended methods. The series of lessons culminates in a group booklet entitled 'How Things Work' aimed at children of their own age, and a companion booklet, 'How Things Work – Junior Edition' for younger Key Stage 2 children. This unit can be organised on a cross-curricular basis with a related geography unit.

Hour	Shared text-level work	Shared word-/ sentence-level work	Guided reading/ writing	Independent work	Plenary
1 Volcano	Reading an explanation text, identifying genre features.		Comparing versions of similar information.	Annotating text for genre features, adding subheadings.	Discussing use of subheadings.
2 An approach to note-taking	Learning a method of taking notes.	Identifying connectives.	Collecting connectives for a 'connectives mat'.	Skimming and scanning to make notes.	Labelling a diagram.
3 How Things Work	Using a checklist to begin writing class explanation book.	Relating key words in children's texts to book glossary.	Researching and writing notes for pages for the class book.	Researching and writing pages for the class book.	Reading each other's notes.
4 Own explanation	Developing diagram notes into text explanation.	Discussing standard English and impersonal style.	Writing their explanation pages.	Writing their explanation pages.	Sharing the texts and combining them into a book.
5 How Things Work – Junior Edition	Discussing how to adapt text for a younger audience.	Discussing how to adapt text for a younger audience.	Simplifying their texts.	Simplifying their texts.	Checking the new texts are uncomplicated.

Key assessment opportunities
● Do the children understand and recognise key features of explanation texts?
● Can they retrieve information and make useful notes?
● Can they use notes to write explanation texts in their own words, using complete sentences?
● Could they simplify their writing for a younger audience?

Volcano

Objectives

NLS
T15: To read a range of explanatory texts, investigating and noting features of impersonal style, eg complex sentences; use of passive voice; technical vocabulary; hypothetical language; use of words/phrases to make sequential, causal, logical connections.
T19: To evaluate texts critically by comparing how different sources treat the same information.

What you need
● Photocopiable page 129 (without annotations)
● other resources on volcanoes.

Shared text-level work
● Explain to the children that they are going to read and write explanation texts.
● Encourage them to help you with a definition and examples: an explanation text tells us how or why something happens, such as how river valleys are formed or why the Romans built roads. Typically such a text describes the subject as an introduction then goes into an explanatory sequence.
● Display and read photocopiable page 129. Repeat the first three sections and ask the children to look for the following key features, which can be jotted on the board (annotate the features as they are identified, using the original of the photocopiable sheet as a guide):

● description or definition
● explanation of how or why
● illustrations and subheadings (in some texts)
● technical vocabulary
● hypothetical 'if... then' constructions (in some texts)
● connectives
● use of passive voice (see below).

● Explain that the passive form emphasises what is done, not who or what did it. Illustrate this by asking the children: What blocked the main vent? (We don't know. Many things could cause a blockage. If we knew, we could use the active voice: a boulder blocked the main vent...)

Guided and independent work
● Work with a group to compare one or two different accounts of how a volcano works from other reference books. Help them to find the key features of explanatory texts and then evaluate the texts by asking Which explanation do you find the most helpful and why?
● Ask the children to work in pairs on the following tasks:

1. Annotate the key features of non-chronological reports on the remaining sections.
2. Annotate words and phrases that make connections, and 'if... then' constructions.
3. Make a list of technical vocabulary, put it in alphabetical order and add definitions.
4. Write a subheading for each paragraph.

Differentiation

Less able
● Give the children a shorter and easier text on the same subject, perhaps from *The Usborne Children's Encyclopedia*.

More able
● Give the children a more difficult text, such as from *Microsoft's Encarta*.

Plenary
● Share and discuss the annotations that the children have added to the rest of the text, writing good suggestions on the display version of photocopiable page 129.
● Ask what subheadings they thought of. Choose the best of these and discuss how they help the reader to see at a glance what the different sections of text are about.

Objectives

NLS
T17: To locate information confidently and efficiently through skimming to gain overall sense of text and scanning to locate specific information.
T20: Notemaking: to discuss what is meant by 'in your own words'.
S8: To construct sentences in different ways, while retaining meaning.

What you need

● Photocopiable page 129
● card 6 from enlarged photocopiable page 130
● A4 sheets with enlarged card 6 in the centre.

An approach to note-taking

Shared text-level work

● Suggest to the children that it will be useful to make notes when retrieving information from reference books for collating and writing in their own words (in the form of a class book on how things work).
● Display card 6 alongside photocopiable page 129 and demonstrate how to use the diagram as a focus for making notes.
● Show the children how to scan the text for key words, and then how to skim the sentence containing the key word to check that it includes the information they need.
● Use the following sequence:

> **Step 1.** Label key parts of the diagram. Read the first two paragraphs with the children and ask them to identify terms that can be used to label the features in the diagram: (*magma chamber, main vent, secondary cone*).
> **Step 2.** Add brief notes to each label. Ask: *What shall we write for 'magma chamber'?* (Build-up of molten rock below Earth's crust.)
> **Step 3.** Number the items in the order in which things happen. *1. magma chamber, 2. main vent.* A secondary cone may or may not form, so it can be referred to at any point in the sequence.

Shared sentence-level work

● Ask the children to look again at the sentence constructions in the text, particularly the use of connectives.
● Ask the children to identify connectives of cause and effect and connectives of time.

Guided and independent work

● Work with a group of children in a guided activity and use this text and others to collect and classify suitable connectives for explanatory writing. Here are some to begin with: *although, as a result of, because, due to, however, later, nevertheless, so, therefore.*
● Ask the children to make a desktop mat of these for the rest of the class to use (an A3 poster that is laminated and placed on each desk for children to do their work on).
● Let pairs of children skim and scan the text to finish labelling and note-making, following the sequence demonstrated in whole class work.

Differentiation

Less able
● Remove more difficult items from the diagrams, such as 'secondary cone' and 'ejecta'.

More able
● Ask the children to make additional notes on the extra information in the text, such as underwater volcanoes, famous volcanoes.

Plenary

● Ask the children to help you to finish off the diagram you began earlier.
● Emphasise how important it is to label the diagram in sequence. Use the diagram to demonstrate the final step:

> **Step 4.** Retell orally and then rewrite the explanation using the numbered sequence and the notes.

● Explain that this approach ensures that the explanation is in your own words, but contains all the important technical information.

How Things Work

Objectives

NLS
T17: To locate information confidently and efficiently through using contents, indexes, sections, headings; skimming to gain overall sense of text; scanning to locate specific information; close reading to aid understanding; text-marking; using CD-ROM and other IT sources.
T20: Notemaking: to discuss what is meant by 'in your own words' and when it is appropriate to copy, quote and adapt.
W9: To search for, collect, define and spell technical words derived from work in other subjects.

What you need
● A4 sheets with each card from photocopiable page 130 in the centre (complete set for each group)
● photocopiable page 131
● access to the school library or a wide range of resources covering the subjects on photocopiable page 131.

Differentiation

Less able
● Allocate the volcano diagram and allow the children to benefit from work done in the shared session.

More able
● Allocate a subject that does not appear on the cards. Explain that the first step in their research will be to find a suitable diagram or draw one themselves. They then follow the same process as everyone else.

Shared text-level work
● Explain to the children that they are going to produce a class book entitled 'How Things Work'.
● Tell them that they will each be given a diagram like the one in the previous session as a basis for their note-taking and writing.
● Explain to the children that their texts will be compiled to form the class book.
● Display photocopiable page 131. Read and talk about the advice for research at the top of the page.
● Take the opportunity to explain to the children the reference system used in the school library and go through the stages of note-taking as given on the checklist.
● Remind the children of the scanning and skimming skills, the importance of notes that are clear (so they can be useful later), and the process of using a diagram as the basis of note-making.
● Explain that the four-point sequence they used in Hour 2 makes up point 4 – *Make clear notes* – on this five-point plan.

Shared word-level work
● Explain that the class book must also contain a contents page and a glossary.
● Briefly revise alphabetical order, and the definition of the term glossary (an alphabetical list of technical terms with definitions, useful when it is not appropriate to include detailed definitions within the main text).
● Explain that the labels and the notes in the labels will form the basis of their glossary (to be compiled in the next lesson).

Guided and independent work
● Organise the children to work in groups of about seven.
● Allocate a different diagram to each child (see note on more able children below).
● Take the children to the library (including internet access and CDs if possible), or provide them with a range of reference materials and ask them to research their subject and to label and annotate their diagrams.
● Remind them how to use contents and index pages, page headings, subheadings and diagrams to locate the details they want.

Plenary
● Let the children exchange their diagrams with a partner and ask some of the partners to show and read out the notes to the class.
● Ask the readers if they think they could write an explanation using those notes.
● Emphasise the message that notes, though concise, must be clear so that they are understood by another person or by the note-maker later.

Own explanation

Objectives

NLS
T22: To plan, compose, edit and refine short non-chronological reports and explanatory texts, using reading as a source, focusing on clarity, conciseness, and impersonal style.
S2: To consolidate the basic conventions of standard English.
S6: To be aware of the differences between spoken and written language.

What you need

● Labelled volcano diagram from the Hour 2 plenary
● the children's labelled and annotated diagrams from photocopiable page 130 from Hour 3
● new copies of photocopiable page 130 may also be needed (see Independent work)
● photocopiable page 131.

Differentiation

Less able
● Ask the children to write to a format: an A3 page folded down the centre, with the diagram on one side and handwriting lines on the other.

More able
● Encourage the children to include additional information based on the more extensive notes they made in Hour 3.

Shared text-level work
● Display the fully-labelled volcano diagram from Hour 2.
● Remind the children that you have used the labels and notes to help you explain orally how a volcano works.
● Explain that this will be the first step that they need to follow when they come to write their own explanations.
● Elicit from the children a similar sentence-by-sentence explanation of the volcano.
● Scribe the best suggestions, demonstrating how the writing is more formal and structured than speech, and is in complete, punctuated sentences.

Shared sentence-level work
● Tell the children that explanation texts should be written in an impersonal style. In other words, explanation texts use a neutral form of standard English that could have been written by anybody. The first step in doing this is to avoid any slang, dialect, chatty phrases or over-familiar contracted forms.
● Taking suggestions from the children, write on the board some examples of slang, dialect and chatty phrases and discuss impersonal alternatives. *Some volcanoes are whopping great big things* or *Some volcanoes are humongous/ginormous* should be *Some volcanoes are very large*.
● Write up some contracted forms, and ask the children what the full form is, for example, 'they are' is used in the text, rather than 'they're'.

Guided and independent work
● Ask the children to write their own explanation pages from their annotated diagrams, using the process modelled in the shared session:

1. Explain the diagram to a partner.
2. Write the explanation, taking any comments into consideration.

● If extra time can be given, it is a good idea to ask the children to redraw the diagrams and add simple labels. If time is limited, provide them with another printed copy of the diagram.
● Remind the children to consider page layout as this is an important feature of this text type.
● Encourage the children to refer to the checklist during writing as a guide, and afterwards to evaluate their work.

Plenary
● Ask some of the children to show and read their explanations to the whole class.
● Evaluate a few of them by using the criteria on the checklist.
● Use a simple binding for copies of the final pages.
● Let children keep their originals and show them what they have achieved by putting the book on display.

How Things Work – Junior Edition

Objective

NLS
T24: To evaluate their work.
S3: To understand how writing can be adapted for different audiences, eg by changing vocabulary and sentence structures.

What you need
● Photocopiable pages 129 and 130
● display version of an explanation text written by a child in Hour 4 (see Shared work)
● the children's explanations from Hour 4.

Shared text- and sentence-level work
● Explain to the children that they are going to adapt their explanation texts for a younger audience and produce a companion volume to the one they made in Hour 4. This new one will be called 'How Thing Work – Junior Edition'.
● Display photocopiable page 129, and explain that it is actually above the independent reading level of the average Year 5 child (so congratulate them on their success with it!). Ask the children which words, sentence structures and so on make it particularly difficult. (Terms such as *geological formation, magma, continental plates*; many sentences contain two or more clauses and about a quarter of the sentences are in the passive form.)
● Display a good example of an explanation text written by one of the children in Hour 4 (making sure that it is simple and reasonably short). Discuss why it is easier to read than the sample text read above. (It is shorter, has fewer technical terms and uses simpler sentences.)
● Finally, discuss how the child's explanation could be made even simpler so that younger children can use it. Perhaps simplify the diagram, trim the explanation to the very basics (don't include secondary cones); cut out as many technical terms and difficult concepts as possible (instead of *magma*, write *molten rock* or even *liquid rock*); keep sentences very short (a complex sentence simply split in two is likely to be easier to follow).

Guided and independent work
● Ask the children to write a shorter and simpler version of their explanation text, for a younger readership.
● If time allows, they should redraw their diagrams, otherwise provide them with another copy.
● They may also want to consider simplifying the layout and using shorter paragraphs.

Differentiation

Less able
● Ask the children to simplify their diagram. Provide a format as Hour 4, but with fewer handwriting lines that are further apart. This will convey visually the need for a simpler text.

More able
● Challenge thechildren to include their extra information but in a simplified form.

Plenary
● Display and discuss some examples of the simplified texts.
● Evaluate them by looking carefully for anything that still seems complicated or too challenging, for example:

> ● words, especially technical terms
> ● sentence structures, especially long sentences and structures like the passive
> ● long paragraphs
> ● over-complex diagrams.

● If possible, try out the texts on a younger class and see if they can understand them.

Volcano

Wise Owl says that a volcano is a geological formation (usually a mountain) where magma (molten rock) erupts through the earth's crust. The study of volcanoes is called volcanology.

A volcanic eruption begins when magma builds up below the earth's crust forming a magma chamber. As a result of this, the pressure builds up and magma in the chamber is forced upwards through the main vent (a tube in the volcano) causing an eruption. The rising magma also ejects rocks, cinders, volcanic ash, dust, steam and sulphurous gas. If the main vent is blocked, then the magma may be forced to the surface by another route. This causes the formation of a secondary cone.

The most noticeable part of a volcano is the crater (a kind of basin at the top of the volcano). The main vent opens into the middle of this crater to allow the magma and other ejecta (the material thrown out by the volcano) to pour out. A crater can be very large and sometimes very deep. Very large craters of this kind are called calderas.

When volcanoes erupt it looks as though they eject smoke and flame, but in fact, the ejecta consist of lava, cinders, volcanic ash, dust, steam and sulphurous gas. What appears to be flame is caused by the glare from red hot magma which reflects off the clouds of dust and gas. In a powerful eruption, lumps of molten rock may also be ejected. These are called volcanic bombs. When magma flows out of the main vent it changes its name to lava. It can flow for several kilometres across the land surface causing great devastation.

from Ask Wise Owl Children's Encyclopedia

illustration/ diagram

Definition/ introduction

technical vocabulary

helpful explanations in brackets

Explanation

connective

passive

hypothetical construction/ passive

technical vocabulary

connectives

technical vocabulary

commas marking list

Diagram cards

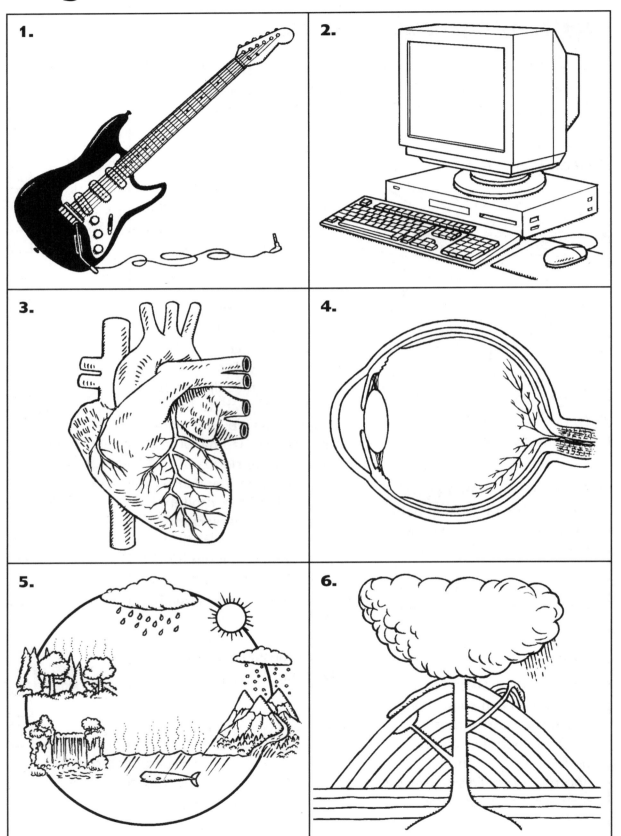

1.

2.

3.

4.

5.

6.

▶SCHOLASTIC

Checklist for explanations and non-chronological reports

This checklist can be used as a reminder when researching and writing, and as a guide for redrafting.
The second part can also be used to evaluate texts.

Research and notemaking

◼ Locate suitable books by using the library referencing system. ▢

◼ Retrieve and rewrite the required information by using this five-point plan: ▢

1. Scan for subheadings and/or key words. ▢

2. Skim to check that the text is what you want. ▢

3. Read it carefully. ▢

4. Make clear notes of key facts, names and dates (see * below). ▢

5. Write your own version, using your notes to help. ▢

– Label key parts on a suitable diagram. ▢

– Add brief notes to each label. ▢

– Number the items in sequence. ▢

Planning

◼ Plan an explanation text by following the numbered sequence on the diagram (see above). ▢

or

◼ Plan a non-chronological report with a spider diagram: ▢

1. Write the name of the main topic in the centre. ▢

2. Draw the spider's legs and write the name of the subtopics at the ends. ▢

3. Add 'baby spiders' for sub-topics. ▢

Writing

◼ Write in your own words as far as possible. *Never copy whole sentences.* ▢

◼ Write as clearly as possible, though you may need to include technical vocabulary and complex sentences. Clarity can be helped by using paragraphs and subheadings. Use diagrams for things that are difficult to explain in words. ▢

◼ Write in an impersonal style, formal style. Use standard English. ▢

Proof-reading

◼ Check for:

clarity ▢

correct use of standard English ▢

correct punctuation and spelling (particularly of technical terms and unusual names). ▢

UNIT 5

Non-chronological report

This unit is designed to complement the work on *The Odyssey* in Unit 3. Children learn to analyse non-chronological reports by working on a text about Homeric Greece. They use their learning to research, plan and write a similar text on Classical Greece which fulfils the National Curriculum history unit: A study of the way of life, beliefs and achievements of the people living in Ancient Greece. However, any topic can be used as the basis for the children's own non-chronological writing. Extra time may be needed to produce a final version of the report, but this could be taken from history time.

Hour	Shared text-level work	Shared word-/ sentence-level work	Guided reading/ writing	Independent work	Plenary
1 Homeric Greece	Reading sections of a non-chronological report, identifying genre features.	Finding connective words and phrases.	Summarising the reordered text.	Noting genre features and connectives; reordering the sections.	Establishing the best sequence of sections.
2 Page designer	Examining layout of reference book.	Noting key words for layout features.	Designing a double-page spread.	Designing a double-page spread.	Evaluating spreads; talking about choices made.
3 Researching Classical Greece	Revising skimming and scanning techniques for research.	Making notes, using abbreviations.	Researching and making notes on Classical Greece.	Researching and making notes on Classical Greece.	Reading and appraising notes.
4 Spiders and baby spiders	Compiling a topic spider diagram.	Comparing active and passive voice.	Constructing spidergram as plan for new double-page spread.	Constructing spidergram as plan for new double-page spread.	Sharing and discussing spidergrams.
5 Double-page spread	Considering adapting texts for different audiences and purposes.	Focusing on impersonal style.	Drafting their reports/ spreads for a certain audience.	Drafting their reports/spreads for a certain audience.	Displaying the spreads.

Key assessment opportunities
● Can the children understand the key features of non-chronological reports?
● Can they locate information confidently, compare sources, and make useful notes?
● Can they plan and write non-chronological reports?
● Do they understand how writing can be adapted for different audiences and purposes?

Homeric Greece

Objectives

NLS
T15: To read a range of explanatory texts, investigating and noting features of impersonal style; technical vocabulary; hypothetical language; use of words/phrases to make sequential, causal, logical connections.
S8: To construct sentences in different ways, while retaining meaning, through: combining two or more sentences; re-ordering them; deleting or substituting words; writing them in more telegraphic ways.

What you need
● Photocopiable page 138.

Shared text-level work
● Explain to the children that they are going to read and write non-chronological reports. Explain that non-chronological means writing that is organised without reference to time sequence. Typically, the text is organised by characteristics and attributes. For example, a report on a town might be organised into population, situation, facilities.
● Display photocopiable page 138 and explain that it contains six sections from a non-chronological report placed in a random order. Later they will be asked to put the topics in a logical sequence.
● Read the first three sections and ask the children to look for the following key features (which can be jotted on the board). Annotate the features on the text as they are identified:

- technical or specialist vocabulary
- complex sentences
- impersonal style
- passive voice.

Shared sentence-level work
● Ask the children: How can you tell that the first section was not first in the original text? (The word also in the first sentence refers to previous text.)
● Ask the children to look for other words and phrases that make connections between items of information, for example, *though unfortunately*, *such as*, *because*. Annotate these as they find them.

Guided and independent work
● Work with a group to write a summary of resource 138 (in its correct sequence) in about one third of its length.
● Ask the children to independently work in pairs to carry out the following tasks:

1. Annotate the key features of non-chronological reports on the remaining four sections.
2. Annotate words and phrases which make connections.
3. Discuss which would be the most effective order for the sections.

Plenary
● Share ideas about the best sequence for the text:

1. *To the Greeks of the 5th century BC...* This is clearly an introduction giving an overview of the text.
2-3. Minoan civilisation came before Mycenaen civilisation, so the Minoan section comes first – a chronological arrangement in a mainly non-chronological text.
4-6. The information about metalwork must come after the information about pottery because of the word *also*. Linear-B could come before or after these linked sections.

Differentiation

Less able
● Less able children and kinaesthetic learners may be helped by physically cutting out the sections and trying them in different orders.

More able
● Ask children, additionally, to annotate the use of colons, semicolons, commas, dashes and brackets as signposts to meaning.

UNIT 5 HOUR 2 ☐ Non-chronological report

Page designer

Objectives

NLS
T17: To locate information through using sections, headings, text-marking.
T19: To evaluate texts critically by comparing how different sources treat the same information.
W9: To search for, collect, define and spell technical words derived from work in other subjects.

What you need
● Photocopiable pages 138 and 139
● double-page spreads from a reference book that include subheadings, illustrations/photographs and diagrams
● computer access.

Shared text- and sentence-level work
● Display a double-page spread from a suitable reference book. Point out the following typical features of non-chronological reports:

● subheadings
● illustrations and labelled diagrams
● careful page design, often based around the double-page spread format
● text in columns (if appropriate)

● Ask the children: What is the advantage of texts designed in this way? (The layout makes them appealing, easy to follow and interesting and quick to read. Illustrations and diagrams are highly informative. Subheadings and labels enable quick navigation/research.)

Shared word-level work
● Jot down key layout and publication terms on the board. Ensure that the children understand the following terms and can spell and use any difficult ones (you will want them to include them in discussions): bold, caption, column, diagram, illustration, italic, subheading, text box, typeface (or font).

Guided and independent work
● Ask pairs of children to design their own double-page spreads using photocopiable pages 138 and 139. Tell them to:

1. Cut out the sections of text and the layout resources.
2. Lay them on a sheet of A3 paper (placed landscape and folded down the middle).
3. Shuffle the items around to achieve an effective design.
4. Paste down.

● Tell the children to allow for a margin all around each page and not put any text across the fold.
● If possible, encourage a group to design double-page spreads using ICT, adapting the above process accordingly.

Plenary
● Ask the children to pin their double-page spreads to a display board (or interactive whiteboard) and allow time for all the class to look at them. Ask them to evaluate each one on three criteria:

1. correct matching of text and subheadings, illustrations and captions
2. clarity of presentation
3 visual appeal.

Differentiation

Less able
● Enlarge all photocopiable pages to A3 size.

More able
● Provide the children with additional text and illustrations so that they have to make selective choices.

● Encourage the pairs to talk about how they made their layout choices.
● Reinforce knowledge of key features of non-chronological texts.

UNIT 5 HOUR 3 ◼ Non-chronological report

Researching Classical Greece

Objectives

NLS
T17: To locate information confidently and efficiently through using contents, indexes, sections, headings; skimming, scanning, close reading; using CD-ROM and other IT sources.
T20: Note-making: to discuss what is meant by 'in your own words' and when it is appropriate to copy, quote and adapt.

What you need
● Photocopiable page 131 [checklist from Unit 4]
● good example of the children's double-page spreads from Hour 2
● access to library or a range of reference books about Ancient Greece
● encyclopedias
● CD-ROM encyclopedia and/or access to the internet (optional).

Differentiation

Less able
● Help the children with the first step by giving them one or two books or directing them to websites that you know contain appropriate information.

More able
● Ask the children to find the same information in different sources and select the most useful.

Shared text-level work
● Remind the children of their work in Hour 2. Explain that they are going to research, plan and write a similar double-page spread about Classical Greece.
● Display photocopiable page 131 and read and discuss the advice for research at the top of the page.
● Remind the children of the reference system used in the school library and emphasise the importance of the five-point plan for research.
● Display the child's double-page spread and demonstrate how you would use it to find information about Linear-B by using these processes.
● Explain that, before you even got to this double page spread in a book you would have looked in the reference section of the library, found the book and consulted the contents and/or index.
● Taking prompts from the children, demonstrate how to scan the page in order to find the subheading Linear-B; skim the text in that section to check that it has the information that you need; read it carefully; and make notes.
● Explain that the final step is to write own version.

Shared sentence-level work
● Demonstrate how you would make notes on the Linear-B passage by writing key information in abbreviated form, for example:

> Linear-B
> syllabic
> found on Crete, Mycenae & other places in Greece
> not deciphered until 1952.

● Elicit from the children how to turn the notes back into a short paragraph written in their own words. (Ensure that you remove the original text.)

Guided and independent work
● Organise the children to work in pairs to research and make notes on Classical Greece.
● Tell them to begin by making a list of the subtopics that they find, for example: architecture, Athens, city states, and then to make brief notes about each subtopic.
● Advise them to consult the checklist to remind them of research techniques.

Plenary
● Ask some of the children to read out their notes.
● Check that they have made a list of subtopics, and that the notes of the subtopics are key facts, names and dates and not mere chunks of copied text.

UNIT 5 HOUR 4 ◼ Non-chronological report

Spiders and baby spiders

Objectives

NLS
T15: To read a range of explanatory texts, noting features of impersonal style, eg use of passive voice.
T22: To plan, compose, edit and refine short non-chronological reports and explanatory texts, using reading as a source, focusing on clarity, conciseness, and impersonal style.

What you need
● Photocopiable page 138.

Shared text-level work
● Explain to the children that you are going to show them how to plan a double-page spread using a spider diagram.
● Draw a large circle in the middle of the board and write 'Classical Greece' in the centre. Draw several lines radiating from it (like a sun, or spider's legs), ready for subtopics to be added.
● Ask the children to suggest labels for subtopics within the topic of Classical Greece (based on their research in Hour 3). These might include: architecture, Athens, city states, democracy, drama, literature, religion, sculpture, Sparta, the Peloponnesian war, war with Persia. Place the more significant subtopics in circles at the end of the spider's legs, for example, city states, and group further subtopics (baby spiders) around those circles, such as Athens, Sparta.
● Explain that the next step is to decide on the order in which each section will appear in the final text on Classical Greece. This should be indicated by numbering the circles around the main spider.
● Then the children will need to consider how best to layout their double-page spread so that the sections of text are read in the order they have established as the best one.

Shared sentence-level work
● Re-read the section on pottery from photocopiable page 138. Point out the construction, *were found*.
● Explain that this is the passive voice. It is used here because we don't know (or it isn't important) who found the pottery.
● Tell the children that the passive voice is often used in non-chronological texts for this reason and because it creates an impersonal style.
● Compare the sentence with one in the active voice: *Bill Bloggs found many fragments of pottery and some complete vases.*

Guided and independent work
● Ask the pairs from Hour 3 to plan the structure of other double-page spreads using spidergrams based on their research into Classical Greece.
● Explain that the first step is to draw the spidergram and the second is to number the subtopic circles in the order in which they will appear in the final text.

Differentiation

Less able
● Ask the children to use a four- or six-legged spider with no babies.

More able
● Encourage the children to plan more detailed sections with several paragraphs (several baby spiders).

Plenary
● Display some examples of the children's spidergrams and discuss the choices they made about the order in which they have placed the paragraphs for their double-page spread.

Double-page spread

Non-chronological report

Objectives

NLS

T22: To plan, compose, edit and refine short non-chronological reports and explanatory texts, using reading as a source, focusing on clarity, conciseness, and impersonal style.

S3: To understand how writing can be adapted for different audiences and purposes, eg, by changing vocabulary and sentence structures.

S&L

53 Group discussion and interaction: To understand and use the processes and language of decision making.

What you need

● Photocopiable page 138
● photocopiable page 131 [from Unit 4]
● the children's notes and spider diagrams
● computers with word-processing or desktop-publishing software
● reference books with good examples of ways of presenting information.

Differentiation

Less able

● The children may benefit from pre-designed spread: a ruled A3 page, with design lines for two text sections and two illustrations per page. Ask them to write for a younger audience.

More able

● Encourage the children to study the layouts of various reference books and experiment with sophisticated design features. Ask them to write for an older audience.

Shared text- and sentence-level work

● Begin by showing the children some good examples of double page spreads in non-fiction texts.
● Discuss the key features of layout:

> ● Everything about the topic or sub-topic fits on the double page
> ● illustrations and diagrams are very important
> ● text is often placed in boxes

● Display photocopiable page 131 and go over the advice for writing non-chronological reports.
● Discuss impersonal style in more detail by re-reading the section on Mycenae from photocopiable page 138. Annotate the following features:

> ● First person, but more general/universal – *we*, not *I* (*We know something about the Mycenaeans...*) *We* refers to everybody.
> ● Third person for most of the text – *they, Mycenae, he, it.* The text is not focused on the author, but on what the author is writing about.
> ● Passive voice – *He was thought to be...* not *I thought he was...* This was a fairly general view, and who held it isn't important.
> ● Formal style; no slang, dialect, chatty phrases or contracted forms.
> ● Discuss how to adapt the double-page spread for different audiences:
> ● A younger audience – simple vocabulary, short sentences, less formal style, less text, more pictures and diagrams.
> ● An older audience – more difficult vocabulary and complex sentences, more formal style, more text and fewer pictures and diagrams.

Guided and independent work

● Ask the children to decide on their intended audience and then to begin the first draft of their non-chronological reports.
● Pairs of children could form larger groups so that each child has only two sections to write. This will require a planning meeting where the group discusses, considers and agrees on the design of the spread and the information to be included. Remind the children to consider all viewpoints and ideas. You may need to join the meeting to ensure fair discussion and compromise, but allow the interaction to be as independent as possible.
● Encourage some groups to produce their double-page spreads by desktop-publishing, or, if ICT resources are limited, children could print text and illustrations for final layout by manual cut and paste.
● Allow time for the children to read and redraft as necessary, referring to the checklist.

Plenary

● Display some of the final double-page spreads and ask the rest of the class to evaluate them by using the checklist.
● Make a permanent display so that children can continue to enjoy and evaluate them after the lesson.

TERM 2

Homeric Greece

The Minoans were excellent metalworkers, though unfortunately, only a few objects remain, such as the Bee Pendant. There is more evidence of Mycenaean metalwork, because they buried precious objects in tombs. These objects include wonderful gold masks and necklaces, silver vases, and highly ornamented bronze swords.

The people of Homeric Greece had a syllabic system of writing called Linear-B. This is very different from the later Greek alphabet or the modern English alphabet. Tablets with Linear-B script have been found on Crete, Mycenae and several other places in Greece. Linear-B was not deciphered until 1952.

Mycenae is the name of an ancient city near the modern town of Mikínai in the south of Greece. We know something about the Mycenaeans because they are the heroes of Homer's two epics poems, *The Iliad* and *The Odyssey*. The civilisation lasted until about 486BC when it was destroyed by an army from Argos. The ruins of Mycenae are impressive and include the famous Lion Gate and the Beehive Tombs.

Little was known about Minoans before the discovery in 1900 of a great palace at Knossos by the British archaeologist Sir Arthur Evans. The palace is decorated with wall

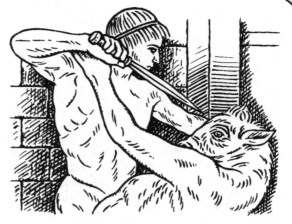

paintings of bull-leaping. This has led many people to think that it is the actual labyrinth in which Theseus slew the minotaur. Minoan civilisation was destroyed by an earthquake in about 1625BC followed by an attack by the Mycenaeans.

There were two major civilisations in Homeric Greece: the Minoan, which was based in Crete; and the later Mycenaean, which developed on the mainland of Greece. Most of what we know about the period comes from myths and legends such as 'Theseus and the Minotaur' (probably set in Knossos) and the Trojan war (launched from Mycenae).

Many fragments of pottery, and some complete vases, were found in the excavations of Knosses and Mycenae. The Minoans, as an island nation, liked to decorate their pottery with marine forms such as fish, octopuses and seaweed. The Mycenaeans preferred to use animals and human figures as decoration.

Layout resources

 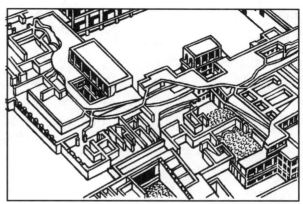

2000BC	Minoan civilisation flourishes
1625BC	Volcanic eruption at Thíra - Minoan civilisation destroyed
1220BC	Siege of Troy
750BC	Homer composes *The Iliad* and *The Odyssey*
5th century BC	The age of Classical Greece

1870	Heinrich Schliemann finds Troy.
1876	Heinrich Schliemann finds Mycenae.
1900	Sir Arthur Evans discovers the palace at Knossos.
1930	Greek archaelogists find evidence of an ancient volcanic eruption on the island of Thíra.

UNIT 1

Narrative: empathy/ point of view

This unit on narrative uses an old West African tale as its main text. It can be supplemented by traditional stories from any source, such as *Moon Tales* by Rina Singh and Debbie Lush (Bloomsbury) and *Stories from Around the World*, chosen by Linda Jennings (Kingfisher), or www.darsie.net/talesofwonder/, which contains traditional tales from around the world. Choose stories that exemplify patterns of relationships, social customs, attitudes and beliefs, and contain characters that create empathy in the reader. The first two hours tie in with Unit 42 in *Grammar for Writing*.

Hour	Shared text-level work	Shared word-/ sentence-level work	Guided reading/ writing	Independent work	Plenary
1 Cultural differences	Reading a West African story; comparing cultural features.	Understanding and finding prepositions.	Exploring uses and meanings of prepositions.	Comparing story with own culture.	Examining and discussing cultural differences.
2 Point of view	Identifying the story's point of view and exploring how it could be changed.	Finding words and phrases that establish point of view and empathy.	Rewriting an extract from a different point of view.	Discussing and rewriting the whole story in pairs.	Sharing drafts of rewritten stories, noting sustained point of view and any conflict .
3 The Man in the Moon	Reading a story from a 'future' culture.	Revising uses of apostrophes.	Reading different tales, noting cultural distinctions.	Reading different tales, noting cultural distinctions.	Taking brief feedback on differences found.
4 Oral presentation	Modelling group presentation from work in Hour 3.		Preparing presentation.	Preparing presentation.	Watching the presentations.
5 Discursive writing	Introducing discursive writing.	Examining sounds and spellings in polysyllabic words.	Writing their own responses to tales read.	Writing their own responses to tales read.	Sharing texts; discussing language differences between oral and written work.

Key assessment opportunities
● Can the children read and recite poems, paying attention to punctuation and rhyme?
● Have they used simple poetry structures to write their own poems?
● Do they use phonological and graphical knowledge to spell words?
● Do they understand that words with the same sounds may be spelled differently?
● Is their knowledge of long-vowel digraphs secure?

Cultural differences

Objectives

NLS
T1: To investigate a range of texts from different cultures, considering patterns of relationships, social customs, attitudes and beliefs.
S3: To search for a range of prepositions; experiment with substituting different prepositions and their effect on meaning.

What you need
● Photocopiable pages 146 and 147
● preposition kits (see Guided reading).

Shared text-level work
● Tell the children that they are going to read a story from another culture. Ask them to look/listen for relationships, social customs, attitudes and beliefs, and to consider how these are similar to or different from their own experience.
● Display photocopiable pages 146 and 147. Read the story to the children, then ask the children what they found.
● Write appropriate annotations based on the children's suggestions, for example, religion, pride in craftsmanship, appreciation of nature, 'traditional' roles, the guardian angel. For each suggestion the children make, ask for comparisons with their own cultures.

Shared sentence-level work
● Discuss and display a definition of the term *preposition*: a word like *at, over, by* and *with*, usually followed by a noun or noun phrase, that indicates position, movement or circumstance.
● Include a list of the 20 most common prepositions: *above, across, along, at, behind, below, between, by, down, from, in, near, on, off, over, past, through, to, under, up.*
● Tell the children to work in pairs to highlight or list all the prepositions they can find in the text. Afterwards, ask the children to report back to the rest of the class.

Guided and independent work
● Use the preposition kit with a group of children. The kit consists of enlarged photocopiable page 146 with prepositions blanked out, and a list of the prepositions used (the number of prepositions should match the number of gaps, so some will need to be listed more than once).
● Help kinaesthetic learners by making a small set of preposition cards. Experiment with substituting different prepositions and ask the children to discuss their effect on meaning.
● Ask the children, independently working in pairs, to make a table comparing old West African culture as presented in *Nyangara, the Fire Python* with their own culture. Ask them to construct a table, for example:

Differentiation

Less able
● Give the children a pre-prepared table with four or five of the main features of old Hawaiian culture in the left-hand column.

More able
● In addition to drawing up the table, ask the children to consider carefully the relationship between Amoafi and the villagers. How does she stand up for herself?

Old West African culture	My culture today
People lived in huts.	People do not live in huts. Huts have no running water or drainage and there is nowhere to plug the television in.

Plenary
● Using the tables that children have made, discuss the differences between different cultures and times.
● Encourage the children to see that life in traditional societies may have some advantages over life in a modern society. For example, traditional societies often have a closer family support network and are much more self-sufficient in that they grow their own food produce.

Point of view

Objectives

NLS
T2: To identify the point of view from which a story is told and how this affects the reader's response.
T3: To change point of view, eg tell incident or describe a situation from the point of view of another character or perspective.

What you need
● Photocopiable pages 146 and 147
● preposition kit from Hour 1.

Shared text-level work
● Explain to the children that every story has a point of view (sometimes called viewpoint or narrative perspective). The point of view is the way the reader sees the action. This can be through the eyes of the main character (which is a bit like real life), or through the eyes of several characters.
● Explain that the point of view of a story is established through the grammatical person in which it is written and partly through empathy.
● Revise personal pronouns for the first person (I/we), second person (you) and third person (he/she/it/they).
● Ask the children which person *Nyangara, the Fire Python* is written in. (Third person. Nearly all traditional tales are narrated in the third person.) Explain that although the narrative is third person, we are often presented with events from Amoafi's perspective, from her point of view.
● Now explain *empathy*. Empathy means *feeling with* a character. It is created by describing in detail how a character feels so that the reader shares his or her feelings.
● Ask which character the reader empathises with in *Nyangara, the Fire Python* and why. (Amoafi, because she is a good character and because we are given detailed information about her thoughts and feelings.)
● Discuss how the story could be changed so that it is told from one of the son's point of view. For example, how would he tell the story of his attempt to rescue his father? Would it be a more sympathetic viewpoint than the use of *humiliated* suggests? What would he think of Amoafi's *bravery*?

Shared word- and sentence-level work
● Ask the children to identify words and phrases that establish the reader's empathy with Amoafi, for example, her timid stutter, her *enchanting* singing, *a small creature*.

Guided and independent work
● Re-read the passage where Amoafi is introduced (from *The villagers were in despair*). Help the children to rewrite the passage in the third person and from one of the brothers' perspective.
● Ask the children to work in pairs to retell the story from the new point of view, telling it orally first (half the story each) and making notes about what things to change.
● The next step is to use their notes to produce a written version (again, half of the story each).

Differentiation

Less able
● Help the children to get started by re-using the first sentences of the original paragraph.

More able
● As an alternative to using another point of view, ask the children to imagine a conflict between Amoafi and her brothers.

Plenary
● Ask the children to share some of their emerging drafts. Give particular praise to those children that most successfully develop empathy with a new character, or develop the conflict between Amoafi and her brothers

UNIT 1 HOUR 3 ■ Narrative: empathy/point of view

The Man in the Moon

Shared text-level work

● Read photocopiable page 148 to the children. Briefly discuss relationships, customs, attitudes and beliefs, and compare them with the children's own cultures.
● Remind them how to write the points in a table:

The Man in the Moon	My culture
The captain and the two duty officers are women. The crew of the Vegas V use a computer to help them.	Women have the same opportunities as men and in the future will be just as successful in the workplace. I often use a computer to help me in my work.

Shared sentence-level work

● Quickly revise the uses of the apostrophe to indicate either omitted letters or possession. Explain:

● We use an apostrophe + s for the possessive form: *my mother's car*.
● With a plural 'possessor' already ending in s (for example, *parents*), an apostrophe is added to the end of the word: *my parents' car*.
● But irregular plurals (for example, *men, children*) take an apostrophe + s: *children's clothes*.

● Display just the first half of photocopiable page 148.
● Ask the children to suggest where apostrophes should be placed, and write them in.
● Encourage the children to explain the apostrophe's use each time. Give particular attention to the use of the apostrophe for possession.

Guided and independent work

● Organise the children to work into groups of four, each group to work on a different tale.
● Ask them to read the tale, discuss, list and look up if necessary any culturally-specific words, then work together to annotate the text as demonstrated in Hour 1.
● Tell the children that their next step is to make a table of cultural differences as in the shared session.

Plenary

● Say to the children that later they will present their thoughts on their tale to the class, but for now ask for brief feedback.
● Explain, if using *Moon Tales* for example, ask what beliefs about the moon their tale presented. Or, what was the single most interesting cultural difference between their tale and their culture?

Oral presentation

Objectives

NLS

T1: To investigate a range of texts from different cultures, considering patterns of relationships, social customs, attitudes and beliefs.
W13: To compile own class/group dictionary using personally written definitions.

S&L
46 Group discussion and interaction: To develop an oral presentation from previous written work.

What you need
● The tales from Hour 3.

Shared text-level work
● Before the lesson, work with one group of children to prepare a three-minute presentation of their tale to use as a model in the shared session. See the structure below for details.
● Explain to the class that they are going to make a presentation of the tales they studied in Hour 3, and that one group is going to give them an example of how to do it.
● State that the presentations should be in two or three parts, involve all of the children in the group, and last approximately three minutes. A suggested structure is:

> 1. A short summary of the story
> 2. The most interesting cultural differences
> 3. If using *Moon Tales*, what this culture believes about the moon.

● Support the chosen group as they give their presentation. After the presentation, clarify any points as necessary.

Guided and independent work
● Ask the groups to prepare a glossary of the culturally specific words that they looked up in Hour 3, for example, *tapa – cloth made from tree bark* (Hawaiian); *moon shuttle – a space ship that goes from the Earth to the Moon*. Tell them that their words and definitions will be collected for compilation by another group.
● Then ask each group to prepare a presentation of the chosen tale. Help the groups to allocate roles where necessary.
● Ask the group that gave the sample presentation to be responsible for collecting the culturally specific words and definitions from the other groups, editing them (putting them in alphabetical order) and making a glossary poster or booklet.

Plenary
● Ask each group to give its presentation. Ask the rest of the class to listen for the plot of the tale and the distinctive cultural aspects the tale reveals.
● Ask the children questions to check listening and understanding. Note significant and interesting cultural differences and similarities.

Differentiation

Less able
● Ask the children to practise their presentation orally.

More able
● Children the should also prepare to discuss the point of view of the tale and explain how empathy is created. Allocate extra time for this.

Discursive writing

Objectives

NLS
T10: To write discursively about a novel or story, eg, to describe, explain, or comment on it.
W4: To spell unstressed vowels in polysyllabic words.

What you need
● The tales from Hours 3 and 4
● the comparison tables from Hour 3
● the children's presentation notes.

Shared text-level work
● Explain to the children that now they are going to write about their stories, including what they have learned during discussion and presentation and what they think of them personally.
● Emphasise that they are going to be writing discursively, so should put forward their own thoughts and views.
● Display a suggested paragraph plan, for example:

1. A short summary of the story
2. The most interesting cultural differences (based on tables done on day 3)
3. If using *Moon Tales*, an explanation of what this culture believes about the moon
4. How point of view and empathy are created
5. A personal response saying what they found interesting about the story.

● Use the plan to model a paragraph or two about one of the stories that the children presented in Hour 4.

Shared word-level work
● Ask the children to identify some polysyllabic words in your model text. Ask why they are often difficult to spell. (Vowels in unstressed syllables are often pronounced as a light *uh* sound.)
● Give them some further examples from *Nyangara, the Fire Python,* such as *enormous* and *humiliated.*
● Ask the children to say how many syllables each word has, which is the stressed syllable, and to suggest a mnemonic to help them to remember the spellings.
● Choose two or three spelling patterns, such as *-able, -tion, -or,* and brainstorm more examples of these words.
● Ask volunteers who suggest words orally to come out and write them on the board.
● Allow other children to prompt with spellings if appropriate.

Guided and independent work
● Ask the children to write about their tales following the paragraph plan modelled in whole class work.
● Explain that they can work in their groups and help each other by discussing the stories and sharing ideas, but they should produce an individual piece of writing.

Differentiation

Less able
● Ask children to omit point of view and empathy.

More able
● Ask children to compare two tales and write a conclusion as part of their personal response on which they prefer and why.

Plenary
● Ask some of the children to read out their work. Praise good structure and interesting points made. Compare different views of the same stories.
● Discuss differences in language and style between the oral presentations of Hour 4 and the written accounts.

Nyangara, the Fire Python

Long, long ago, Nyangara the python lived in a cave at the top of a mountain. He was the only creature at that time to have fire, which he shared with no one. In fact, he used it to scare off the people who lived in the village below. They steered well clear of him, that is, up until their chief fell ill. Medicine men and women came from far and near with oils and ointments, potions and poultices. They danced and sang, wove spells and chanted, but to no avail.

Then one day, in hobbled a wise old woman. She went past the group of elders gathered under a palm tree, straight into the chief's hut. Observing him closely, she pronounced: "Only Nyangara, the fiery one can cure him now. Send for Nyangara."

The news spread like wild fire. *Send for Nyangara?* Who was there brave enough to go up the mountain and fetch Nyangara down?

The chief's eldest son volunteered. He was a hunter, brave and strong, famous throughout the region. "I'll go" he boasted, "I'll hunt Nyangara down." Up the mountain he went, approached the mouth of the cave and called out to the python "Nyangara, Nyangara, Nyangara!"

Angrily the huge python uncurled his enormous body and slithered towards him. At the sight of Nyangara, the brave hunter turned and fled. With a huge gusty breath, the python sucked in all his clothes and ornaments. The hunter arrived in the village shaken and ashamed.

The chief's second son stepped forward. He was a handsome athlete and dancer.

"I'll go," he said, flexing his biceps. But he ran off as soon as he heard Nyangara moving in his cave. He too had his clothing sucked off his body and he arrived back in the village with blood-curdling accounts of his struggle with the fearsome python.

Naturally, the third son, a gifted woodcarver, felt obliged to try and save his father. "I will entice Nyangara down," he said softly. Of course, he suffered the same fate as his brothers. One by one all the brave young men of the village tried, only to return humiliated.

The villagers were in despair. Their chief would surely die. Then to everyone's amazement, up stood Amoafi, the chief's only daughter. Timidly, she stuttered: "Pl... pl... please, may I go?" This was greeted by peals of mocking laughter. "You, a girl, who stutters too. You would go where all these brave young men have gone and failed!" But as Amoafi persisted in her request, the elders gave in.

"Go then daughter and may the spirits of the ancestors protect you," they said.

Up and up the mountain she climbed, got as near the mouth of the cave as she dared, took her courage in her hands and sang gently to the python.

Nyangara, tie ha (come here)
Nyangara, tie ha.

Three times she called to him in this way. The sound of Nyangara's name echoed enchantingly over the valley, rousing him. What a surprise he had to see the small creature, who had woken him so pleasantly from his sleep. He was even more surprised that she hadn't run away as had all the others before her. The happy result was that Nyangara withheld his fiery breath. Amoafi was thus able to explain her father's condition and especially what the old woman had said. Nyangara was silent for what seemed like a hundred years and then he boomed "I will come with you on one condition."

"What's that?" she asked.

"You will have to carry me down," replied the python.

"I will," agreed Amoafi, without thinking.

And so, ever so gently, the huge python wrapped himself around the girl's neck, shoulders and waist, way past her feet. Up till this day, no one knows just how she managed this heavy burden down the mountainside right up to her father's bed. Indeed, Nyangara *was* able to revive the chief. There was great feasting and rejoicing. Before returning to his cave, Nyangara offered a gift to Amoafi as a reward for her bravery – a lighted torch. "Take this torch. Use it wisely so no harm comes to you and your people, for it holds much danger." With that, he went up the mountain, back into his cave, where, for all we know he might still be asleep today.

Well, the torch did cause a lot of envy and bickering among the villagers but they have kept it burning from generation to generation.

Jane Grell

The Man in the Moon

"**A**ttention all crew members! This is your captain…" Miriam Masters couldn't help smiling when she said these words. After ten years, she was now captain of the Moon Shuttle Vegas V. "We have the following readings:

Temperature in landing zone: – 173°C

Surface of landing zone: volcanic rock

Status of landing zone: safe

Landing sequence starts in ten minutes. All Duty Officers please report to the bridge."

Pilot Officer Helen Harris put down her book and turned to her instrument panel.

"Whats that youre reading?" asked Captain Masters.

"Oh, its nothing," muttered Helen, slightly embarrassed.

"Let me look."

The books title was *Myths and Legends of the Moon* and its contents page listed stories such as 'The Man in the Moon', 'Green Cheese' and 'The Chinese Lantern in the Sky'. "Youll never make captain if you read this rubbish," the captain laughed, tossing Helens book back to her. "Id recommend this – *Facts about the Solar System* – much more useful than nonsense about the man in the moon and green cheese isnt it?"

"But its not very poetic," muttered Helen under her breath.

Luckily, Captain Masters wasnt listening. "Wheres Navigation Officer Walters?" she asked, looking around anxiously. "Shes supposed to be on the bridge. Call the officers mess, and see if shes there. If not, try the crewpersons cafe."

Just then, the bridge door slid open and Sally Walters hurried in.

Captain Masters announced, "All Duty Officers in position. Fasten seat belts. Prepare for deceleration."

This was the most difficult point of the journey – particularly for Helen, who had to pilot the ship. All eyes were glued to the ships main screen. Helens skilful hands flicked over the controls. Suddenly, an unexpected message came up:

Temperature in landing zone: 98.4°C

Surface of landing zone: green cheese

Status of landing zone: DANGER – BLACK HOLE

The Vegas was soon out of control, and as it spiralled into the black hole, Helen didnt know whether to panic, or be pleased that there was still some poetry left in the universe.

As for the Man in the Moon, he had had enough of humans crawling over his face like irritating insects and decided to put an end to it. So he opened his mouth – and swallowed.

UNIT 2

Poetry

For this unit a wide selection of poetry suitable for performance will be needed. Good anthologies include *Unzip Your Lips* chosen by Paul Cookson (Macmillan) and *Words Alive!* by Barry Wilsher and Jill Wilsher (Cambridge reading scheme). The latter contains helpful advice on the performance of oral poetry. Aim to plan the week on a rotational pattern with as much time as possible given to rehearsal and performance. Hour 1 is based on guidance for oral performance, while Hours 2 to 5 each begin by exemplifying a different type of oral poetry. However, children should be given access to a wide variety of poems and should be encouraged to make their own choices.

Hour	Shared text-level work	Shared word-/ sentence-level work	Guided reading/ writing	Independent work	Plenary
1 A poetry performance	Watching poetry performance, discussing techniques.		Annotating poem for performance.	Discussing and choosing poems for performance.	Revealing choices and talking about reasons for choices.
2 Fairground	Reading a poem and discussing how to perform it.		Textual analysis of another poem.	Preparing their choice of poem for performance.	Performing the poems for evaluation.
3 Old Mother Laidinwool	Reading and analysing an older poem.	Learning unfamiliar words; picking out dialect words and phrases.	Continuing work on poetry performance.	Continuing work on poetry performance.	Performing shared text and other poems.
4 Dialect poetry	Reading poem extracts from several dialects.	Distinguishing between accent and dialect.	Continuing work on poetry performance.	Continuing work on poetry performance.	Performing shared text and other poems.
5 That's a rap!	Reading and analysing a humorous rap poem.		Writing new verses to chosen poem, for constructive criticism by partners.	Writing new verses to chosen poem, for constructive criticism by partners.	Enjoying and evaluating added verses.

Key assessment opportunities
- Can the children choose and perform poems?
- Did they explore the challenge of older poetry?
- Did they investigate dialect through poetry?
- Can they use performance poems as a model for their own poems?

UNIT 2 HOUR 1 ▢ Poetry

What you need
● Sample of oral performance (recorded or live – see Shared work below)
● wide range of poems suitable for performance.

A poetry performance

Shared text-level work

● Show the children an example of how to perform a poem. This can be done by playing a video or audio tape of performances by published poets or other children, or by helping a group to prepare a performance in advance.
● Discuss the techniques and features that made the performance successful, such as, clarity, expression, variation in tone and pace, drama, music.
● Talk through different techniques of presentation, relating them to the performance you have just watched. The six main ones suggested by Barry and Jill Wilsher in *Words Alive* are:

> ● Pace
> ● Pause (leaving 'space' where appropriate)
> ● Pitch
> ● Power (loud, soft, shout, whisper and so on)
> ● Emphasis (stress)
> ● Inflection.

● The most important point is *variety*. Other ideas include orchestration (using several voices) and adding sound effects and/or music.
● Discuss and write up the list as a poster for display throughout the rest of the week.

Guided and independent work

● Help a group of children to annotate their own choice of poem for performance. Begin by brainstorming ideas, then decide who will say what, what actions are needed, and what sound or lighting effects could be used to enhance the performance. If you are able to make copies, encourage the children to make performance/production notes in the margins of their texts.
● Organise the children into groups of four to work independently, ask them to browse through the selection of poetry and to discuss and agree the choice of three poems which they would like to prepare for performance.
● Ask them to look for three poems which are as different as possible, for example, funny, sad, dialogue-based, action-based, older literature, modern, and to prepare a short explanation about why the group chose each one.
● Tell the groups that you will be asking which poems they have chosen and what initial ideas they have about how to perform them.

Plenary

● Ask each group which poems they have chosen and the reasons for their choices.
● Encourage the children to give you a few initial ideas about how to perform the poems. Did these ideas inform their choice?

Differentiation

Less able
● Guide less able children towards suitable poems.

More able
● Ensure the children choose appropriately challenging poems, for example, classic poems (see Hour 3).

Fairground

Objectives

NLS
T4: To read, rehearse and modify performance of poetry.
W11: To explore onomatopoeia. Collect, invent and use words whose meaning is represented in their sounds, eg splash, plop, bang, clash, smack, trickle, swoop.

S&L
40 Drama: To comment constructively on performance, discussing effects and how they are achieved.

What you need
● Photocopiable page 155
● the children's choices of poems from Hour 1.

Shared text-level work
● Explain to the children that poetry has been called *the mother tongue of mankind*. It exists in every culture, even in those which have no system of writing.
● Tell the children that today they are going to read a poem which is based on the sounds, sayings, instructions and shouts of delight which can be heard in any fairground.
Explain that the poem was specially written to be performed by three solo voices supported by a chorus who support their words with actions.
● Talk with the children about their own experiences in fairgrounds. Ask: What sounds did they hear? What noises did the rides make? What noises did the people on the rides make? What sounds did they make when they were on a scary ride?
● Read photocopiable page 155 and then discuss how the poem could be performed and brought to life using ideas from the previous discussion.

Shared word-level work
● Remind the children of the meaning of the term onomatopoeia - a word whose meaning is represented in its sound, for example, splash, plop, bang.
● Tell the children that 'Fairground' contains many such words and ask them to find them, and underline appropriate suggestions.
● Discuss with the children how to say these words to emphasise their onomatopoeic quality.

Guided and independent work
● Help a group to analyse one of the three photocopiable poems more fully (encourage the group to choose which) by revising work from Term 1. For example, ask them to look for word play, the expression of feeling, metaphors, similes, and well-chosen words.
● Help these children to annotate the features in the margins on the sheet.
● Ask other groups to work independently on their chosen poems and to have at least one ready for performance at the end of the lesson. Remind them to consult the poetry performance poster for ideas.

Differentiation

Less able
● Children may find the use of sound effects or percussion instruments supportive.

More able
● Ask children to annotate chosen poems with production notes and to add speakers' names in front of lines, in the manner of a playscript.

Plenary
● Begin with the performance of 'Fairground'.
● Ask the rest of the class to evaluate the performance constructively, using the poetry performance poster as a checklist. How well did the group use PPPPEI, orchestration and sound effects?
● Continue with more performances followed by evaluation.

Old Mother Laidinwool

Objectives

NLS

T6: To explore the challenge and appeal of older literature through: listening to older literature being read aloud; reading accessible poems; discussing differences in language used.

W12: To use dictionaries efficiently to explore spellings, meanings, derivations, eg by using alphabetical order, abbreviations, definitions with understanding.

S&L

44 Speaking: To tell stories using voice effectively.

What you need

● Photocopiable page 156
● the children's chosen poems
● dictionaries.

Shared text-and word-level work

● Aim to allow time in the plenary for all of the groups' performances.
● Display photocopiable page 156 and ask the children what they can tell you about Rudyard Kipling (1865–1936, author of *The Jungle Book*, *Just So* stories, and many poems).
● Read 'Old Mother Laidinwool' and question the children to check their overall understanding.
● Ask the children questions like: Why did she want to return from the dead? What was she worried about? What did she find? Why did she go back to her grave?
● Discuss the tone of the poem. Is it frightening or humorous? What makes it funny?
● Look at the language used in the poem. Ask the children to indicate any vocabulary that they don't understand, and work together to annotate the text with the meanings, using dictionaries as necessary.
● Ask the children to identify grammatical structures, words and abbreviations that suggest the country dialect of the poem, for example, *hops <u>was</u> doing well* (instead of <u>*were*</u> *doing well*), *an'* (*and*), *lads* (*boys*), *'em* (*them*), *grand* (*well*).
● Re-read the poem and then discuss how it could be performed.
● Elicit performance ideas from the children, and write good points on the board. In terms of personnel, these may include:

> ● one child to be the narrator
> ● one child to be Old Mother Laidinwool, act out her movements and say her words
> ● other children to act out the movements of other characters in the poem, for example, the Parson, Old Mother's daughters
> ● Two or more children, possibly those also acting character movements, to chant the refrain (which could be recited after every stanza).

Guided and independent work

● Ask each group to continue working on their chosen poems and to have one ready for performance at the end of the lesson.
● Ask the guided group from previous lessons to practise performing 'Old Mother Laidinwool' or one of the poems they have analysed.
● Remind the children to take into account the evaluation given in last lesson's plenary.

Differentiation

Less able
● The children may find the use of sound effects or percussion instruments supportive.

More able
● Ask the children to write an extra section for their chosen poem.

Plenary

● Begin with the performance of 'Old Mother Laidinwool'.
● Ask the rest of the class to discuss whether the performance helped them to understand the poem a little better and enjoy it more.
● Continue with more performances followed by evaluation using the performance poetry poster as a checklist.

Objectives

NLS
T4: To read, rehearse and modify performance of poetry.
W9: To understand how words vary across dialects.

What you need

- Photocopiable page 157
- the children's chosen poems for performance.

Dialect poetry

Shared text-level work

- Display photocopiable page 157, with the glossary covered.
- Read each poem with the children and ask them if they know or can work out what the dialect words mean. After they have taken several guesses, reveal and go through the glossary.
- Discuss any surprises, or praise the children for their accuracy.
- Read the poems again.
- Ask the children to match the poems to the dialects (the first is Yorkshire, the second Caribbean, the third, Cockney), and discuss how they can tell.
- Discuss how the poems could be performed. For example, one or two other children could provide a context for the speaker, such as a miner speaking to his friends in a pub.
- Explain that of course, the key element of any performance here will be an imitation of the accent. Sometimes the spellings or rhymes will help with this.
- Remind the children to consult the poetry performance poster for further ideas.
- Ask for three groups to volunteer to perform one of the poems each at the end of the lesson.

Shared word-level work

- Ask the children if they know the difference between the terms *accent* and *dialect*.
- Elicit or explain the following definitions:

> *accent* – features of pronunciation that vary according to the speaker's regional and social origin.
> *dialect* – a variety of a language used in a particular area, distinguished by certain features of grammar or vocabulary.

- Ask the children to brainstorm dialect words and make a list on the board along with their standard English equivalents.
- Explain for example, *beck, brook* and *stream* are all words for a small river. *Brook* is a dialect word used in the Midlands, Yorkshire and Lancashire, and *beck* is used further north.

Guided and independent work

- Ask the groups to continue working on improving and practising the performances of their chosen poems ready for another performance at the end of the lesson.

Plenary

- Begin with the performances of the dialect poetry.
- Ask the rest of the class to enjoy, discuss and evaluate each of the different group's performances.
- Continue with more performances followed by evaluation using the performance poetry poster as a checklist.

Differentiation

Less able
- Encourage the children to include sound effects or percussion instruments.

More able
- Ask the children to write performance notes for their chosen poem.

UNIT 2 HOUR 5 📄 Poetry

That's a rap!

Objectives

NLS
T11: To use performance poems as models to write and to produce poetry in polished forms through revising, redrafting and presentation.

S&L
60 Group discussion and interaction: To understand and use a variety of ways to criticise constructively and respond to criticism.

What you need
● Photocopiable pages 155–158
● the children's chosen poems
● electronic music keyboard (optional).

Differentiation

Less able
● Ask the children to write a short rap in simple couplets.

More able
● Ensure that the children choose a suitably challenging poem as a model.

Shared text-level work
● Ask the children if they like rap, and explain that rap is the most recent expression of oral poetry, extremely popular with young people in particular. Unfortunately, many rap and hip-hop lyrics, are unsuitable for children because of the violent and offensive images and bad language they contain. However, there are some enjoyable rap poems written especially for children, of which 'Gran Can You Rap?' is one.
● Ask for volunteers to read the poem, preferably in rap style with a musical background (the auto-accompaniment on an electronic keyboard is ideal). Then ask the children what is funny about the poem (for example, comparing Gran to a typical rap star, and the way the poem drifts off at the end as Gran raps on out of earshot).
● Analyse the verse form by asking children to indicate the rhyme scheme. The rhyme scheme is a a b b c c, or in other words, couplets. Ask them to count the number of stressed syllables in each line by reading the poem with emphasis (there are four and that this is important to create the strong rhythm of the poem). Note too that it should be read quickly (partly indicated by all the fast *action* in the story of the poem).

Guided and independent work
● Ask the children to choose one of the poems they have performed during the week and use it as a model for writing a similar poem or additional stanzas.
● Tell the children to analyse the verse form, content and theme, as demonstrated in whole class work and to adapt these for their new ideas.
● Explain that the next step is to write a draft of the new poem or extra stanza(s) and read it to other group members, asking them to listen carefully to check that the rhyme and rhythm, vocabulary and phrasing continue the form of the rest of the poem.
● Remind listeners to offer *constructive* criticism, and encourage writers to use it!

Plenary
● Ask some of the children to perform their poems. A good way to do this is to ask them to perform the model first, and then their poem based on it.
● Ask the audience to evaluate how well the model has been followed or adapted.
● If time allows, allocate additional lessons for the redrafting and presentation of the poems both orally and in writing.
● An interesting follow-up wolud be to investigate the vocabulary of rap. For this, some examples of real rap lyrics will be needed.
● Choose these lyrics with care to ensure that they are free from bad language, racists and sexist stereotypes or excessive violence. A good place to start would be 'Rappers Delight' by the Sugarhill Gang which contains words such as boogie, hip hop, mix, knicks, groove and mellow.

FAIRGROUND!

INTRO (THREE SOLO VOICES)
SOLO 1 Fairground!
SOLO 2 Merry-go-round!
SOLO 3 Ride the Carousel

V.1   Let's go........ on the Waltzers!
    Grip the bar! Hold tight!
    Spinning, flipping
    Reeling, dipping!
    Laugh and scream
With fright!

CHORUS (WITH ACTIONS AND MOVEMENTS)

Fairground! Merry-go-round! Ride the Carousel.
Try your luck on hook a duck! The coconut shy as well.
Fairground! Merry-go-round! The ghost train makes us yell.
Fairground! Merry-go-round! Ride the Carousel.

V.2   Let's go..... on the bumper cars!
    Grab the wheel! Hold tight!
    Skidding, bashing,
    Dodging, crashing,
    Laugh and scream
    With delight!

CHORUS (WITH ACTIONS AND MOVEMENTS)

Fairground! Merry-go-round! Ride the Carousel.
Try your luck on hook a duck! The coconut shy as well.
Fairground! Merry-go-round! The ghost train makes us yell.
Fairground! Merry-go-round! Ride the Carousel.

V.3   Let's go........ on the Roller Coaster!
    Grasp the headrest! Hold tight!
    Rolling, roaring,
    Swooping, soaring,
Laugh and scream
With fright and delight!

CHORUS (WITH ACTIONS AND MOVEMENTS)

Fairground! Merry-go-round! Ride the Carousel.
Try your luck on hook a duck! The coconut shy as well.
Fairground! Merry-go-round! The ghost train makes us yell.
Fairground! Merry-go-round! Ride the Carousel.

Campbell Perry

Old Mother Laidinwool

Old Mother Laidinwool had nigh twelve months been dead.
She heard the hops was doing well, an' so popped up her head,
For said she: 'The lads I've picked with when I was young and fair,
They're bound to be at hopping and I'm bound to meet 'em there!'

> *Let me up and go*
> *Back to the work I know, Lord!*
> *Back to the work I know, Lord!*
> *For it's dark where I lie down, My Lord!*
> *An' it's dark where I lie down!*

Old Mother Laidinwool, she give her bones a shake,
An' trotted down the churchyard-path as fast as she could make.
She met the Parson walking, but she says to him, says she: —
"Oh, don't let no one trouble for a poor old ghost like me!"

'Twas all a warm September an' the hops had flourished grand.
She saw the folks get into 'em with stockin's on their hands;
An' none of 'em was foreigners but all which she had known,
And old Mother Laidinwool she blessed 'em every one.

She saw her daughters picking an' their children them-beside,
An' she moved among the babies an' she stilled 'em when they cried.
She saw their clothes was bought, not begged, an' they was clean an' fat,
An' Old Mother Laidinwool she thanked the Lord for that.

Old Mother Laidinwool she waited on all day
Until it come too dark to see an' people went away —
Until it come too dark to see an' lights began to show,
An' old Mother Laidinwool she hadn't where to go.

Old Mother Laidinwool she give her bones a shake,
An' trotted back to churchyard-mould as fast as she could make.
She went where she was bidden to an' there laid down her ghost...
An' the Lord have mercy on you in the Day you need it most!

> *Let me in again,*
> *Out of the wet an' rain, Lord!*
> *Out of the wet an' rain, Lord!*
> *For it's best as You shall say, My Lord!*
> *An' it's best as You shall say!*

Rudyard Kipling

Dialect poems

◖ Match these dialects to the following poems: Caribbean, Cockney, Yorkshire.

Ex-miner's song

I'll tell thee all a **yarn**
Of how I once went down
In **yonder** pit for t'coal
Wi' **mickle** sweat an' toil.

I **dursn't** look for fear –
'Twere terrible down there!
'Twere **muckier** than a barn –
I wish I'd not gone down!

I couldn't gi'o'er puking
Though all the men were
looking,
It nearly was me ruin –
Tomorrer – I'm not going!

Itanami

One morning **de**
captain wake.
Captain wake, he wake de
boatman,
Boatman wake, he wake de
bowman,
Bowman wake **wid** de paddle in he
han:
All ah wan is a lang an strang...
Lang and strang is too much for me,
Lang and strang is Itanami!
Itanami, Itanami
Itanami, Itanami oh!

Captain, captain, put me ashore!
Ah don wan to go any more!
Itanami **gon fighken** me,
Itanami gon wuk me belly,
Itanami gon too much for me!
Itanami, Itanami
Itanami, Itanami oh!
Anon

Anon

Wot a Marf

Wot a marf' e'd got
Wot a marf,
When 'e wos a kid,
Goo' Lor' luv'll
'Is pore old muvver
Must 'a' fed 'im **wiv a shuvvle**.

Wot a gap 'e'd got,
Pore chap,
'E'd never been known to **larf**,
'Cos if 'e did,
It's a penny to a **quid**
'E'd 'a' split 'is **fice in 'arf.**
Anon

Glossary
story
that (over there)
much
dare not
dirtier
stop being sick
Itanami – dangerous rapids on
the river Potaro
the
with hand
all I want is long and strong
is going to frighten
is going to give me stomach-
ache
What a mouth he'd got
Good Lord love him
His poor old mother
with a shovel
laugh
pound
face in half

Gran Can You Rap?

Gran was in her chair she was taking a nap
When I tapped her on the shoulder to see if she could rap.
Gran can you rap? Can you rap? Can you Gran?
And she opened one eye and she said to me, Man,
    I'm the best rapping Gran this world's ever seen
    I'm a tip-top, slip-slap, rap-rap queen.

And she rose from her chair in the corner of the room
And she started to rap with a bim-bam-boom,
And she rolled up her eyes and she rolled round her head
And as she rolled by this is what she said,
    I'm the best rapping Gran this world's ever seen
    I'm a nip-nap, yip-yap, rap-rap queen.

Then she rapped past my dad and she rapped past my mother,
She rapped past me and my little baby brother.
She rapped her arms narrow she rapped her arms wide,
She rapped through the door and she rapped outside.
    She's the best rapping Gran this world's ever seen
She's a drip-drop, trip-trap, rap-rap queen.

She rapped down the garden she rapped down the street,
The neighbours all cheered and they tapped their feet.
She rapped through the traffic lights as they turned red
As she rapped round the corner this is what she said,
    I'm the best rapping Gran this world's ever seen
    I'm a flip-flop, hip-hop, rap-rap queen.

She rapped down the lane she rapped up the hill,
And as she disappeared she was rapping still.
I could here Gran's voice saying, Listen Man,
Listen to the rapping of the rap-rap Gran.
    I'm the best rapping Gran this world's ever seen
    I'm a –
        tip-top, slip-slap,
            nip-nap, yip-yap,
                hip-hop, trip-trap,
                    touch yer cap,
                        take a nap,
                            happy, happy, happy, happy,
                            rap—rap—queen.

Jack Ousbey

▪SCHOLASTIC

UNIT 3

Narrative: author style

This unit on author style offers an approach to the classic novel. It is based on *The Secret Garden* by Frances Hodgson Burnett, but can be adapted for use with any classic novel. It is recommended that you read the novel with the class two or three times per week over a half term. After most, though not necessarily all readings the children could be asked to complete a reading journal entry. Two to four scenes should be analysed in detail. In this unit, one of the scenes focuses on character and one on language. When the reading is complete, or nearly so, ask children to write creative responses then draw upon all the work they have done to write discursively. Hour 4 covers objectives in Unit 35 of *Grammar for Writing*.

Hour	Shared text-level work	Shared word-/ sentence-level work	Guided reading/ writing	Independent work	Plenary
1 Reading journal	Reading first chapter; modelling reading journal entry.	Picking out words from other languages.	Using etymological dictionaries.	Beginning reading journals.	Discussing journal entries.
2 Character and setting	Annotating an extract for character introduction and setting description.	Revising spelling patterns for words ending in *y*.	Annotating another extract in similar way.	Annotating another extract in similar way.	Examining extract for character points.
3 Language	Reading another extract, noting language features.	Revising understanding of dialect and accent.	Annotating another extract for language features.	Annotating another extract for language features.	Examining extract for notable language features.
4 Creative responses	Discussing different ways to adapt or write about a text.	Exploring how to simplify a text for younger audience.	Adapting a text for younger children.	Choosing a creative response for one extract.	Sharing responses; discussing how responses help understanding of text.
5 Discursive writing	Planning structure of discursive text about story.	Revising connectives.	Drafting discursive essays about the novel.	Drafting discursive essays about the novel.	Discussing responses to the novel.

Key assessment opportunities
● Are children noting personal responses in a reading journal?
● Have they successfully explored older literature?
● Can they respond creatively to a text?
● Can they write discursively about a novel?

UNIT 3 HOUR 1 ◗ Narrative: author style

Reading journal

Objectives

NLS
T6: To explore the challenge and appeal of older literature through: listening to older literature being read aloud; reading accessible stories and extracts; discussing differences in language used.
T8: To record predictions, questions, reflections while reading, eg through the use of a reading journal.
W8: To identify everyday words such as spaghetti, bungalow, boutique which have been borrowed from other languages, and to understand how this might give clues to spelling.
W11: To use a range of dictionaries and understand their purposes.

What you need
● *The Secret Garden* (or other classic novel)
● etymological dictionaries

Differentiation

Less able
● Give the children a 'what to do' list for writing entries to paste inside the front cover of their journals.

More able
● Add more categories to explore, such as how characters are presented through dialogue, action and description; sentence construction; use of description (adjectives, adverbs, figures of speech).

Shared text-level work
● Read chapter 1 of the chosen novel, briefly discuss interesting points and personal responses, then model a good way to write a reading journal entry. Begin by writing the following headings on the board, then ask the children to suggest what they might write under them. For example:

● *Reflections* – It is very unusual for the main character of a novel to be an unpleasant person, but I think Mary is like this because…
● *Questions* – What was it like to have lessons at home from a governess?
● *Predictions* – I think that Mary will get more love in her uncle's family and that will make her a nicer person. Also, the fresh air might improve her complexion.
● Interesting words (see below).

Shared word-level work
● Explain that many of the interesting or unusual words in this novel are *loan words*; they have been loaned, relatively recently, from another language. Many languages and dialects are spoken in India, two of the most important being Hindi and Urdu. These, and other Indian languages, are the source of many English words. Ask the children to look out for interesting loan words as they read, and also to investigate loan words from India on the internet.

Guided and independent work
● Help the children to use an etymological dictionary (most large dictionaries contain etymological information).
● Explain that etymology is the study of the origin and history of words. Dictionaries use abbreviations to show which language a word comes from. The abbreviations used in different dictionaries may differ slightly, but they will be similar to the following:

L–Latin Gk–Greek F–French G–German H–Hindi It–Italian Urd.–Urdu ME–Middle English (c. 1200–1500) OE–Old English (c. 700–1200).

● Ask them to look up each of the words listed in the reading journal entry and make notes about their origins and definitions.
● Ask the children to independently complete their own reading journal entry for this chapter, using the four headings listed in the shared session.
● Encourage them to express themselves fairly freely within those headings.
● Explain that after future readings, you will expect the children to know what to do when they are asked to write a reading journal entry.

Plenary
● Encourage all of the children to share some of their entries, particularly their personal responses and develop this into a conversational discussion.

UNIT 3 HOUR 2 ▭ Narrative: author style

Character and setting

Objectives

NLS
T6: To explore the challenge and appeal of older literature.
W5: To investigate and learn spelling rules: words ending in *y* preceded by a consonant change *y* to *ie* when adding a suffix.

What you need
● Photocopiable page 165 (if you are using a different book, choose a scene that introduces a major character)
● copies of another scene, which reveals new things about the character or describes another main character, such as Colin or Dickon (add the prompt box from photocopiable page 165).

Shared text-level work
● Read photocopiable page 165 to the children.
● Then annotate the text: take each prompt, turn it into a question, and use the children's answers as the basis for annotations.
● Focus particularly on character and setting. For example:

> ● How is Mary presented through dialogue? (She speaks in a haughty tone to the servant.) How else is she described?
> ● Where is the story set? What adjectives and adjectival phrases describe the setting? (For example, *one frightfully hot morning*.)

● Tell the children that they will be analysing a different extract in the same way, to explore character and setting in particular.

Shared word-level work
● Draw attention to the word *parties* on line 14 of photocopiable page 165. Ask the children: *What is the singular form of this word?* See if they know the spelling rule, or remind them:

> Words ending in *y* preceded by a consonant change *y* to *ie* when adding a suffix, for example *flies, tried* – except for the suffixes *ly* or *ing* (*shyly, flying*).

● Ask the children to brainstorm more examples of this rule.

Guided and independent work
● Organise the children to work in pairs to read, discuss and annotate the second chosen extract in the way that was modelled in whole class work.
● Remind them to talk about and note down use of dialogue in character presentation and use of powerful adjectives in any description of the setting.

Plenary
● Display and read the extract that the majority of children have been working on and ask them to suggest annotations, focusing on character and setting.
● Afterwards, ask the children to predict how the character may develop in the rest of the story.

Differentiation

Less able
● Ask the children to annotate photocopiable page 165.

More able
● Ask the children to read and annotate a longer extract, of about 600 words.

UNIT 3 HOUR 3 ▣ Narrative: author style

Language

Objectives

NLS
T6: To explore the challenge and appeal of older literature.
W9: To understand how words vary across dialects.

What you need
● Photocopiable page 166 (or other scene that exemplifies interesting features of language)
● another scene that reveals similar features of language, for example, Ben Weatherstaff's conversation with Mary earlier in Chapter 10.

Shared text-level work
● Explain to the children that the main focus of this lesson is to examine the use of language in the text, but that they will begin with a brief discussion about Dickon's character.
● Display photocopiable page 166. Read the extract to the children, then explore:

> ● how the character of Dickon is presented through dialogue, action and description
> ● the features of language in older literature by examining vocabulary (difficult/unusual/archaic words) and sentence construction (long/short, simple/ complex)
> ● how the Yorkshire dialect differs from Standard English in vocabulary and grammar (see shared word-level work).

● Explain to the children that they will be investigating and annotating a similar passage.

Shared word-level work
● Revise the terms *accent* and *dialect* (see Unit 2, Hour 4).
● Make a list of differences in vocabulary, for example, *flight* – frighten; *tha'rt* – you are.
● Make a list of differences in grammar: *slow, gentle* (standard English would use the adverbs *slowly* and *gently*); *is* (standard English would use *are* because *wild things* is plural.)
● Investigate how spellings have been modified in the dialogue to represent the Yorkshire dialect, particularly the use of apostrophes, for example *tha', 'em, an'*.
● Relate the dialect words to the setting of the story, by asking the children: *Why does Dickon speak in dialect?*
● Finally, discuss how place has an influence on language. Discuss the children's own linguistic variety including other languages as well as dialects.

Differentiation

Less able
● Ask the children to write their own annotations for photocopiable page 167. The discussion that took place in the shared session will support them.

More able
● Ask the children to examine how conjunctions are used to link statements in longer sentences by highlighting the conjunctions.

Guided and independent work
● Ask the children to work in pairs to annotate their second extract for characterisation and notable language features.
● Suggest that one of them reads aloud while the other listens for how the characters are presented through dialogue, action and description, and unusual and effective words, phrases and sentence constructions.

Plenary
● Display the extract that the children have been working on and ask them to suggest and explain annotations relating first to character, and then to language. Identify the key features of the Yorkshire dialect: vocabulary, grammar, and the way spelling has been changed. Compare Ben or Dickon's language with that of Mary. She speaks standard English, but often uses words from India.

Creative responses

Objectives

NLS
T7: To write from another character's point of view, eg retelling an incident in letter form.
S2: To understand how writing can be adapted for different audiences and purposes, eg by changing vocabulary and sentence structures.

What you need
● Photocopiable pages 165 and 166
● photocopiable page 44 [creative response menu from T1, *Kensuke's Kingdom*] (ideally, adapted for *The Secret Garden*).

Shared text-level work

● Display photocopiable page 44 and briefly discuss each section of the creative response menu.
● Ask the children for suggestions about how each idea might be developed with reference to *The Secret Garden*, for example, adapting photocopiable page 166 into a playscript.
● Choose one of the items from the menu to develop into a piece of creative writing.
● Begin with ideas, then formulate a plan, followed by the beginning of a first draft.

Shared sentence-level work

● Explore with the children how the vocabulary and sentence structure of photocopiable page 165 (or an extract from your chosen text) would change if the story were adapted for younger children.
● Explain, for example, that for younger children simpler language, shorter and less complex sentences could be used, as well as fewer 'loan' and dialect words and consistent tenses. If possible, compare the result with a simplified version of the text, such as the Ladybird version.
● Now investigate with the children how the vocabulary and sentence structure would change if the story were retold in different *forms*, but for readers of roughly the same age, reading level and cultural background as themselves.
● Tell the children that if the story were retold in diary form, the story would be written in the first person, exclusively from Mary's viewpoint, and in the informal, personal style of a diary.

Guided and independent work

● Work with a group in a guided writing session to adapt photocopiable page 165 or 166 (or an extract from your chosen text) for younger children.
● Ask the children to choose an extract they have examined in this unit and write one of these additional ideas:

● Update a scene so that the main characters are 21st-century children – the language and style of writing should also be updated.
● Change the setting to an ordinary suburban house (no servants). What plot features will have to change?
● Rewrite a scene in which dialect is used, and change the dialect.
● Put the characters in new situations and write about what happens. Include dialogue.

Differentiation

Less able
● Ask a group to compile a glossary as this will help their comprehension of the book. Allow them to gather words and definitions from all the children's reading journals.

More able
● Ask the children to choose a creative response that requires writing in the same style as the author. Remind them of their analysis of Burnett's style in Hour 3 and encourage them to imitate it.

Plenary

● Ask the children to share with the rest of the group their own creative responses.
● Explore how the process of examination and exploration or textual analysis has contributed to a deeper understanding of the author and her work.

Discursive writing

Objectives

NLS
T10: To write discursively about a novel or story, eg to describe, explain, or comment on it.
S7: To use connectives to link clauses within sentences and to link sentences in longer texts.

What you need
● Photocopiable pages 166 and 167 (with annotations)
● all of the children's work so far, including reading journals
● connectives mats, if made, from Term 2, Unit 4.

Shared text-level work
● Tell the children that they are going to bring together all the work they have done on *The Secret Garden* (or other novel) by writing a discursive essay about the book.
● Brainstorm some thoughts about the story, then display a paragraph plan with prompts like the following. Elicit ideas about how to begin the introduction and each paragraph and write helpful words and phrases in column 3.

Shared sentence-level work
● Tell the children that they are now going to revise connectives from Term 2 as these will be useful when writing their essay. Ask the children which connectives they can remember and add them to column four of the table. Discuss in what contexts they will be particularly useful.

Paragraph	Content	Helpful phrases	Connectives
Introduction	This could be a very brief summary of the story	*The Secret Garden* is a story about...	although, as a result of, because
A paragraph on characters	A description of Mary, Dickon and/or Colin	The main character in the book is...	
A paragraph on language and style	About the author's use of loan words from India and dialect	The author uses several words from India, for example...	
Conclusion	A personal response to the characters and the story.	I thought that... I really enjoyed the scene where...	

Guided and independent work
● Ask the children to use their work from the week to write a short discursive essay on *The Secret Garden*. Tell the children that the first step is to plan their paragraph structure (see suggested plan in shared work), then write a first draft.
● Encourage them to discuss ideas and recall the story and its features in their group, but to produce an individual piece of work, including their personal likes and dislikes and critical comments on the novel (plot, character, setting and author style). Explain that the nature of a discursive text means that the writer can put forward a point of view, perhaps to be challenged, or agreed with, by a reader.

Differentiation

Less able
● Specify that the children should write three paragraphs: introduction, *one* of the characters, personal response.

More able
● Ask the children to write four or five paragraphs, including one on language and style.

Plenary
● Ask the children to share their emerging drafts, giving particular attention to the way in which they have built up paragraphs and linked ideas using connectives.
● Discuss the opinions expressed in the concluding paragraph, and, if there is time allow a few minutes of debate and discussion about the novel.
● Ask the children to add to their reading journals.

Scene from *The Secret Garden*

What to look for:
◾ Point of view (first or third person, story, letter, diary form...)
◾ How characters are presented through dialogue, action and description (direct and indirect speech, adjectives, adverbs)
◾ How settings are described (adjectives, synonyms)
◾ How the story is told (powerful verbs, adverbs)
◾ Vocabulary (difficult/unusual words)
◾ Sentence construction (long/ short, simple/complex)

When Mary Lennox was sent to Misselthwaite Manor to live with her uncle. Everybody said she was the most disagreeable-looking child ever seen. It was true, too. She had a little thin face and a little thin body, thin light hair and a sour expression. Her hair was yellow, and her face was yellow because she had been born in India and had always been ill in one way or another. Her father had held a position under the English Government and had always been busy and ill himself, and her mother had been a great beauty who cared only to go to parties and amuse herself. She had not wanted a little girl at all, and when Mary was born she handed her over to the care of an Ayah, who was made to understand that if she wished to please the Mem Sahib she must keep the child out of sight as much as possible. So when she was

a sickly, fretful, ugly little baby she was kept out of the way, and when she became a sickly, fretful, toddling thing she was kept out of the way also. She never remembered seeing familiarly anything but the dark faces of her Ayah and the other native servants, and as they always obeyed her and gave her her own way in everything, because the Mem Sahib would be angry if she was disturbed by her crying. By the time she was six years old she was as tyrannical and selfish a little pig as ever lived. The young English governess who came to teach her to read and write disliked her so much that she gave up her place in three months, and when other governesses came to try to fill it they always went away in a shorter time than the first one. So if Mary had not chosen to really want to know how to read books she would never have learned her letters at all.

One frightfully hot morning, when she was about nine years old, she awakened feeling very cross, and she became crosser still when she saw that the servant who stood by her bedside was not her Ayah.

"Why did you come?" she said to the strange woman. "I will not let you stay. Send my Ayah to me."

Frances Hodgson Burnet

Scene from *The Secret Garden*

What to look for:
◧ Point of view (first or third person, story, letter, diary form...)
◧ How characters are presented through dialogue, action and description (direct and indirect speech, adjectives, adverbs)
◧ How settings are described (adjectives, synonyms)
◧ How the story is told (powerful verbs, adverbs)
◧ Vocabulary (difficult/unusual words)
◧ Sentence construction (long/short, simple/complex)

A boy was sitting under a tree, with his back against it, playing on a rough wooden pipe. He was a funny looking boy about twelve. He looked very clean and his nose turned up and his cheeks were as red as poppies and never had Mistress Mary seen such round and such blue eyes in any boy's face. And on the trunk of the tree he leaned against, a brown squirrel was clinging and watching him, and from behind a bush nearby a cock pheasant was delicately stretching his neck to peep out, and quite near him were two rabbits sitting up and sniffing with tremulous noses – and actually it appeared as if they were all drawing near to watch him and listen to the strange low little call his pipe seemed to make.

When he saw Mary he held up his hand and spoke to her in a voice almost as low as and rather like his piping.

"Don't tha' move," he said. "It'd flight 'em."

Mary remained motionless. He stopped playing his pipe and began to rise from the ground. He moved so slowly that it scarcely seemed as though he were moving at all, but at last he stood on his feet and then the squirrel scampered back up into the branches of his tree, the pheasant withdrew his head and the rabbits dropped on all fours and began to hop away, though not at all as if they were frightened.

"I'm Dickon," the boy said. "I know tha'rt Miss Mary."

Then Mary realized that somehow she had known at first that he was Dickon. Who else could have been charming rabbits and pheasants as the natives charm snakes in India? He had a wide, red, curving mouth and his smile spread all over his face.

"I got up slow," he explained, "because if tha' makes a quick move it startles 'em. A body 'as to move gentle an' speak low when wild things is about."

He did not speak to her as if they had never seen each other before but as if he knew her quite well. Mary knew nothing about boys and she spoke to him a little stiffly because she felt rather shy.

"Did you get Martha's letter?" she asked.

He nodded his curly, rust-colored head.

"That's why I come."

He stooped to pick up something which had been lying on the ground beside him when he piped.

"I've got th' garden tools. There's a little spade an' rake an' a fork an' hoe. Eh! they are good 'uns. There's a trowel, too. An' th' woman in th' shop threw in a packet o' white poppy an' one o' blue larkspur when I bought th' other seeds."

Frances Hodgson Burnett

UNIT 4

Persuasion 1

This first unit on persuasive texts is based on a mock leaflet from the Stop Animal Testing Society. Children explore the different types of argument and the persuasive devices in the leaflet and use them as a model for their own debate speeches. In Hour 3, the children participate in group debates as a preparation for a whole-class debate. The best way to introduce this session is to ask a small group to prepare a debate to demonstrate the process. A different group should be asked to prepare debate speeches for the whole-class debate in Hour 4. In Hour 5, the children write their own persuasive articles based on group debate topics from earlier in the week. Hour 2 links to Unit 43 in *Grammar for Writing*, and Hour 5 links to Unit 35.

Hour	Shared text-level work	Shared word-/ sentence-level work	Guided reading/ writing	Independent work	Plenary
1 Stop animal testing!	Reading persuasive text and discussing issue.		Finding common arguments in text.	Annotating text for persuasive features.	Identifying persuasive devices and seeing their effect.
2 Persuasion planner	Discussing an example of how to structure an argument.	Choosing connectives to link points.	Researching and making notes.	Preparing for small group debates.	Talking about speech plans.
3 Group debate	Explaining the debate procedure.		Preparing and holding group debates.	Preparing and holding group debates.	Voting on one of the topics discussed.
4 Class debate	Explaining the organisation of whole-class debate.		Holding the debate.	Holding the debate.	Talking about the issue and what has been learned.
5 Persuasive writing	Exploring differences between spoken and written arguments.	Examining differences in sentence structure and textual organisation.	Writing persuasive magazine article.	Writing persuasive magazine article.	Comparing debate speech and article on same issue.

Key assessment opportunities
● Can the children recognise persuasive devices?
● Can they research and make notes to support an argument?
● Can they link points in a persuasive text with appropriate connectives?
● Have they participated in group and class debates?

UNIT 4 HOUR 1 ■ Persuasion 1

Stop animal testing!

Objectives

NLS
T14: To select and evaluate a range of texts, in print or other media, for persuasiveness, clarity, quality of information.
T15: From reading, to collect and investigate use of persuasive devices: eg words and phrases: persuasive definitions, rhetorical questions; pandering, condescension, concession; deliberate ambiguities.

What you need
● Photocopiable page 173 (with annotations removed).

Shared text-level work
● Read through the leaflet on photocopiable page 173 together.
● Ask the children what they think about the issue raised and then ask them to identify how the leaflet tries to persuade them to join the campaign against animal testing.
● Test the children's understanding of the leaflet and explore their responses with questions like the following:

● In the section entitled 'The Facts', four reasons are given for animal testing. Do you think any of these is a good reason?
● Look at the list of animals used for testing. Do you think it is acceptable to test on some animals but not on others?
● In the second section, three arguments against animal testing are given. Which do you think is the most powerful and why?
● What is the Draize eye test, and why is it described in the leaflet?
● The leaflet says that there is something that you can do to help – what is it?
● After reading the leaflet, has your opinion benn changed or made stronger.

● Develop this discussion to identify some of the types of arguments used and the inclusion of persuasive language, for example, emotive words like *hurt, killed* and *suffering*; a rhetorical question, the contrast between *life-saving drugs* and *trivial things,* such as *shampoo*, the effect of the pictures and captions.
● Help the children to annotate the different types of arguments and persuasive language they identified using those on the photocopiable sheet as a guide.

Guided and independent work
● Give the children the following list of commonly-used arguments and persuasive devices and ask them to see if they can find any in the text:

● facts or statistics
● examples
● appeals to the emotions
● rhetorical questions
● expert opinion
● pictures and captions.

● Ask the children to work in pairs independently and produce their own textual analysis by annotating the text for persuasive language and powerful arguments as modelled in the shared session.

Plenary
● Identify the persuasive devices found in the text.
● Discuss if children's opinions have been changed by the text. If so, which arguments were responsible for the change of opinion? Has anyone learned more about the topic that has reinforced their existing point of view?

Differentiation

Less able
● Ask the children to annotate the slogan, pictures and captions and to explain their persuasive effect.

More able
● Ask thechildren to include in their annotations brief explanations of the persuasive effect of these features.

Objectives

NLS
T16: Note-making: to fillet passages for relevant information and present ideas which are effectively grouped and linked.
T19: To construct an argument in note form to persuade others of a point of view.
S7: To use connectives to link clauses within sentences and to link sentences in longer texts.

S&L
50 Group discussion and interaction: To plan and manage a group task.

What you need
● Photocopiable pages 173 and 174
● access to library and/or internet
● poster of common connectives.

Persuasion planner

Shared text-level work
● Display photocopiable page 174. Explain that it is a guide to help plan persuasive speeches and articles, using examples from the fur trade. Read column 1, relating each point to the example in column 2.
● After reading through the section on arguments, ask the children which argument they find the most persuasive and why. How could they develop each argument more fully? For example, the paragraph on sea otters could be extended by giving examples of more species threatened with extinction, such as the snow leopard or whooping crane.

Shared sentence-level work
● Point out that the examples on photocopiable page 174 do not form a continuous text. The arguments are not in any order. Ask the children which order they would put the arguments in and which connective words and phrases they would use to link them. For example, *Another point is that the RSPCA say… Even though some people say…*

Guided and independent work
● Make notes for an argument on a topic from this list (or others):

> ● Animal testing
> ● Cosmetic surgery
> ● Crisps, fatty snacks and fizzy drinks should be banned from school lunchboxes
> ● Fur trading
> ● It should be illegal for parents to smack children
> ● Smoking should be made illegal
> ● TV can seriously damage your brain.

● Tell the children that they should look for information, facts and statistics that can be used as arguments. If researching the food topic, for instance, they will need to find nutritional information.
● Demonstrate how to skim and scan for relevant information and how to note it down briefly. Emphasise the importance of selecting a few facts and statistics that will be useful, rather than trying to make notes about everything.
● Ask the children to work in groups of four to prepare for small group debates by:

> ● choosing a topic (see list of suggestions above)
> ● deciding which two group members will speak for and which two will speak against the topic
> ● researching important facts and statistics
> ● making notes for the speeches.

Plenary
● Go through photocopiable page 174 again, asking children to relate it to the topics they have been researching. For example, *Thomas and Amanda, what will you say for your introduction?*

Differentiation

Less able
● Use photocopiable page 173 or the fur trading example in 174 as a starting point.

More able
● Ask pairs to speak on the more difficult or least popular side of the argument. In the case of fur trading, for example, it is harder and less popular to make the case for it.

Group debate

Objectives

NLS
T19: To construct an argument in note form to persuade others of a point of view and present the case to the class or a group.

S&L
55 Speaking: To present a spoken argument, sequencing points logically, defending views with evidence and making use of persuasive language.

What you need
● The children's notes from Hour 2.

Shared text-level work
● The ideal model for this session is a sample group debate that has been prepared in advance by a group of children, or a recorded group debate.
● Show/watch the exemplar group debate and use it to explain the following debate procedure (if watching a video, watch the whole debate first, then watch it a second time, pausing at each part):

> ● Speaker 1 presents the case for the topic (introduction, statement, one or two logically sequenced arguments).
> ● Speaker 2 presents the case against the topic.
> ● Speaker 3 continues the case for the topic (restating the point of view, one or two arguments, conclusion).
> ● Speaker 4 continues the case against the topic.
> ● Freewheeling discussion of the topic to which everyone can contribute to make points and ask questions.

● Display this procedure for use during group work.
● Emphasise the importance of speaking from notes rather than just reading a written speech, and to use gesture, make eye contact with the audience, and speak in an interesting and varied tone of voice.
● Remind the children they are trying to convince people of a viewpoint not send them to sleep!

Guided and independent work
● Ask the groups to use their notes made in Hour 2 to prepare and give two-minute (approximately) speeches for and against their chosen topic.
● Remind the children to follow the debate procedure discussed in whole class work.
● Advise the groups that the speakers should be allowed to speak uninterrupted for a set time, and to save counterpoints and questions until afterwards.
● Allow about ten minutes preparation time and ten minutes for the group debate.

Plenary
● Ask one or two groups to re-run their discussion while the rest of the class try to identify the types of arguments and the persuasive devices they have used.
● Ask the class to vote on which side of the argument they favour after listening to the debate.
● Choose the debate topic which created most interest and most diversity of opinion, and ask the group to develop their speeches (by adding more arguments and examples) for a full debate in Hour 4.

Differentiation

Less able
● Help the children to rehearse speaking from notes.

More able
● Ask the second speaker to try to expose weaknesses in the other team's arguments.

UNIT 4 HOUR 4 📄 Persuasion 1

Class debate

Objectives

NLS
T19: To construct an argument in note form and evaluate its effectiveness.

S&L
55 Listening: To analyse the use of persuasive language.

What you need
● Chosen debate topic (see note in plenary of Hour 3)
● the main speakers' prepared speeches.

Shared text-level work
● Tell the children that you are going to hold a formal class debate and explain how a formal debate is organised:

> ● The topic is presented as a motion giving one point of view, for example: Animal testing becomes: This house believes that animal testing should be abolished.
> ● The speakers are paired as in Hour 3, but are now referred to as proposer and seconder – one how puts forward the viewpoint and the second who supports it.
> ● After the speeches, the topic is opened up to the floor for general discussion.
> ● Two votes will be taken: a vote for and against the motion; a vote for the best pair of speakers.

Guided and independent work
● Reorganise the classroom for a class debate. Position the chairperson (you or a more able child) and the four speakers at the front of the class.
● Explain that you will be chairing the debate, keeping it structured and watching the time, and that after the speeches you will call on volunteers individually to ask questions of the speakers or to contest their viewpoint.
● Remind the children not to interrupt the speakers and to listen carefully to other questions and points that are raised during the discussion.
● End with two votes, one for the best speaker, and one for the motion. Is it carried?

Plenary
● Praise all speakers and contributors and evaluate the debate by asking:

> ● Has anyone learned any more about the issue?
> ● Has anyone changed their mind about the issue?
> ● How close was the vote on the motion? What does that tell us about the issue? (Perhaps opinion is divided or surprisingly one-sided.)
> ● What have you learned about making a persuasive speech? How might you change certain aspects of the next persuasive speech you give?

Differentiation

Less able
● Ensure all of the children are allowed to contribute.

More able
● Ask a more able child to chair the meeting.
● Encourage the children to 'think on their feet' when asking or answering questions to keep the debate moving.

Persuasive writing

Objectives

NLS
T19: To construct an argument in note form or full text to persuade others of a point of view.
S2: To understand how writing can be adapted for different audiences and purposes, eg by changing vocabulary and sentence structures.

What you need
● Photocopiable page 174
● the children's notes from Hour 3
● connectives mats or poster.

Shared text-level work
● Explain to the children that now they are going to write a persuasive article for a magazine for young people about the topic of their group debate from Hour 3.
● Display and re-read photocopiable page 174 and relate it to the debate in Hour 4.

Shared sentence-level work
● Discuss the differences in audience and purpose between a debate speech and a persuasive magazine article on the same subject.
● Draw a table and brainstorm some of the differences.
● Consider how the differences will affect the organisation, vocabulary and phraseology of their texts.

Debate speech	Persuasive text
Known audience, direct contact with audience. Tone of voice and gesture can be used to help get the message across. Certain words and phrases sound too formal in a speech.	No direct contact with audience. Only language can be used to get the message across, so it is sometimes more detailed and complex. Written language uses a wider range of vocabulary and sentence structures.

● Finally, remind the children that they have been using notes to speak from but must develop these into linked and structured sentences and paragraphs for their written article.

Guided and independent work
● Ask the children to write their persuasive magazine article following the plan on photocopiable page 174.
● Tell them to use the notes they made for the group debate speech in Hour 3 as the basis for their article.
● Encourage the children to recall and discuss the notes as a group before writing their articles individually.
● Remind them of the work done in Hour 2 on expanding and connecting discussion points.
● Also remind the children of the persuasive devices they examined in Hours 1 and 2 and to use these in their texts. If they are able to use IT, encourage the children to experiment with effective layout features and to include emotive pictures if possible.

Differentiation

Less able
● Ensure that the children make use of a connectives mat or poster.

More able
● Ask the children to write for a specific audience and purpose, for example, a campaign leaflet similar to photocopiable page 173.

Plenary
● Ask one of the children who gave a class debate speech or modelled the group debate in Hour 3 to read out their persuasive article on the same subject.
● Discuss the issue and the differences between the speech and the article.
● Go back to the table from whole class work, and illustrate each point with specific examples.

SATS (Stop Animal Testing Society) says

STOP ANIMAL TESTING!

The facts

Every year in the UK over 2.7 million animals are hurt or killed in scientific tests. Official statistics show that 31% of tests are for biological research, 24% are for testing drugs and 18% are tests for the safety of foodstuffs, household products and agricultural chemicals. The remaining 27% include testing for a wide range of purposes, for example, genetic testing. Most of the tests are done on mice, rats, guinea pigs and rabbits, but horses, pigs, dogs, cats, hamsters, birds, monkeys and many other animals are used.

Why animal testing is wrong

First, the tests are cruel and cause animals a great deal of suffering, especially as 60% of the tests are given without any anaesthetic. An example is the Draize eye test in which a concentrated solution is dripped into the eyes of rabbits over a period of 7–18 days. Pain-relieving drugs are not usually given because experimenters claim their use would interfere with test results.

Secondly, the majority of the tests are not for life-saving drugs or important medical advances, but for trivial things, such as whether a new shampoo is safe if it gets into the eyes. Of course, no one wants to be harmed by shampoo – but do we really want animals to suffer just to add another brand to the supermarket shelves?

Finally, the tests are outdated and unnecessary. Modern science offers a range of tests that are more reliable and more humane, including chemical analysis and computer models. For example, the Draize eye test can be effectively replaced by using corneas from eye banks.

What you can do

Join SAT. We are a non-violent organisation working to change the law through legal means, such as raising public awareness, leafleting and political lobbying. Sign up at www.sats.org. Membership is free, though donations are welcome.

Eye-catching slogan stating the aims of the organisation

Facts – powerful argument because of the numbers involved

Surprising facts

Example is a powerful argument because it gives us precise details of a cruel test

Persuasive word – this suggests doubt

'Experimenters' rather than 'scientists'

Another argument – tests are for trivial purposes

Some concession, then persuasive phrase

Examples to back up argument

An appeal to the 'experts', here, 'scientists'

Persuasive word

Emotive picture

Caption plays on reader's feelings

Persuasion planner

Plan	Example
Introduction State your point of view/argument.	Farming or killing animals for their fur is wrong.
Statement Explain your subject clearly.	Many animals are hunted for their fur. For example, foxes, lynx, otters and seals. The fur is not needed to keep humans warm, it is just a fashion accessory.
Arguments Give at least two arguments to support your point of view. Put them in a logical order. These are some of the types of argument you could use: ◼ facts and statistics ◼ examples ◼ appeal to emotions of reader/ listener ◼ reference to expert opinion ◼ consider the best arguments on the other side and attack them ◼ illustrations, captions, charts, tables, slogans	◼ Over 20 million animals are killed for their fur every year. ◼ Have you ever seen a sea otter? Probably not because they have been hunted to extinction by fur traders. ◼ Animals that are killed for their fur are strangled or beaten to death so that the fur is not damaged. ◼ The RSPCA say that many species are endangered because of fur trading. ◼ Some people say they have a right to wear what they want – but not if it causes animals to suffer or species to become extinct.
Conclusion Restate your point of view in a memorable way.	For these reasons, it is wrong to kill animals for their fur and it should be made illegal.

UNIT 5

Persuasion 2

This unit raises issues surrounding the development of a wind farm. Though the project is fictional, it is based on a number of real-life projects such as those at Scout Moor in Cumbria and Nympsfield in Gloucestershire. In the course of the simulation, the children role-play the different interest groups: developers, local residents and a range of individual interests. While in role, they collaborate to write protest letters and participate in a public meeting. The simulation can be further developed by linking to Geography, PSHE and Citizenship.

Hour	Shared text-level work	Shared word-/ sentence-level work	Guided reading/ writing	Independent work	Plenary
1 The plan	Reading a formal letter; discussing issue raised.		Developing roles and points of view.	Developing roles and points of view.	Reporting on role-play discussions.
2 The arguments	Raising arguments for and against to be supported by research.		Discussing arguments and deciding importance.	Researching points for arguments.	Sharing information found.
3 Letter of complaint	Planning a letter of protest.		Examining features of business letters.	Writing a letter of protest/complaint.	Reviewing the letters in role.
4 Planning for the public meeting	Discussing the use and organisation of protest meeting.		Helping group representative to prepare a presentation for the meeting.	Helping group representative to prepare a presentation for the meeting.	Considering how to give a good presentation.
5 The public meeting	Holding the meeting.				Adopting new roles to consider points raised in the meeting; taking a vote.

Key assessment opportunities
● Can the children read and evaluate official letters?
● Can they discuss an issue in role and sustain their roles?
● Can they write letters of protest?
● Have they participated in whole class debate?

UNIT 5 HOUR 1 ▫ Persuasion 2

The plan

Objectives

NLS
T12: To read and evaluate letters, eg from newspapers, magazines, intended to inform, protest, complain, persuade, considering how they are set out, how language is used, eg to gain attention, respect, manipulate.
S6: To investigate clauses.

S&L
54 Drama: To reflect on how working in role helps to explore complex issues.

What you need
● Photocopiable pages 181 and 182.

Shared text-level work
● Display photocopiable page 181 and explain that it is an example of the kind of letter that a local council sends to residents when new building is planned.
● Explore what the children already know about wind turbines and wind farms.
● Read the letter then look at layout and language. Draw attention to:

> ● heading, logo and 'mission statement'
> ● line breaks between paragraphs
> ● contact details and references.

● Ask the children to find formal/official words and phrases, such as, *in accordance with*.
● Ask: Which paragraph attempts to manipulate the reader into agreeing with the wind farm proposal? (Note phrases like, *These needs can be met.*)
● Briefly examine the conventions of opening and closing a formal letter.
● Display photocopiable page 182 and relate the plan to the landscape.
● Briefly discuss advantages and disadvantages of wind energy and how the proposal will affect local residents.
● Explain to the children that they are going to role-play different groups of people who live in the area to take part in discussions and write letters and articles about the proposed wind farm. Organise the children into the following mixed-ability groups: residents of Edenthorpe, residents of Whitfield, residents of Barnsdale, managers of WindPower Holdings, environmentalists in favour of wind power.
● Discuss what the views of the different groups might be.

Guided and independent work
● Within the groups, each child should choose an individual identity to represent a range of views, for example, bird watcher, journalist, landscape painter, mother, pensioner, poet, rambler, sheep farmer, shopkeeper, the custodian of Lammermoor Castle, unemployed builder. Help the children to choose their identity and ensure that it is appropriate (a sheep farmer would be unlikely to live in Barnsdale), and that there is a good range.
● Ask the residents to imagine that they have just received the letter from the council and are holding their first meeting to discuss it. Encourage them to mark photocopiable page 182.
● Ask the managers and environmentalists to discuss the arguments they will use to counter protests from residents.

Differentiation

Less able
● The children may find it easier to get into role if they have role cards describing the characters they are playing.

More able
● Allocate more challenging individual roles, such as poet.

Plenary
● Ask some groups to report back on their initial reactions to the plans. What do they think the next step would be? (For example, find out more about wind farms, contact other protest groups, write to the council.)

The arguments

Objectives

NLS

T13: To compare writing which informs and persuades, considering, eg the deliberate use of ambiguity, half-truth, bias.
T16: Note-making: to fillet passages for relevant information and present ideas which are effectively grouped and linked.
W12: To use dictionaries efficiently to explore meanings.

What you need

● Photocopiable page 183
● access to library and/or internet, or a range of reference materials
● dictionaries.

Shared text-level work

● Divide the board into two sections: For and Against, and ask the children to brainstorm arguments for and against wind farms, scribing good points on the board.
● Explain to the children that this is just a starting point, and that the next step is for them to do further research into the arguments 'For and Against'.
● Remind the children how to skim and scan a text for relevant information and how to make brief notes of key information. For example, show the case study at www.scoutmoor.com/casestudy.htm and look for information to be used in the argument against wind power, for example, the turbines are creating terrible noise.
● Emphasise the importance of selecting a few facts or statistics that will be really useful to support their side of the argument.
● Now read photocopiable page 183 and compare the lists with the children's own ideas. It may prompt further debate and argument.

Guided and independent work

● Carry out some guided reading work with a group to evaluate the arguments on photocopiable page 183 by discussing them and putting them in order of importance (this may be affected by the role or point of view). For example, visual blight is a greater concern than interference with television signals. (Or is it? How bad is the interference? Some children may take the opposite view!)
● Ask the children, in role, to independently research additional arguments to support their case. For example, the residents groups could find more information about the problems caused by wind farms.
● Ask them to choose from the reference material provided in the classroom and/or the library or begin with these suggested websites before looking for others: www.windustry.com (For), www.scoutmoor.com/facts.htm (Against).
● Warn the children that sites such as these, may be biased, and may include opinion disguised to seem like fact. Tell them to look out for this and be careful when making notes.
● Encourage the children to use dictionaries for difficult and/or technic`al terms.

Differentiation

Less able
● Allocate a specific book page, or website as a starting point.

More able
● Encourage open-ended research – browsing the library or internet to find their own sources of information.

Plenary

● Ask the children what new information they have found and add them to the arguments on the board.
● Explain that a full debate (in role) will take place later in the week, but that you are going to allow five minutes for a brief discussion of the information which has been written into the two sections, *For and Against.*
● Explain to children that you will 'tidy up' the ideas on the board, separating them into the correct sides of the argument, for use later in the week. (The tidied up version can either be photocopiable page 183 or an adapted version of it.)

Letter of complaint

Objectives

NLS

T17: To draft and write group letters for real purposes, eg put a point of view, comment on an emotive issue, protest; to edit and present to finished state.

S&L

56 Group discussion and interaction: To understand different ways to take the lead and support others in groups.

What you need

● Photocopiable page 181
● several real business letters.

Shared text-level work

● Begin the following plan on the board and work with the children to plan a letter to the council.

Opening/addresses	Follow the layout and punctuation of the council's letter. Remember to include reference.
Introduction acknowledging letter received; explaining what the letter is about and who you are	For example, Thank you for your letter about the proposed wind farm at Lammermoor. We, the residents of Edenthorpe, are writing to let you know our objections.
A number of paragraphs explaining why you object to or why you support the plans	3 or 4 strong points clearly explained are more effective than lots of points, especially if some are trivial.
A polite and expectant conclusion	For example: We hope that you will consider our objections carefully, and look forward to hearing your reply.
Closure	*Yours faithfully* - if addressed to Sir/Madam *Yours sincerely* - if addressed to named person, for example, Mr/Ms Clouds

● Display photocopiable page 181 to demonstrate the standard layout and punctuation and the opening and closure of a formal letter.
● Note that the layout is much simpler than most real business letters, but see Guided reading, below.

Guided and independent work

● Ask the children to investigate a range of real business letters. Examine the information contained in the opening, for example, their address, your address, telephone and fax numbers, a reference number, a company logo. Note the way they are punctuated and laid out and any abbreviations used. Discuss the tone and formality of the language. Are there long sentences with multiple clauses? Is there unusual/archaic vocabulary or subject-specific terminology? Check forms of salutation and closure.
● Ask each group to independently plan and write a letter to the council. It will be best to subdivide the groups into twos or threes who have similar points to make. Tell the children to follow this process:

1. Discuss which points you want to include in the letter.
2. Consider the wording of each paragraph.
3. Write a draft of the letter.
4. Read and talk about the draft with a view to making improvements.

Differentiation

Less able
● Make sure the children can contribute to the discussion, but let others scribe.

More able
● Ask confident speakers to ensure all the children are involved in the discussion.

Plenary

● Ask the children to read out their letters.
● Ask the rest of the class to imagine that they are councillors and to evaluate the letters. Which did they find most persuasive? Why? Were the points raised valid and worthy of consideration? How might they respond?

Planning for the public meeting

Objectives

NLS
T19: To construct an argument in note form to persuade others of a point of view and present the case to the class or a group.
55 Speaking: To present a spoken argument, sequencing points logically, defending views with evidence and making use of persuasive language.

Shared text-level work

● Tell the children that part of the process of a major planning application, such as the proposed wind farm, is a public meeting that would be held after the planning department has considered all the information about the planning application, including letters from residents. Explain the proceedings:

> ● You will play the Chief Planning Officer and chair the meeting.
> ● The Chief Planning Officer will briefly explain the future electricity needs of the Barnsdale area and the two alternatives (the wind farm, or an extension to the coal-fired power station near Barnsdale).
> ● Managers of WindPower Holdings will present their plan – with a positive spin.
> ● A representative of the Edenthorpe residents speaks against the plan.
> ● A representative of Whitfield residents speaks against the plan.
> ● A representative of Barnsdale residents expresses a range of views.
> ● An activist from the environmentalist group speaks for the plan.
> ● Individuals, such as a farmer, landscape painter, parent, express their views.
> ● General discussion. Tell the children that this is where they will have the opportunity to ask questions of group representatives and that they should think of a question in advance, and also listen carefully to the proceedings in case their question has already been answered or is not relevant.

What you need
● All the resources and notes from the week.

Guided and independent work

● Ask each group to choose a representative and then to discuss what they want their representative to say based on their notes and previous discussions and letter.
● Tell each group to help its representative to prepare a short presentation, for example, by offering suggestions about the order of ideas, the use of emotive language and persuasive examples, and finally, by helping the representative to make useful notes.
● Ask every individual (except group representatives) to prepare at least one question to ask any of the representatives, and a short comment to make in the general discussion if appropriate.

Plenary

● Using one of the representatives' notes as an example, give advice on how to speak to an audience with the use of notes.
● Emphasise the importance of speaking (rather than reading) and of making eye contact with the audience.
● Encourage everyone to practise what they are going to say as homework.

Differentiation

Less able
● As Hour 1.

More able
● Ask the children to use their research from Hour 2 to think of a really challenging question for one of the representatives.

The public meeting

Objectives

NLS
T14: To evaluate texts, in print or other media, for persuasiveness, clarity, quality of information.

S&L
52 Speaking: To use and explore different question types.

What you need
● Photocopiable page 182
● the children's resources from the week.

Whole class work
● Most of this lesson will be taken up by the meeting.
● Ask the group representatives to join you at the front of the classroom and announce that the public meeting is about to begin.
● Remind the children that they should listen carefully to all the speakers and questioners as you expect them to comment on what they have heard during the debate.
● Begin the meeting with a short introductory speech in role as the Chief Planning Officer. Explain the purpose of the meeting and introduce each of the representatives. Then, using photocopiable page 182, remind the audience of the details of the proposed wind farm.
● Ask each representative to speak.
● Then ask for any questions or comments from the audience. Remind the children to remain in role, to stand up when asking their question and to address it to the appropriate representative.
● Open up the meeting to allow general debate. Encourage children to challenge points that have been made and facts that have been presented, as appropriate.
● Close the meeting. Thank the representatives for speaking and the residents for attending. End with a short speech in which you state that all the views expressed at the meeting will be carefully considered.

Plenary
● Explain to the children that they are now going to adopt other roles in order to take a vote. They are now planning officers and local councillors at a meeting of the Barnsdale District Council Planning Department. In role, as the Chief Planning Officer, introduce this summary discussion by reminding the officers and councillors that they are going to discuss and then vote on the following question:

> Should the energy needs of the Barnsdale area be met by the proposed wind farm, or by adding an extension to the coal-fired power station near Barnsdale?

Differentiation

Less able
● Make sure all of the children are able to participate and are listened to fairly.

More able
● Remind the children to remain in role.
● A more able child could work with you as a senior member of the planning department.

● Remind the children that, as public officers and councillors, they have a duty to take a wider view: the needs of everyone, not just one pressure group.
● Take them through the main points put forward by each group and invite brief discussion.
● Finally, ask the Council to vote on how to proceed.

Letter from the council

Barnsdale District Council
Serving the Community

Barnsdale District Council
Planning Department
Cavendish Place
Barnsdale BM1 2GL
tel: **01999 123645**
fax: **01999 123647**

Ref: BDCHICWHPP775aE1

7 July 2005

Dear Resident

WindPower Holdings have applied for permission to build a wind farm on Lammermoor, covering 950 acres near the villages of Edenthorpe and Whitfield. In accordance with Regulation 55b of the Town and Country Planning Directives, I wish to draw your attention to the following information.

The wind farm will consist of 12 turbines 80 metres high placed on Lammermoor Ridge on either side of a Service Road.

The Service Road will follow the route of the B6291 through Whitfield where the road will be widened. All the buildings to the east side of the road will have to be demolished. Compensation will be paid at market rates.

A new viaduct will carry the road across the Lammer valley.

30 kilometres of pylons will link the wind farm to the National Grid.

It is important to point out that the energy needs of the Barnsdale area will increase in the next 10 years. These needs can be met by the proposed wind farm or by adding an extension to the environmentally-harmful coal-fired power station near Barnsdale.

A plan and a computer-generated view of the wind farm are attached at Annex A. If you have any comments which you would like the council to take into consideration you must contact this office within one month, quoting the above reference number.

Yours faithfully,

HI Clouds

HI Clouds
Chief Planning Officer

Annex A

Plan of proposed wind farm at Lammermoor

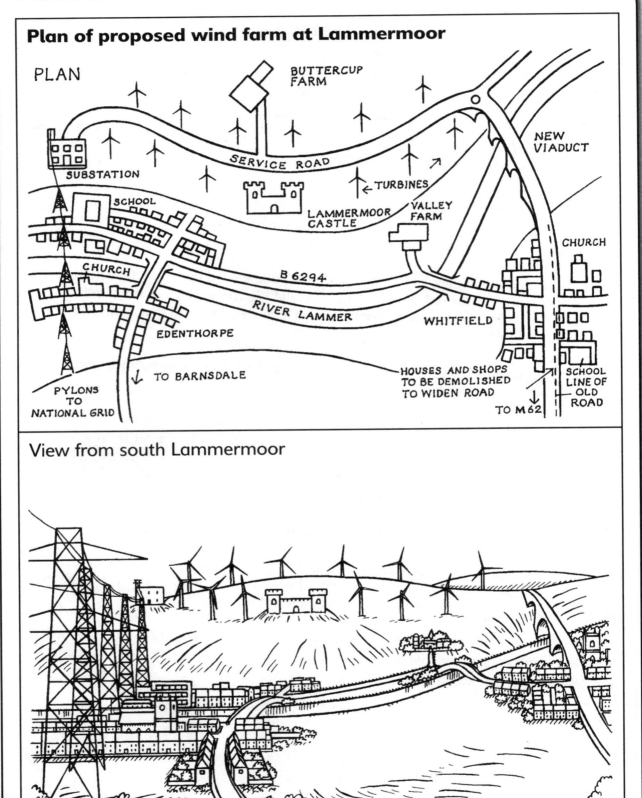

PLAN

BUTTERCUP FARM

SERVICE ROAD

SUBSTATION

SCHOOL

NEW VIADUCT

TURBINES

LAMMERMOOR CASTLE

VALLEY FARM

CHURCH

CHURCH

B 6294

RIVER LAMMER

WHITFIELD

EDENTHORPE

↓ TO BARNSDALE

HOUSES AND SHOPS TO BE DEMOLISHED TO WIDEN ROAD

SCHOOL LINE OF OLD ROAD

PYLONS TO NATIONAL GRID

TO M 62

View from south Lammermoor

Arguments for and against wind farms

For

✔ It is essential to find additional sources of energy. Our reliance on fossil fuels has caused serious problems, including global warming and acid rain. Wind energy is one of the best alternatives.

✔ Wind energy is clean, free and renewable. This means people can enjoy cheaper electricity and cleaner air.

✔ A wind farm is much safer than a nuclear power station. There is no danger of a Chernobyl-type explosion, or any problems with the disposal of nuclear waste.

✔ Communities where wind farms are built should take the wider view and avoid nimbyism (NIMBY = not in my back yard). There are benefits for local communities:

✔ A wind farm will develop the local economy by providing a wide range of jobs including meteorologists, construction workers, mechanics and operators.

✔ A wind farm will lead to improvements in local facilities, such as roads and railways, and will stimulate the local economy and local property market.

Against

✘ Wind farms are noisy. The wind turbine at Nympsfield in Gloucestershire, which is one of the quietest available, creates a noise level of 99dB (a pneumatic drill creates a noise level of 110dB).

✘ Visual blight. There are now 87 wind farms in Britain, many of them in places of great natural beauty. In a recent poll in *Country Life* magazine they were voted the worse eyesore in Britain.

✘ Not one nuclear or coal-fired power station has been closed down because of wind energy. Why? Because we still need other sources of energy for days when the wind is not blowing.

✘ Though not as dangerous as nuclear power stations, wind turbines can be harmful to wildlife, especially birds, and they can frighten farm animals.

✘ There is little benefit to local economies. Construction requires many workers, but only a handful are needed to keep them running.

✘ Not all environmentalists support wind farms. For example, green campaigner Dr David Bellamy led hundreds of people on to the moors to protest against plans for a wind farm at Scout Moor, near Rochdale.

UNIT 6

Persuasion 3

This unit is based on an article about healthy eating and can be linked to units in Science, PSHE and PE. After exploring the persuasive devices used in the article, the children investigate the topic for themselves, first by learning about the five food groups and then by conducting a lunchbox survey. They use their findings to write letters replying to the article and to write their own balanced commentary on what children should eat at school. Hour 1 links to *Grammar for Writing* Unit 43.

Hour	Shared text-level work	Shared word-/ sentence-level work	Guided reading/ writing	Independent work	Plenary
1 Food fascists	Reading a newspaper article; noting persuasive devices and balance.	Revising uses of connectives.	Categorising persuasive words and phrases.	Adapting article for a new audience and context.	Evaluating rewritten articles.
2 My daily diet	Reading a food chart.	Noting telegraphic language.	Adapting the text for new audience and context.	Compiling a food diary.	Looking for patterns in children's eating habits.
3 Lunchbox survey	Comparing recommended foods with children's lunches.	Noting telegraphic language.	Using situation cards to discuss balanced diets; creating healthy lunchbox menus.	Using situation cards to discuss balanced diets; creating healthy lunchbox menus.	Persuading others of good lunchbox menus.
4 Promoting healthy eating	Discussing features of web pages.	Brainstorming topic buzz words.	Producing a web page to promote healthy eating.	Producing a poster to promote healthy eating.	Displaying and discussing web pages and posters.
5 Balanced commentary	Re-reading news article to note genre features.		Experimenting with connecting clauses.	Writing balanced commentaries on the topic.	Evaluating articles; overview of topic.

Key assessment opportunities
● Can the children recognise and use a range of persuasive devices?
● Can they write a balanced commentary on an issue they have researched?
● Can they use connectives to link phrases and sentences?

Objectives

NLS
T15: From reading, to collect and investigate use of persuasive devices: eg words and phrases; persuasive definitions; rhetorical questions; pandering, condescension, concession; deliberate ambiguities.
S7: To use connectives to link clauses within sentences and to link sentences in longer texts.

What you need
● Photocopiable page 190.

Food fascists

Shared text-level work
● Display photocopiable page 190. Ask the children to identify what type of text it is. (Newspaper article.)
● Read the headline and briefly explain the word fascist. Ask the children what effect the word has when applied to an article about school food. (It is emotive and highly exaggerated.)
● Read the text, then clarify understanding by asking questions like 'What is Mrs Malcolm angry about?'
● Consider the persuasive devices used in the article and ask the children to find examples of persuasive words and phrases as you re-read it. A fun way to begin is to look for 'purr' words and 'snarl' words. Do this by asking the children to help you to complete a table like this:

Purr words – words and phrases with good associations	Snarl words – words and phrases with bad associations
duty	fascists
healthy eating	naughty
right-thinking	unhealthy
wholesome	obesity

● Go through the article again and make a list of other persuasive words and phrases, for example, *claimed, threatening, exaggerated, surely.*
● Ask the children to consider the way in which the author of the article presents the different arguments. Does she favour one side of the argument? (Both sides of the argument are presented but there is clear bias on the side of Mrs Malcolm. This is particularly evident in the headline and the conclusion.)

Shared sentence-level work
● Briefly revise work on connectives from Unit 4 and ask the children to identify connectives in the text, for example, however, on the other hand, as a result. Note how they link phrases and sentences together in a logical way.

Guided and independent work
● Work with a more able group to sort the persuasive words and phrases collected in shared work into the categories listed in the NLS text-level objective.
● Ask the children to work in pairs to use the information in the article to reconstruct it for the school's newsletter. They will need to make it shorter and simpler, and shift the bias towards the school's point of view (that the article about naughty and nice foods was helpful) by writing a new headline and leaving out negative information such as Dr Manson's comments, and the protest. Advise them to use photocopiable page 190 as a model for the use of persuasive words and phrases, quotations, connectives and paragraph structure.

Plenary
● Read some of the children's examples and ask them to consider how well each article has changed the bias of the original article.

Differentiation

Less able
● Ask the children to begin by highlighting on photocopiable page 190 all the relevant information.

More able
● See Guided and independent work.

UNIT 6 HOUR 2 ▭ Persuasion 3

My daily diet

Objectives

NLS
T14: To select and evaluate a range of texts, in print or other media, for persuasiveness, clarity, quality of information.
S2: To understand how writing can be adapted for different audiences and purposes, eg by changing vocabulary and sentence structures.

What you need
● A table/chart of the five basic food groups including recommended daily servings and foods.

Shared text-level work
● Display the food chart and read it with the children.
● Ask: Why is it clearer to give the information in this form rather than writing it out in sentences and paragraphs? (The eye can travel easily and quickly across and up and down for information and explanations and to compare food groups. The information is basically made up of lists so sentences would be unsuitable.)
● Ask the children if they recognise all the foods mentioned. Explain any that they are unsure of.
● Elicit which foods the children particularly like or dislike.

Shared sentence-level work
● Re-read the chart, asking children to look for telegraphic language – shortened/abbreviated sentences, similar to headlines, from which inessential words have been omitted, such as *1 glass milk* (instead of, one glass of milk) – the subject of the sentence (Grains are..., or These are...) has been left out. Ask the children to find other examples.
● Ask the children why telegraphic language has been used. (To save space in the table, and because this type of text does not require full sentences.)

Guided and independent work
● Work with a group in a guided writing session to experiment with other ways of presenting the information.
● Ask the children to think first about the intended audience, such as young children, parents reading the school newsletter, patients in a doctor's waiting room, and then to consider which form would be most appropriate: an article, a list, a table, a poster and so on.
● Ask the children to work independently to complete a food diary of *What I ate and drank*.
● Tell them to use the same abbreviated style as the food chart and to be as specific as possible in listing exactly what they ate yesterday.
● Use the following table as an example:

Group	Foods included	What I ate and drank on...
Grains	Breakfast cereals, muesli, rice, pasta, bread, oats, noodles – all other foods made from flour and grains. Healthiest are less refined types.	2 servings (1 bowl) of Country Store for breakfast. 4 servings of bread at lunchtime (two sandwiches)

● Finally, ask the children to add up the daily servings and check if they were over or under the recommended amounts.

Plenary
● Ask the children to feed back on their food diaries. List each child's number of servings as they are called out.
● Ask the children if they can see any patterns, such as too much sugar and fat, too little fruit.

Differentiation

Less able
● Help the children to add up the daily servings.

More able
● Challenge the children to try to remember everything they ate and drank, including snacks, sweets and drinks.

Lunchbox survey

Objectives

NLS
T13: To read other examples, eg newspaper comment, headlines, adverts, fliers. Compare writing which informs and persuades, considering eg the deliberate use of ambiguity, half truth, bias; how opinion can be disguised to seem like fact.
S2: To understand how writing can be adapted for different audiences and purposes, eg by changing vocabulary and sentence structures.

What you need
● Chart of food groups
● photocopiable page 191 cut into cards.

Shared text-level work
● Display the food chart. Read through the list of example foods and ask the children how many of them have the recommended foods in their own lunchboxes.
● Children who have school meals should work in a group to evaluate the balance of foods in school meals.

Shared sentence-level work
● Continue as Hour 2, but looking for examples in the list of recommended foods.

Guided and independent work
● Organise the children into groups of six and ask them to follow this process:

1. Shuffle the cards from photocopiable page 191 and deal them out.
2. Each child takes it in turns to tell the group the contents of the lunchbox on his/her card.
3. The group then discusses these questions:
● Which lunchbox would you most like to have and least like to have?
● Which contain the most balanced diets? (3 and 5.)
● Which contain the most unhealthy foods? (2 and 4.)
● Which is dangerously low in nutrition? (4.)
4. The group discusses and chooses one of the following labels for each lunchbox: Balanced diet, Everything beginning with p, Fast food addict, Gourmet, Health fanatic, Snack scoffer.

● Then ask each child to design a lunchbox that is both healthy and appealing. Encourage them to use the list of recommended foods on the food chart as a guide to healthy choices.
● In addition, let them add one treat of any kind, for example, a chocolate bar, a fizzy drink.
● Finally, ask them to write a short description of their lunchbox in a way that would persuade other children to choose it.

Differentiation

Less able
● Ask the children to select one item from each food group for their ideal lunchbox.

More able
● Ask the children to analyse their ideal lunchbox and then see if there are ways of improving the healthiness of the lunchbox without reducing its appeal.

Plenary
● Share ideas about the ideal lunchbox and the way they would persuade children to choose it. This could be made into a kind of competition in which the children present their lunchboxes and the class votes for the healthiest and most appealing.

◻ **187**

Promoting healthy eating

Objectives

NLS

T18: To write a commentary on an issue on paper or screen, (eg as a leaflet); to use structures from reading to set out and link points, eg numbered lists, bullet points.

S2: To understand how writing can be adapted for different audiences and purposes.

W2: To use known spellings as a basis for spelling other words with similar patterns or related meanings.

What you need

● The children's resources used so far
● interactive whiteboard (if appropriate)
● access to computers with web editing software (optional).

Differentiation

Less able

● Ask the children to produce a poster. Suggest that a few well-chosen sentences, perhaps using bullet points, along with a slogan and an illustration will be most effective.

More able

● Ask the children to produce a leaflet (such as four pages consisting of one folded A4 or A3 page). Suggest that the first page should be eye-catching, but that the inside pages should contain detailed dietary information and advice.

Shared text- and sentence-level work

● Explain to the children that they are going to write a web page, poster or leaflet to persuade children to ask for healthy foods in their lunchboxes.
● Tell the children that the title will be 'Yum, Yum and a Healthy Tum'.
● Say that the emphasis must be on healthy foods. and that they must be careful not to lose their focus by all the information they have acquired in the last few days.
● Ask the children to suggest what kind of persuasive devices would work best on a web page, poster or leaflet.
● Discuss devices such as 'Buzz' words, phrases and slogans; bullet points; appealing illustrations or photographs; attractive layout.
● Using the favourite lunchbox from the last lesson, begin a model based on the children's suggestions for clear, simple wording; persuasive language and attractive layout.
● Remind them that it is aimed at children of their own age.
● Draw a rough page layout, and demonstrate how to use bullet points, images and different sizes and colours of text.

Shared word-level work

● Have fun brainstorming buzz words and phrases to make the text exciting and appealing to younger people.
● Encourage the children to come up with appealing or even made-up words, for example, crunchy, mega bites, munch munch your healthy lunch, scrumptious, vegilicious.

Guided and independent work

● Work with a group to produce the web page to promote healthy eating. This can be done using a word processing or desktop publishing package that allows ordinary documents to be saved as web pages.
● Encourage the children to include photographs and experiment with moving the page elements around for maximum appeal and ease of use. Remind them to keep text brief and to use a 'screen-friendly' format (bulleted list, for example).
● Ask the children to independently work in groups of two to four to discuss, design and produce a poster or leaflet entitled 'Yum, Yum and a Healthy Tum'.
● Remind them of their audience and purpose and the persuasive devices they suggested earlier.

Plenary

● Display the finished posters and leaflets and the web page if possible.
● Ask the class to evaluate each one and to shortlist five which they consider are the most effective. Discuss which persuasive devices worked the best.
● Ask the ICT co-ordinator to make the web page available on the school network.

Balanced commentary

Objectives

NLS
T18: To write a commentary on an issue on paper or screen, (eg as a news editorial, leaflet), setting out and justifying a personal view; to use structures from reading to set out and link points.
S6: To investigate clauses through: identifying the main clause in a long sentence; investigating sentences which contain more than one clause; understanding how clauses are connected.

What you need
● Photocopiable page 190
● the children's resources used throughout the week.

Differentiation

Less able
● Organise the children to work in groups of three, with one child being responsible for the first draft of each section. Ask them to work together to revise the draft.

More able
● Encourage the children to think of their own headline and plan their own framework.
● Remind them to use the detailed research they did in Hour 3.

Shared text- and sentence-level work
● Explain to the children that they are going to complete their work on healthy eating by writing a balanced article further to that on photocopiable page 190.
● Read the text again and ask the children to note:

> ● use of quotes from key people involved and/or experts
> ● subheadings
> ● captioned illustration/photograph
> ● key quote pulled out from the body text
> ● persuasive words and phrases
> ● connectives.

● Display and read the following suggested title/headline and structure. Invite questions from the children.

> **Food researchers recommend balance**
> ● One-paragraph introduction explaining the problem – that many people are worried about children's unhealthy food habits.
> ● Next two or three paragraphs present one side of the argument – how the 'food fascists' believe that all unhealthy foods should be banned.
> ● Closing two or three paragraphs to use investigations in Hours 2 and 3 to present the other side of the argument. For example, you could use Dr Manson's quote from photocopiable page 190 and show that you have researched that it is fine to include small treats at lunch as long as it is part of a balanced diet.

Guided work and independent work
● Give the group of children the following three clauses:

> ● chocolate is best avoided
> ● it contains high levels of fat and sugar
> ● a small amount is not harmful as part of a balanced diet.

● Ask the children to make one sentence from the three clauses by joining them with appropriate conjunctions. Ask: Which is the main (most important) clause? (*Chocolate is best avoided.*)
● Ask the children to try to join the clauses using two conjunctions between the clauses (*because, but*), then to try to join them using one initial and one central conjunction (*Although chocolate is best avoided because it contains high levels of fat and sugar, a small amount...*)
● Tell the children to write down their balanced commentaries following the suggested fra,e

Plenary
● Share examples of the articles and ask the class to evaluate them in terms of persuasive devices, use of research, style and balance.
● Finish by asking if any children have been persuaded by any of their work to change their eating habits.

TERM 3

Food fascists ban 'naughty' foods

Education editor, **Margaret Soames**, reports

Mrs Malcolm, a parent at Langton Primary in Pembroke, claimed that 'food fascists' were threatening to take junk food and fizzy drinks from children's packed lunches. However, headteacher Helen Holbrooke said that the claim was exaggerated. "No teacher has the right to take food from children. On the other hand, it is our duty to encourage healthy eating."

A junk food junky at 9 years old

She went on to explain that every right-thinking person was worried by the rise of obesity in young children. As a result, the staff decided to take part in the government's Healthy Schools programme set up in 1998 by the Department for Education. The programme covers road safety, personal hygiene and healthy eating. To encourage healthy eating, the school has begun a programme of advice to children and their parents. In addition, the school canteen will replace harmful fatty foods such as chips and burgers with healthy, wholesome foods such as pasta, fresh vegetables and fruit.

Naughty or nice?

It appears that the trouble began with an article in the school newsletter which labelled some foods as 'naughty', for example chips, chocolate and crisps, and others as 'nice', for example carrots, nuts and fruit. Despite the school's good intentions, some parents felt insulted. One mum said, "Surely this is the parents' responsibility! The teachers should stick to education. I provide a healthy, balanced diet at home, so what's wrong with a bar of chocolate at lunch time?" Another parent objected to the word 'naughty'. "This could cause some children to feel guilty about eating, leading to illnesses such as bulimia."

> ## "No-one but a complete idiot would try to force children to eat healthy foods..."
> Dr David Manson

A spokesperson from Pembroke Education Committee said, "The real truth is that Mrs Malcolm misunderstood the article. Yes, the article was strongly critical of harmful foods, and did call them 'naughty', but it didn't say that anything would be taken away from children. The Committee strongly supports the school's campaign for healthy eating."

Counterproductive

But Dr David Manson, director of the Langton Health Centre, said "No-one but a complete idiot would try *force* children to eat healthy foods. It would only make them rebel by stuffing themselves with crisps and chocolate when the 'food police' are not looking. Rather, you should try to win them over by teaching them about the effects of different kinds of foods and allowing them to make informed choices. An occasional treat is fine."

Crisp-in protest

In the meantime, Mrs Malcolm is organising a 'crisp-in'. She is encouraging all parents to put a bag of crisps in their children's lunchboxes every day until the school agrees to adopt a more balanced approach to its healthy eating campaign.

In this series:

ISBN 0-439-97164-0
ISBN 978-0439-97164-5

ISBN 0-439-97165-9
ISBN 978-0439-97165-2

ISBN 0-439-97166-7
ISBN 978-0439-97166-9

ISBN 0-439-97167-5
ISBN 978-0439-97167-6

ISBN 0-439-97168-3
ISBN 978-0439-97168-3

ISBN 0-439-97169-1
ISBN 978-0439-97169-0

ISBN 0-439-97170-5
ISBN 978-0439-97170-6

To find out more, call: 0845 603 9091
or visit our website www.scholastic.co.uk

Lunchbox cards

1

Vegetable soup in a small flask
Pear
6 carrot sticks
Cucumber sandwich
Fresh fruit drink

2

Double bacon cheesburger with extra
cheese smothered in tomato sauce (cold)
Fries (cold and soggy)
Fizzy drink
Packet of chewing gum

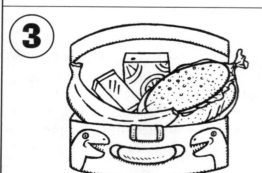

3

Chicken and salad in wholemeal roll
Banana
Fresh fruit drink
Cereal bar

4

Two bags of crisps
Diet Fizzy Drink
Chocolate bar
Bag of salted peanuts

5

Pitta bread
Frankfurter sausages
Nectarine
Small bunch of seedless grapes
Cereal bar

6

Pasta and tuna salad
Pear
Peppers (sliced)
Packet of popcorn
Peach tea drink